Restorative Free Will

Restorative Free Will

Back to the Biological Base

Bruce N. Waller

LEXINGTON BOOKS
Lanham • Boulder • New York • London

Published by Lexington Books
An imprint of The Rowman & Littlefield Publishing Group, Inc.
4501 Forbes Boulevard, Suite 200, Lanham, Maryland 20706
www.rowman.com

Unit A, Whitacre Mews, 26-34 Stannary Street, London SE11 4AB

British Library Cataloguing in Publication Information Available

Library of Congress Control Number: 2015949521
ISBN: 978-1-4985-2238-0 (cloth)
ISBN: 978-1-4985-2240-3 (pbk.)
ISBN: 978-1-4985-2239-7 (electronic)

Contents

Preface and Acknowledgments

Restorative free will is a new way of looking at free will, but in some respects it is a very old view of free will: some of the free will pieces that the account fits together have been observed and celebrated and elaborated for centuries. But rather than viewing these elements as competitors, restorative free will attempts to show how they function together—and serve vital symbiotic functions—when free will is viewed as an important capacity of complex biological organisms such as humans but also other species. Trying to understand the functioning of the heart in isolation from the rest of the organism, or as if the heart must be the defining essence of the organism, is not a promising path to understanding how the heart functions. The same applies if we attempt to understand the need for open alternatives, or the need for control, or the need for reflection, as if these are the defining features of free will, such that free will can be explained by exclusive reference to that essential element. The major accounts of free will have provided great insights; but those insights have been treated as competitors, rather than as mutually supportive elements of the free will of human animals. Rather than seeking *the* essential element of free will, a better approach is to examine the full range of essential elements of a well-functioning free will in organisms similar to ourselves, and how those elements work together for the benefit of the organism. Furthermore, studying the human heart under the assumption that hearts are the exclusive property of humans is not a promising method of understanding how the heart functions; the same rule applies to treating free will as a uniquely human capacity.

Discovering—what I take to be—the combined symbiotic elements of free will was not the result of any brilliant insight or deeper inquiry or clearer perspective. To the contrary, those discoveries were all but forced upon me, while I struggled vigorously but unsuccessfully to avoid seeing them. They were discoveries that happened in the course of a very different quest:

a quest aimed at destruction. My goal was to destroy moral responsibility, drive a stake in its heart, and bury it at the crossroads; and I was quite willing to destroy the free will accounts—nothing better than accomplices, in my view—that were providing aid and comfort to moral responsibility. This destructive quest resulted in discoveries I had not anticipated: the arguments in favor of moral responsibility still seem fatally flawed; but the accompanying accounts of free will—while they fail to establish claims of moral responsibility—contain rich insights into the nature of free will, which I could not avoid appreciating even when my goal was to attack them. When they are liberated from the impossible task of supporting moral responsibility, those insights can be better appreciated: rather than competing accounts of moral responsibility they are essential and harmonious elements of animal free will.

The goal of this book is not only to show that free will can survive the demise of moral responsibility; rather, to show that our understanding of free will can flourish and expand and deepen when it is freed from the dead weight of moral responsibility, and our understanding of free will can be enhanced by remarkable studies in psychology, neuropsychology, biology, primatology, sociology, and anthropology. We do not lose free will when moral responsibility is rejected; to the contrary, we gain a better understanding and appreciation of free will, as well as better understanding of ways to enhance and enrich and protect free will.

This is not an argument against moral responsibility. I believe that moral responsibility cannot survive in a world without miracles, and that our natural world is devoid of any plausible niche that will support moral responsibility. Most contemporary philosophers are compatibilists, who insist that moral responsibility can survive and flourish in a purely natural, even deterministic, environment. But moral responsibility is not the focus of this book. I have spent many years developing the best arguments I could muster against moral responsibility (Waller 1990, 2011, 2015) in the fervent hope of destroying moral responsibility, root and branch. Many others (such as Derk Pereboom, Galen Strawson, Neil Levy, Thomas Nadelhoffer, and Gregg Caruso) have been allies in that effort. But whether the walls of moral responsibility are broken or standing, the question here is not moral responsibility, but the nature of free will. Given the long history of philosophical efforts to link free will and moral responsibility, it will not be possible to leave moral responsibility entirely out of the discussion. (And given my obsession with destroying moral responsibility, I doubt that I could manage to leave it out of the discussion in any case.) But my hope is that even those who are fervent supporters of moral responsibility will find *some* part of the restorative free will account appealing. It would be surprising if they do not, since restorative free will embraces insights from compatibilists and libertarians who are dedicated champions of moral responsibility; and not only embraces them, but incorporates them, and claims that they are allies rather than adversaries.

In the years that I have been writing about free will and moral responsibility, the most frequent target of my arguments has been the work of Daniel Dennett. In one way, that seems strange, since Dennett is among the philosophers whose work I most admire; and Dennett's work on the importance of control—together with his seamless integration of empirical studies with philosophical investigation—has had an enormous influence on my own approach to issues of free will and moral responsibility. In another sense, it is not surprising: Dennett has developed a variety of the strongest and clearest and most creative arguments for moral responsibility, and anyone who seriously questions the legitimacy of moral responsibility must carefully address those powerful arguments. But while I have often criticized Dennett's views, I trust it is clear that I regard his work on free will and on the importance of control as profoundly insightful, and that Dennett is a philosopher to whom I am deeply indebted.

Other major targets of my argumentative efforts include Harry Frankfurt, Susan Wolf, and John Martin Fischer. Again, their arguments concerning moral responsibility are targeted because I take them very seriously: they rank among the strongest advocates of moral responsibility, and anyone who denies moral responsibility must endeavor to deal with their powerful arguments. But I hope that it is clear that I believe that not only have they made rich contributions to the debate concerning free will and moral responsibility, but also that they have enriched our understanding of some of the vital elements of free will.

Many years ago I was offered the opportunity to review a book by Robert Kane: *Free Will and Values*. When I agreed to write the book review, I thought it would be an easy task: all I knew of the book was that it offered a libertarian account of free will and moral responsibility, and I was confident that any libertarian account could be swiftly demolished. I soon discovered that demolishing the views of Robert Kane would require much heavier artillery than I carried. I had come to scoff; and while I did not quite stay to pray, I certainly stayed to respect the profound insights Robert Kane had achieved into the nature of free will. That respect has only grown deeper over several decades: no one has struggled more honestly or productively with these thorny issues than Robert Kane. I have not had as many opportunities to sit and talk with Bob as I would like; but the few occasions when we have discussed these questions—sometimes for several hours of intense examination of the issues—stand out as among the most enjoyable and edifying philosophical conversations of my lifetime.

Richard Double—both in conversations and in his writing—has long been an invaluable resource for understanding the enormous complexity, connections, and implications of the various and sundry views on free will.

Gregg Caruso, in conversations and correspondence and in his published work, has helped me to see connections and problems that I had entirely overlooked, and I greatly admire his critique of moral responsibility. The question of whether free will should be eliminated (along with moral responsibility) is one of the very few philosophical issues on which we disagree, so discussing "free will eliminativism" with him has certainly sharpened the entire issue. My hope is that Gregg can be turned back from this sinful path of free will eliminativism, and become a fervent free will preservationist; but whether that happens or not, I am indebted to him for very helpful discussions of this question.

I am particularly indebted to Thomas Nadelhoffer, not only for his insightful work on free will and moral responsibility but also for managing his remarkable blog, *Flickers of Freedom*. For thoughtful, productive, insightful, and respectful discussion and debate on issues related to free will and moral responsibility, there is no forum anywhere that comes close to its value.

Thanks also to Thomas W. Clark, for his important writings on this area as well as for his very valuable website, Naturalism.org, that posts a wide range of excellent work: an essential resource for keeping up with important publications on this subject.

I hope that a few philosophers will be convinced that this is a promising approach to free will, but that would be a nice bonus; I mainly wrote this book to convince my friends Fred Alexander, Lauren Schroeder, and Luke Lucas that free will can flourish in a purely natural world devoid of gods and miracles. Even if they are not convinced, I am indebted to them for many years of rich conversations, tips on improving my poker game (which needs all the help it can get), and for providing the powerful motivation to actually write this book.

Very special thanks to my friend Homer Warren, with whom I have shared a weekly lunch for many years, and who has been a wonderful listener, an insightful critic, and a very rich resource of new perspectives on this ancient subject; and to my friend and colleague Brendan Minogue, with whom I have shared many sessions of wonderful debate and conversation on this and many other philosophical subjects, some delightful evenings of Irish music, and more gin and tonics than I care to mention.

My greatest piece of philosophical luck was landing in the philosophy and religious studies department at Youngstown State University, where I have spent an enjoyable and stimulating quarter century. No academic could ask for better colleagues. Each and every one of them—Tom Shipka, Chris Bache, Brendan Minogue, Tess Tessier, Mustansir Mir, Gabriel Palmer-Fernandez, Victor Wan-Tatah, Deborah Mower, Mark Vopat, Alan Tomhave, and Michael Jerryson—does serious scholarly work, and they are all remarkably supportive and encouraging. They are not only amazing resources on a wide range of questions but also wonderfully patient and kind in answering my questions and straightening out my confusions. Many of our adjunct faculty—Julie Aultman, Walter Carvin, Sarah Lown, Sister Nancy Dawson, Arnold Smith, Lynette Stratford, Jeff Limbian, Lou D'Apolito, Vince Lisi, Bernie Oakes, Joseph Schonberger, Donna Sloan, and Richard White—also have special areas of expertise, ranging from bioethics to the Gnostic Gospels to the criminal law, and not only have they done a wonderful job teaching our students but also have enriched my understanding of a wide variety of subjects. Very special thanks indeed to Mary Dillingham: she is absolutely the Platonic Ideal of a departmental administrator. Neither I nor the department would have survived my years as department chair without her remarkable efficiency, her gentle manner of fixing my many mistakes, and her warm cheerfulness in all weathers. Thanks also to Nicole Pavlansky, our brilliant and dedicated student worker who always does superb work, often in the midst of chaos. Finally, I am deeply indebted to my students at YSU; not only is it especially gratifying to watch our students from this tough rust belt city go on to great success in graduate studies at Harvard and Yale and many other elite universities, but also their enthusiastic participation in philosophical discussions constantly reminds me of the importance and fascination of philosophical questions.

Many others have stimulated my interest in questions about free will and other philosophical issues during many delightful conversations, and among those are my friends Jane Kestner, Charles Singler, Jim Morrison, Ikram Khawaja, Howard Mettee, Paul Sracic, Keith Lepak, Lia Ruttan, and Stephen Flora.

Everyone at Lexington has been efficient, pleasant, and accommodating. They have made all the laborious grungy publishing details as smooth and painless as they could possibly be. Special thanks to my editor, Jana Hodges-Kluck, whose enthusiasm for this project has been a constant and kind source of motivation.

My greatest debt, always, is to my family: my wife, Mary, whose knowledge of clinical psychology is a great help to my work and whose loving patience with an often distracted and exasperating philosopher exceeds that of Job; my delightful son, Adam, who not only guides me patiently in all things music and computer related, but also gives me more joy and pride than he could ever imagine; Russell, my mathematical and philosophical son, whose work always amazes me and whose constant kindness astounds me; Russell's wife, Robyn, who is the best mother for a grandson any adoring grandfather could possibly imagine, and whose superb philosophical writing and teaching is a source of great pride to her father-in-law; my grandson, Nathanael Carmine, the most brilliant and amazing and wonderful child in the entire cosmos; and Bruno the wonder dog, whose affection never wavers no matter how many stupid things I do.

Chapter 1

Introduction

Free will is the capacity to effectively explore alternative paths in response to a combination of environmental contingencies and internal motives, and essential elements of that capacity include the ability to discriminate among and evaluate alternatives and the ability to adjust the level of behavioral variability to environmental conditions. That is a gritty mundane account of free will as it exists among foraging animals that evolved in a changing world. Natural evolved free will inspires neither poetry nor religious devotion. Free will is not the quality that makes us godlike, nor is it the special gift of God to his last and favorite creation. Free will is not unique to humans, it does not require a high level of reflective rationality, it does not support moral responsibility, and it does not involve any special *causa sui* powers.

This is not a revisionist account of free will; rather, it is a *restorative* view of free will, which restores free will to many species that have been denied free will under accounts contrived by humans to claim exclusive rights to free will. Free will is common to many species, and various species manifest free will in a variety of ways. All of those manifestations, however, share common features and serve similar functions. On the restorative view, the free will powers enjoyed by human animals are basically similar to those of other animals, and free will—including the human variety—is better understood by examining the common elements of free will shared by many species, rather than focusing on the distinctive *enhancements* of free will that are unique to humans. In order to support moral responsibility and uniquely human free will, the picture of human free will has been distorted to make it appear more godlike; when we view it through the broader lens of animal behavior—the behavior of many species, with which humans have more in common than with gods—we can see free will more clearly, rather than looking through a glass darkened by *conscious* claims of human uniqueness and moral responsibility and *non*conscious belief in a just world.

Revisionist accounts of free will (such as Vargas 2013) generally insist that the new revised account successfully preserves some form of moral responsibility (perhaps a "forward-looking" anemic version of "moral responsibility," in which "being morally responsible" merely means that sanctions have the potential to improve future behavior). But moral responsibility is a distorting addition that was added late and has nothing to do with free will. It's as if we were planning the restoration of an ancient Greek temple to which a Christian church had been added in a later century, and in carrying out the restoration we insist that the church must be preserved. Such a revision will never achieve a clear view of the original temple. The *restorative* account restores free will to its larger role in animal behavior, and eliminates the human uniqueness and moral responsibility claims that distort our understanding of animal free will.

The project of this book is *not* an attack on moral responsibility. My arguments against moral responsibility can be found in Waller (1990, 2011, 2015); better arguments against moral responsibility are available in Pereboom (2001, 2014); Strawson (1986); Levy (2011); and Caruso (2012). This book does not add any further arguments to those. Rather, this is an attempt to understand free will when it is not encumbered by the insistence that it support moral responsibility.

To make sense of free will we must find its real value for animals like ourselves: animals that are not unique, but closely related to other species; animals that have reason, but not reason that sets them radically apart; animals that are not morally responsible. We must return to where accounts of free will took a wrong turn toward human uniqueness, and to a point before free will—conceived as uniquely human—was drafted for service in defense of uniquely human moral responsibility (in support of a moral responsibility that could rationalize deep belief in a just world).

Restorative Free Will offers an account of free will, and claims that it is the most plausible and workable of all the accounts on offer. That is an arrogant claim. Philosophers are notorious for being arrogant, but this claim ranks particularly high on the arrogance scale. After all, the competing philosophical accounts of free will are legion, and they continue to multiply. George Wright, a professor of law at Indiana University's Robert H. McKinney School of Law, gives a sobering but accurate assessment of the current situation:

> Schools of thought on free will and criminal responsibility have multiplied and proliferated at a remarkable rate. It would not be much of an exaggeration to say that at this point, nearly every serious academic philosopher in the field is developing, at a certain level of detail, his or her own slightly distinctive

approach to free will and moral responsibility, or the lack thereof. At this point, nearly every imaginable variation on the basic themes of free will, responsibility, and their meaning and roles has been articulated by at least one philosopher. If an approach can be imagined, it has likely been advocated. (2014, 227–8)

So why should anyone suppose that the free will account proposed here is any more plausible than the multitude of accounts already available?

This restorative account of free will does not add one more "imaginable variation" to the fascinating variety of free will accounts developed by philosophers. Rather, it is an attempt to discover the roots of free will in not only human behavior, but also in the free will behavior of animals other than humans, including animals that benefitted from free will long before humans arrived on the scene to claim exclusive dominion over free will. To appreciate the nature and value of free will, it is important to go back to where it started: back to the evolutionary processes that shaped free will in a rich variety of species. Human free will has some distinctive features; but focusing exclusively on human free will results in a distorted account: we treat the distinctive features of *human* free will as the essentials of free will, when in fact they are only enhancements. Valuable enhancements, certainly, but not the vital center of animal free will. If we wish to understand the human heart, first we start with the study of hearts in many species, and from that study we discover the basic structure and function of the heart; then we can go further, and study what is distinctive about the human heart. The same process is our best approach to free will: study the common basic function of free will in many species; and then study how distinctively human free will fulfills that function, and any special human adaptations to enhance the functioning of free will.

This is not a revisionist account of free will. It is not an account of how the folk think of free will. It is not an account that traces free will back to the views of ancient philosophers. It is not an account of free will found in popular religions or ancient myths. Rather it is an account of free will writ large and deep: the free will that many species enjoyed and practiced long before humans evolved, the free will deeply rooted in adaptive animal behavior, and the free will that humans share with a variety of other species. This is not an account of uniquely human free will, except in arguing that "uniquely human free will" designates an empty set.

Is it an account of *free will* at all? Is it an account of anything that either philosophers or the folk could recognize as free will? Yes. Libertarians have long championed open alternatives as the key element of free will, while the opposing compatibilist camp has celebrated control. Restorative free will not only incorporates *both* elements, but also explains how they work together and why both are essential. That explanation is the task of this book.

PHILOSOPHICAL ACCOUNTS OF FREE WILL

Studying philosophical accounts of free will is like watching a tennis match from midcourt: following the action requires pivoting from one side to the other. For Aristotle free will means following the single path of intellectual virtue, but Lucretius insists that free will requires a random and inexplicable swerve. The Stoics view perfect rationality guiding us along the single true path as the only genuine freedom, while Alexander of Aphrodisias requires absolutely open alternatives. With the development of Christianity, genuine freedom becomes again a single track path, though now the path is defined by devotion to God rather than devotion to reason. Come the Renaissance, Pico della Mirandola identifies free will with a godlike power to make ourselves in a wide range of forms (ranging from beasts to gods). David Hume again switches directions, with free will now being perfectly compatible with determinism. William James derides the "freedom" of a determinist block universe (1897), and insists free will requires genuinely open alternatives (1907); William Barrett (1958) concurs. But Harry Frankfurt (1971) claims that reflective commitment is the essence of free will, and open alternatives are not needed; and John Martin Fischer agrees, insisting that I have free will so long as I live my life "my way" (2006). Robert Kane (1985, 1996, 2007) insists there can be no genuine free will without open alternatives—open alternatives generated by random forces—that make possible our ultimate free self-defining choices. In bright contrast, Susan Wolf (1990) maintains that the only genuine free will consists in rationally following the single true path for the right reasons.

This conflict between two basic models of free will has raged for many long centuries. On the one side, free will requires open alternatives and free choices among such alternatives; on the other, genuine free will is found in following the single true path. Both of these views come in several varieties, of course. On the open alternatives view, the alternatives are sometimes provided by random motions and at other times by some special power of will: the will may even be miraculous, as in Pico and Chisholm (1964). On the single path view, free will typically requires special rational powers to recognize and follow the True and Good, but on some views it requires simple-minded devotion to the will of God. For Frankfurt the single path is one that is reflectively approved (even if the path favored is a self-destructive one, such as drug addiction), while for Fischer (2006) it requires only that the path taken be approved as genuinely one's own that is followed "my way" (Frank Sinatra, Mother Teresa, and John Martin Fischer can each freely follow distinctively different paths, so long as each does so in his or her own way). In contrast to Frankfurt and Fischer, for Susan Wolf free will requires following the *single* narrow path of the True and Good.

There are variations within the camps of those who favor open alternatives and those who champion a single path, but the basic divide is between those competing views. These two perspectives—call them the alternatives and authenticity perspectives—face off across a deep divide, and there seems to be no way of reconciling the conflict. That contemporary philosophical positions on free will have hardened into such an intractable dispute should not surprise us. The contemporary effort to make sense of free will has two deep problems. First, it incorporates the principle that free will must set humans distinctly apart from the rest of the natural world, including all other species; and while that may have been a plausible belief for Aristotle and Augustine and Pico and even Descartes, it is difficult to square with our post-Darwinian perspective. Second, it is assumed that free will must support moral responsibility; and while the miracle-working free will of Pico might work (with miracles one can "prove" anything), and the exaggerated semi-miraculous view of human rational powers might prove adequate for the task, it is a difficult project indeed when we take a more naturalistic perspective on human abilities. We encounter problems when trying to forge a naturalistic account of free will that can support beliefs belonging to a different era altogether: an era of gods and miracles, of humans crafted in God's image with godlike rational powers, a pre-Darwinian era with gods and godlike humans on one side and all the rest of creation of a completely different nature. Fitting a godlike uniquely human account of free will into a post-Darwinian naturalist world is like trying to run Photoshop on a TRS 80, and the resulting breakdowns are not surprising.

The single track, fixed path model of free will results from our most basic misconception of human animal free will: free will sets us apart from the world of animals and makes us special and godlike rather than animal-like. What is the nature of God's free will, which human free will emulates? This question concerns the free will of the God of Aristotle, and the later Christian God that incorporated the features of the Aristotelian God (not the short-tempered and capricious God of Abraham and Moses). First and foremost, God is absolutely self-sufficient and perfect, and changes not (any change would be a step down from perfection). God knows everything, and knows everything eternally and absolutely. God is immutable: God never changes, wonders, or wanders; has no needs whatsoever; and obviously has no use for exploring open alternatives, since there is nothing he lacks. Aristotle recognizes, of course, that we are not gods; but we are *like* God, we are distinct from the rest of the grubby world, and our good lies in emulating God to the best of our abilities:

> The activity of our intelligence, inasmuch as it is an activity concerned with theoretical knowledge, is thought to be of greater value than the others, aims

at no end beyond itself, and has a pleasure proper to itself . . . ; and that the
qualities of this activity evidently are self-sufficiency, leisure, as much freedom
from fatigue as a human being can have, and whatever else falls to the lot of a
supremely happy man; it follows that the activity of our intelligence constitutes
the complete happiness of man. . . .

However, such a life would be more than human. A man who would live it
would do so not insofar as he is human, but because there is a divine element
within him. This divine element is as far above our composite nature as its activity is above the active exercise of the other [practical] kind of virtue. So if it is
true that intelligence is divine in comparison with man, then a life guided by
intelligence is divine in comparison with human life. We must not follow those
who advise us to have human thoughts, since we are men, and mortal thoughts,
as mortals should; on the contrary, we should try to become immortal as far as
that is possible and do our utmost to live in accordance with what is highest in
us. For though this is a small portion, it far surpasses everything else in power
and value. One might even regard it as each man's true self, since it is the controlling and better part. (Aristotle 1925, Book X, 7)

So for godlike humans the truly proper life, the truly free life, is the life
of theoretical knowledge: a life of self-sufficiency, contemplating the fixed
and unchanging truth. The closer we come to this ideal of perfection, the
more godlike and unchanging we become; and the less need we have for
anything outside our own intellects, and the less need for open options. Free
will—which makes us godlike and unique—is linked to the idea that genuine
freedom consists in following the one true path of rational reflection, and
alternative open paths are useless (or worse than useless, since they tempt us
from the one true path).

It is not surprising that this Aristotelian view of free will should be attractive to medieval Christians. For Christians, humans are God's special favored
creation, and our only true freedom consists in following God's will. We are
God's artifacts, made for one purpose; and that purpose requires no open
alternatives, but only single-minded devotion to God. Susan Wolf drops the
godliness, but retains the basic outlook. For Wolf, genuine freedom requires
perfect rationality that recognizes the one true path, and freedom is following
that straight and narrow path. Alternatives are useless: ". . . we can state the
condition of freedom and responsibility more directly by referring outright
to the ability to act in accordance with (and on the basis of) the True and the
Good" (1990, 73). Because true freedom consists in devotion to the straight
and narrow path of the True and the Good, open alternatives hold no charms:

To want autonomy [in the sense of genuine alternatives], then, is not only to
want the ability to make choices even when there is no basis for choice but to
want the ability to make choices on no basis even when a basis exists. But the

latter ability would seem to be an ability no one could ever have reason to want to exercise. Why would one want the ability to pass up the apple when to do so would merely be unpleasant or arbitrary? (1990, 55)

Since the alternative paths are irrational deviations from the True and Good, the ability to explore such paths "is a very strange ability to want, if it is any ability at all" (1990, 56).

PHILOSOPHERS AND OPEN ALTERNATIVES FREE WILL

Though Solomon was reputed to have exceeded all others in wisdom and was thus a good candidate for the joys of Susan Wolf's single true path, he was sadly aware that a world with nothing new to explore and no forking paths is not the world of human happiness:

> All the rivers run into the sea; yet the sea is not full; unto the place from whence the rivers come, thither they return again. . . . The thing that hath been, it is that which shall be; and that which is done is that which shall be done; and there is no new thing under the sun. Is there any thing whereof it may be said, See, this is new? It hath been already of old time, which was before us. (Eccl. 1: 7, 9-10)

And there being nothing new, no open alternatives to explore, causes depression in Solomon as it does in Seligman's (1975) dogs and in those of us having significantly less wisdom than Solomon: "I have seen all the works that are done under the sun; and, behold, all is vanity and vexation of spirit" (Eccl. 1: 14). For foraging animals that evolved in a changing world, the prospect of no new possibilities is deeply disturbing.

Stagnant stability and single-path certainty may have their charms; but those charms are not the charms of free will. William James had healthy grounds for renouncing the certainty and stability and comforts offered by an omnipotent deity:

> Suppose that the world's author put the case to you before creation, saying: "I am going to make a world not certain to be saved, a world the perfection of which shall be conditional merely, the condition being that each several agent does its own 'level best.' I offer you the chance of taking part in such a world. Its safety, you see, is unwarranted. It is a real adventure, with real danger, yet it may win through. . . . Will you trust yourself and trust the other agents enough to face the risk?"
>
> Should you in all seriousness, if participation in such a world were proposed to you, feel bound to reject it as not safe enough? . . .

Of course if you are normally constituted, you would do nothing of the sort. There is a healthy-minded buoyancy in most of us which such a universe would exactly fit. . . . It would be just like the world we practically live in; and loyalty to our old nurse Nature would forbid us to say no. (1907, 139–40)

If truth is final and fixed, what can you add to it? If omnipotent God fights on the side of goodness, then the triumph of goodness is inevitable—and the efforts of puny humans are irrelevant.

There is a remarkable poetic parallel to William James in the Islamic tradition; and perhaps it is not a coincidence that William James and Muhammad Iqbal were contemporaries. Iqbal (1877–1938)—a great poet as well as an outstanding philosopher—writes of "The Houri and the Poet," describing a poet who has arrived in eternal unchanging heavenly bliss, but who is dissatisfied and wishes to continue his quest:

My heart is restless,
Like the west wind in a field of tulips. . . .
In the spark I seek a star, in the star a sun;
I have no wish for a destination,
For if I stop I die.* (Iqbal 1990, 82)

The quest, even the uncertainty of the quest, is essential to free will. If one has found the final truth—as religions often claim—then change is a danger and novelty a threat: in the Catholic tradition, curiosity is a sin. But for white-footed mice, chimpanzees, and humans—who evolved in a changing challenging world—the exploration of new paths and possibilities is vital for survival, and its value is deeply ingrained. The fascinating arguments of Harry Frankfurt and Susan Wolf and John Fischer notwithstanding, open alternatives are a fundamental requirement of free will. This power of generating and pursuing open alternatives is not a product of human reason, nor is it C. A. Campbell's power of uniquely human contra-causal free will, nor is it (as in Pico Della Mirandola's account) a mysterious and miraculous gift from God to His last and favorite creation. It is instead a basic but valuable capacity that humans share with white-footed mice, polar bears, and even flies.

THE BASICS OF RESTORATIVE FREE WILL

The restorative model of free will starts by *restoring* free will to a wide variety of species (or more precisely, acknowledging the existence of free will

---

Tulip in the Desert, published by Iqbal Academy, Pakistan, 2000, is used by permission of Mustansir Mir, translator.

in those species), and then examines free will writ large in animal behavior. Many centuries ago, humans—a powerful, resourceful, and somewhat ruthless species—claimed exclusive rights to free will. This was the result of two trends: First, a remarkable arrogance that insisted on a super specialness for the human species; not just human uniqueness (since each species is unique) but a special sort of uniqueness that sets humans on one side of the animal kingdom and all other species on the other side, with a huge chasm between. The special power of reason seemed the best way of marking that divide, and that power of reason—the unique property of humans—seemed a good foundation for a special uniquely human capacity of free will. Second, after humans became deeply convinced—in our bones, if not in our conscious intellects—that the world is just, we needed a way to make punishment and reward, as well as different stations in life, appear just. Moral responsibility seemed to be the ticket, and as we came to believe that only humans could be morally responsible, free will (a uniquely human capacity) seemed a good candidate for the support of uniquely human moral responsibility. This view proved very convenient. Other species have neither free will nor moral responsibility, and thus they fall outside the sphere of moral consideration. And whenever cruelty to another group of humans became impossible to justify—the treatment of Native Americans, slaves, Vietnamese civilians during the Vietnam War—it was convenient to simply classify them as non-humans and consign them to the category in which questions of justice do not apply.

The goal of this book is to restore free will to its rightful owners, and break the human monopoly over free will. The cost is that humans must share something—something of great importance—to which we have long believed we held exclusive title. But there are benefits. By examining free will writ large in the needs and behavior of a wide variety of species, we gain a better understanding of free will, and begin to understand how the various elements of free will (which we had thought to be in irreconcilable conflict) actually fit together to form a richer picture of our shared animal free will. This broader examination reveals the value of both the alternatives and the authenticity perspectives, and how their value depends on their being allies rather than competitors—which is precisely the way animal free will functions.

This is not a *descriptive* account of how the folk or philosophers have understood free will; it is not a *revisionist* account of how we should understand free will in the light of advancing knowledge; rather, it is a *restorative* account of free will, that attempts to restore our understanding of free will to its basic elements, and strip away the accretions that have been added in a futile effort to make free will something that can support moral responsibility. The cumbersome and patched together notion of free will that is the result of these unfortunate additions not only fails to support moral responsibility, but also transmogrifies free will into something of little use for either man or beast.

By studying the roots of free will in the adaptive behavior shared by many species we can understand the real value of free will; and we can identify the distorting and stultifying attachments that must be eliminated if free will is to function well for humans (and other animals). This account will examine how the distortions came about, why they were added, and why they are impediments. Returning to the deeper roots of free will in widely shared animal behavior yields a clearer understanding of what human animals really want from free will. From that broader perspective, basic elements of free will that appeared to be in conflict are seen to be not only compatible but complementary. When we *restore* free will to its rightful owners and its rightful place we eliminate the distortions that have resulted from claiming free will as the exclusive property of humans.

Both philosophers and folk—with some exceptions—take it as obvious, almost axiomatic, that free will is the exclusive possession of humankind; so the fact that the restorative understanding of free will matches neither the folk nor any of the major philosophical views should not be a surprise. The test of restorative free will is not whether it fits either folk or philosophical assumptions, but whether the restorative model can provide a clearer and more comprehensive account of free will: an account that is a better fit with our naturalistic world view while incorporating the broadly recognizable features of free will.

Chapter 2

Human Uniqueness

Humans are unique. Of course every species is unique, but in the case of the human species that uniqueness sets humans radically apart: humans on one side, animals on the other. Humans occupy one category, and all the rest of the animal kingdom are in a distinctly different category. Between humans and all other animals, there is a vast chasm. Our myths emphasize human uniqueness: we are god's favorite creation, we are made in the image of God, we are ourselves godlike (we are partially gods), we have the potential to become gods, gods enter into sexual relations with humans and produce offspring, gods sometimes take human form. To class a human as an "animal" is the ultimate way of demeaning that individual. If there is a desire to treat another group of humans in an especially cruel manner, that cruelty is often justified by first transferring that group to the animal class.

Belief in human uniqueness is deep in our bones. It is the central element in the popular Hebraic creation myth. The Christian fundamentalists—in their fierce struggle against Darwinism—have directed attention away from the real meaning of the story. The point is not the process of creation: that is only the stage setting. Its relative insignificance can be seen from the fact that two creation stories are told, and the author can't be bothered to reconcile them—in one, God creates male and female humans simultaneously, while in the second the man is created first, is apparently lonely, and so God makes a "help meet for him" from one of Adam's ribs. The story is tangentially about creation, but it primarily concerns the special unique status of humans. The Hebraic creation myth "explains" why humans are not quite gods but are nonetheless very similar to gods: certainly more like gods than like any other Earthly creature:

And God said, Let us make man in our image, after our likeness, and let them have dominion over the fish of the sea, and over the fowl of the air, and over the cattle, and over all the earth, and over every creeping thing that creepeth upon the earth. So God created man in his own image, in the image of God created he him; male and female created he them. And God blessed them, and God said unto them, Be fruitful, and multiply, and replenish the earth, and subdue it; and have dominion over the fish of the sea, and over the fowl of the air, and over every living thing that moveth upon the earth. (Genesis 1:26-28)

Ordered by God not to eat of the tree of the knowledge of good and evil, humans can and do make their own choices, and defy God, and eat the fruit that gives them—like the gods—knowledge of good and evil. In the Garden of Eden story, the only difference between Adam and Eve and the gods that created them is that Adam and Eve did not also get their hands on the fruit of the tree of life, which would have made them immortal gods: "And the Lord God said, Behold, the man is become as one of us, to know good and evil: and now, lest he put forth his hand, and take also of the tree of life, and eat, and live for ever" (Genesis 3:22), man must be driven from the Garden and prevented from gaining access to the tree of life by "a flaming sword which turned every way, to keep the way of the tree of life" (Genesis 4:24).

This explains why humans—who are almost gods, and certainly godlike rather than beastlike—fall just short of being divine immortals. And in case the special godlike status of humans should be overlooked, there is an account of sexual relations between "the sons of God" and "the daughters of men," and their offspring are "giants in the earth" and "men of renown," suggesting that humans and the gods are so closely related—essentially the same species—that they can produce offspring:

And it came to pass, when men began to multiply on the face of the earth, and daughters were born unto them, that the sons of God saw the daughters of men that they were fair; and they took them wives of all which they chose. . . . There were giants in the earth in those days; and also after that, when the sons of God came in unto the daughters of men, and they bear children to them, the same became mighty men which were of old, men of renown. (Genesis 6:1-2, 4)

That marks the similarity of humans and gods as very close indeed. The creation of the earth and the heavens and "all that dwell therein" is merely a backdrop for the main point: humans are special, humans are unique, humans are godlike.

The special distinctness of humans is a theme that continues for millennia—indeed, to the present day. In the Renaissance, Pico wonders what is it that makes humans so special, and sets them apart, and he insists that:

> I have come to understand why man is the most fortunate of creatures and consequently worthy of all admiration and what precisely is that rank which is his lot in the universal chain of Being—a rank to be envied not only by brutes but even by the stars and by minds beyond this world. . . . Man is rightly called and judged a great miracle and a wonderful creature indeed. (1486/1948, 223)

The reason for humankind's remarkably special status (envied not only by the brutes but also by the angels) is that God grants to humans the uniquely human power of free choice:

> The nature of all other beings is limited and constrained within the bounds of laws prescribed by Us [God]. Thou, constrained by no limits, in accordance with thine own free will, in whose hand We have placed thee, shalt ordain for thyself the limits of thy nature. We have set thee at the world's center that thou mayest from thence more easily observe whatever is in the world. We have made thee neither of heaven nor of earth, neither mortal nor immortal, so that with free-dom of choice and with honor, as though the maker and molder of thyself, thou mayest fashion thyself in whatever shape thou shalt prefer. Thou shalt have the power to degenerate into the lower forms of life, which are brutish. Thou shalt have the power, out of thy soul's judgment, to be reborn into the higher forms, which are divine. (1486/1948, 224–5)

We have the power to become gods by our own choices and efforts; or sink into bestiality, down to the level of the despised animals. Only humans have this remarkable power of *choosing ourselves* and *making ourselves*—divine or bestial—by our own special power of thought and choice.

Pico's picture of the special powers of humans—powers that set us distinctly apart from the rest of the world—seems a rather extraordinary indulgence of Renaissance imagination; but in fact, Pico merely adds a fascinating story to a basic belief that persists (in philosophers and folk alike) to this day. Roderick Chisholm's story is not quite as colorful and imaginative as Pico's, but the moral of the story—humans have unique and amazing powers—is the same:

> If we are responsible, and if what I have been trying to say is true, then we have a prerogative which some would attribute only to God: each of us, when we really act, is a prime mover unmoved. In doing what we do, we cause certain events to happen, and nothing and no one, except we ourselves, causes us to cause those events to happen. (1982, 32)

Though Sartre (1946/1989) casts the distinction in secular form, he draws the same distinction that is dramatized in the Garden of Eden story: Humans, and only humans, are the special self-creating "being-for-itself," while all other animals are merely "being-in-itself."

Darwin's account of natural selection disturbed people on many levels. Not so much because it contradicted a literal reading of Scripture (though that still bothers Christian fundamentalists): After all, people had long since accepted the disturbing and heretical Copernican account, though it plainly contradicts Scripture (at the battle of Jericho, God makes the Sun stand still in the heavens, rather than making the Earth stop turning, so that the Israelites will have sufficient daytime to slay all their enemies). Part of the Darwinian disturbance, as Darwin himself recognized and as Stephen Jay Gould emphasizes (1977), is that the Darwinian view is materialist. But the biggest factor is that Darwin demolishes the cherished divide between humans and other animals: After Darwin all the other species belong to our family tree, and some are very close relatives indeed.

BREAKING THE UNIQUENESS BARRIER

Humans are unique. So are chimpanzees, canyon mice, and dung beetles. The differences that distinguish humans from other species, and the differences among the many distinct species, are a constant source of fascination and edification. Or rather, those differences are edifying until and unless human uniqueness becomes a justification for grossly exaggerating the differences and supposing that humans must have absolutely unique properties and must be studied in a totally different manner. We know this to be false. We study sensation seeking in bees, learning in rats, self-control in pigeons, emotions in monkeys, peace making in chimpanzees, and cooperative behavior in bonobos. But that inconvenient fact does not shake our visceral belief in human uniqueness.

The scientific discoveries that have been most troubling and most disputed have challenged our traditional belief that humans are unique and very special. Copernicus moved us off center stage, no longer the pivot point of the universe. Giordano Bruno and Galileo showed that our Sun is just one of many more Suns. Bruno went even further (and was burned at the stake for doing so): Each of the stars might be the center of its own solar system, and each might contain planets with their own special god-favored beings; and thus humans might not enjoy the unique status of being God's favorite creation. Darwin's evolutionary account knocked humans off our special separate pedestal, and established that humans have a variety of close relatives on the other side of the divide. Why such controversy over learning experiments—conducted by B. F. Skinner and other researchers—yielding parallel results between humans and nonhumans? Because they showed a fundamental similarity, rather than a vast divide, between the learning processes and behavioral causes in human and nonhuman animals. Humans respond to various schedules of reinforcement in patterns that mirror the results from studies of rats and mice and pigeons. Human slot machine players fervently press a lever or button to obtain rewards on a variable interval schedule of reinforcement: a schedule first discovered in studies of pigeon bar pressing.

Joseph Wood Krutch (1967) detested this scientific study of human and nonhuman behavior, arguing that the traditional human uniqueness view fits with Hamlet's evaluation of humankind, "How like a god!" In contrast, Krutch complained, the behavioral sciences look at humankind and conclude: "How like a dog." And Krutch was precisely right: Scientific research, from Darwin to Skinner to de Waal, has piece by piece eroded away the barrier between humans and nonhumans. Consider the intense and ongoing controversy over the question of language capability in species (such as chimpanzees) other than humans. It's an interesting question: because chimpanzees are very similar to humans but are somewhat limited in the range of sounds they can produce, might they be more adept at learning language if they used sign language instead? The question of whether chimpanzees actually learned language is one issue: they certainly learned many signs and sign combinations, taught them to others in their group, used them spontaneously, combined them in unique ways, and could use their signing to communicate concerning objects that were not present (Fouts 1997); but did they really develop a syntax? The second interesting question is why this line of research generated such remarkable hostility and controversy. That question has a relatively easy answer: language is one of the special capacities that supposedly sets humans radically apart from all other species, and a chimpanzee learning language would break down one of the last barriers protecting human uniqueness. As de Waal notes, "language research on apes has served to sharpen the definition of language, if only because of the desire of linguists to keep their domain free of hairy creatures" (1996, 111). And one effect was to make language even more complicated than it is, with an enormous range of rules that must be learned, and even a theory that must be tested (Waller 1977). This is an old philosophical trick: take something difficult, and make it impossible. And since humans have powers to achieve the impossible—through our godlike powers, if all else fails—that is a good way of keeping human powers uniquely human.

Use of tools and the possession and transmission of culture were two powers often celebrated for separating humans from our nonhuman relatives; the crumbling of those two barriers has been swift and decisive. Chimpanzees not only use a wide variety of tools, but also make and preserve them. Furthermore, the construction and use of such tools is a defining mark of distinctive chimpanzee *cultures*: the use of a specific tool is discovered within one culture, transmitted to other members of that culture, taught by adults to the young of that culture, and not found in other chimpanzee cultures existing in similar environments. As Christophe Boesch notes:

The chimpanzees in the Tai forest not only use tools but use them almost daily for a good part of the year. During a typical day . . . [they] use tools to access hard-to-reach insects. Even during the nut-cracking season, they use sponges [which they make from leaves] to drink water out of holes in tree trunks, prepare wands to dip for ants, fashion short, stout sticks to extract grubs from the nests of wood-boring bees, prepare different twigs to uncover grubs inserted under the bark in the wood of large dead tree trunks or to inspect holes and different cavities in the forest, make small sticks to get at bone marrow in their colobus monkey prey, and make long sticks to dip for honey in large beehives found in tree hollows. (Boesch 2012, 53)

In a field project to study chimpanzees in Loango National Park in Gabon, and following the lead of one of his students at the project, Boesch found an impressive variety of tools that chimpanzees prepared and used for securing honey from a bee nest (a nest protected by a very hard resin). There were larger branches used as pounders to open the nest, thinner sticks to break open chambers within the nest, sticks to extract the honey, as well as some sticks used both for breaking chambers and extraction. All of the sticks of various sizes—over one hundred in all—had been cut at both ends to make them a suitable length, and the side branches removed; while the extractors had brushed ends (Boesch 2012, 61–2).

Perhaps the most impressive tool use is fashioning a hammer for cracking nuts, developing the skill to crack the nuts with just the right force, and use of an "anvil" rock on which the nuts are placed for cracking and which is made flat by the use of stones placed beneath it. Chimpanzees not only make tools for specific purposes—different tools for cracking nuts—but they also save their tools for use in the future (Mucalhy and Call 2006), which indicates an impressive degree of planning for future events. In the case of a favored and well-crafted nut hammer, the chimpanzee may guard it carefully against theft. The hammer is, after all, an important tool: it must be taken from the right kind of tree, a limb must be found of the right shape and length and weight, and the limb must be carefully crafted. It's not designing a suspension bridge or planning an expedition to the North Pole, but it is planning and problem solving (including tool use). The extensive chimpanzee use of tools—and cultural influences on which tools are used—is no longer in doubt.

CHIMPANZEE CULTURES

Distinctive patterns of tool use among various chimpanzee groups is the most obvious and impressive type of cultural difference among nonhumans, but there are many others occurring in a variety of species. Among chimpan- zees, a comprehensive study among leading primatologists found 39 specific behavioral patterns that were culturally distinct and culturally transmitted

(Whiten et al. 2001), including ant-fishing (using a probe to extract ants), termite-fishing (in two different cultural forms), knuckle-knocks (and in other cultures, branch-slaps) to attract attention, a rain dance (a slow display at the start of rain), and use of a nut-hammer to break nuts. Some of these cultural practices were found in several cultures but never in all (similar environmental conditions notwithstanding), but each distinctive culture contained a variety of cultural practices. As noted by Andrew Whiten and Christophe Boesch, different chimpanzee cultures are unique and identifiable:

> Chimpanzees, though, do more than display singular cultural traits: each community exhibits an entire set of behaviors that differentiates it from other groups. As a result, we can talk about "Gombe culture" or "Tai culture." Indeed, once we observe how a chimpanzee behaves, we can identify where the animal lives. For instance, an individual that cracks nuts, leaf-clips during drumming displays, fishes for ants with one hand using short sticks, and knuckle-knocks to attract females clearly comes from the Tai Forest. A chimp that leaf-grooms and hand-clasps during grooming can come from the Kibale Forest or the Mahale Mountains, but if you notice that he also ant-fishes, there is no doubt anymore—he comes from Mahale.
>
> In addition, chimpanzee cultures go beyond the mere presence or absence of a particular behavior. For example, all chimpanzees dispatch parasites found during grooming a companion. But at Tai they will mash the parasites against their arms with a finger, at Gombe they squash them onto leaves, and at Budongo they put them on a leaf to inspect before eating or discarding them. Each community has developed a unique approach for accomplishing the same goal. (Whiten and Boesch 2001)

The distinctive cultural practices of chimpanzees have been the most extensively studied, but cultural practices have also been observed in other species. Wild vervet monkeys learn and transmit to other members of their cultural group distinct food preferences (De Waal, Borgeaud, and Whiten 2013). While culturally distinct vocal patterns have been recognized in humpback whales for some time (Noad et al. 2000, Garland et al. 2011), recent study of a particular method of "lobtail feeding"—in which a whale strikes the surface of the water several times with its fluke before proceeding to the more common bubble-feeding process—indicates that this specific manner of feeding was transmitted and sustained by members of a specific cultural group (Allen et al. 2013).

MAKING PLANS

It is sometimes suggested that only humans can make plans for the future. The fact that chimpanzees can craft tools for future use—and save them for subsequent use—makes it clear that there are animals other than humans that can formulate goals and make plans to accomplish those goals in the future. But there are many examples other than tool-making. As Frans de Waal notes:

> It is often thought that animals are captives of the here and now, but . . . planning is in fact well developed in the apes. Other examples include wild chimps collecting a bundle of tall grass stems, which they carry in their mouths for miles until they arrive at the termite hills where the stems serve as fishing tools. Similarly, zoo chimps may gather armfuls of straw from their night cage before going outside where it is cold. But the best-known case for planning is undoubtedly provided by Santino, a male chimp at a Swedish zoo. Every morning, before the visitors arrived, he'd leisurely collect rocks form the moat around his enclosure, stacking them up into neat little piles hidden from view. This way, he'd have an arsenal of weapons when the zoo opened its gates. Like so many male chimps, Santino would several times a day rush around with all his hair on end to intimidate the colony. Throwing stuff around would be part of the show, including projectiles aimed at the public. Whereas most chimps find themselves empty-handed at the critical moment, Santino had prepared his rock piles for this purpose. He had done so at a quiet moment, when he was not yet in the adrenaline-filled mood to produce his usual spectacle. (De Waal 2013, 205; Santino is described in Osvath 2009)

De Waal also describes his own observation of a chimpanzee going to an area with large stones, carefully selecting a large stone, and carrying the stone back to the group for use in a well-planned intimidation display against a rival:

> Research has taught us that chimpanzees have memories like the proverbial elephants and are capable of planning ahead; observation of their social life suggests that they use these capacities all the time. An adult male may spend minutes searching for the heaviest stone on his side of the island, far away from the rest of the group, weighing the stone in his hand each time he finds a potentially bigger one. He then carries the stone he has selected to the island's other side, where he begins—with all his hair on end—an intimidation display in front of his rival. Since stones serve as weapons (chimpanzees throw fairly accurately) we may assume that the male knew all along that he was going to challenge the other. This is the impression chimpanzees give in almost everything they do: they are thinking beings just as we are. (1989, 38–9)

De Waal (2001, 65) describes a particularly mischievous chimpanzee— Georgia—who lived at the Yerkes Primate Center where De Waal worked. When visitors arrived, Georgia would rush to the water spigot and collect a mouthful of water, then mix casually with the other chimpanzees while holding the water in her mouth (sometimes for several minutes). Georgia did nothing to betray her intention (as de Waal notes, "not even the sharpest observer will notice anything unusual")—she was a practiced deceiver—until the visitors came within range, at which time she would spray the visitors with water, which she and the other chimpanzees found hilarious.

The power of purposeful deception has also been suggested as a uniquely human capacity. Georgia's casual and "innocent" approach to visitors, with the purpose of spewing them with water, shows that being purposefully deceptive is not a talent confined to humans. But deception, and efforts at deception, are not confined to chimpanzee practical jokers. When Puist (another chimpanzee observed by de Waal) practices deception, the purpose is deadly serious:

> If Puist is unable to get a hold of her opponent during a fight, we may see her walk slowly up to her and then attack unexpectedly. She may also invite her opponent to reconciliation in the customary way. She holds out her hand and when the other hesitantly puts her hand in Puist's, she suddenly grabs hold of her. This has been seen repeatedly and creates the impression of a deliberate attempt to feign good intentions in order to square accounts. (De Waal 1982, 55)

A CHIMPANZEE THEORY OF MIND

Chimpanzees can create and use tools, act purposefully, plan their acts (whether making the right tool for an intended job of nut cracking or planning an intimidation display or planning a "practical joke" on visitors), and develop and transmit cultural practices. They can act with careful plans and powerful intentions; but can they recognize the intentions of others? Can they recognize that others *have* intentions, and take those intentions into account in planning their own activities? Or as this question has typically been framed: Do chimpanzees have a *theory of mind*? Can they attribute intentions to others? Can they distinguish purposeful from accidental behavior in others? Do they have the necessary categories and sophistication to draw such a distinction?

Do chimpanzees have a theory of mind? This question was posed to primatologists in a famous paper that was published almost 40 years ago, by Premack and Woodruff (1978). As several primatologists recently stated (in a striking understatement): "As for Premack and Woodruff's original question about chimpanzees, there has been controversy from the beginning" (Kaminski, Call, and Tomasello 2008, 224). The answer that was given by most primatologists—and of course, by almost everyone outside of primatology—was decisively negative. But primatologists are perhaps more willing to change their views than are philosophers. Taking account of new observational and experimental studies, many primatologists who had initially rejected the chimpanzee "theory of mind" changed their own minds. Michael Tomasello is clear concerning his own changed conclusion:

> Since 1994, we have learned much more about chimpanzee social learning and the cognitive skills that underlie it, mostly from laboratory experiments. . . . Importantly, my particular hypothesis from 1994—that chimpanzees do not engage in true imitative learning because they do not analyze behavior in terms of its goals as differentiated from its behavioral means—has been proved false. A number of studies now have documented that chimpanzees do understand the actions of others in terms of goals; specifically, they differentiate intended from accidental actions that both produce the same external result, and they differentiate trying (and failing) to transform an object from acting on it in similar nontrying ways. (Call and Tomasello 1998; Call et al. 2004; Tomasello 2009, 215–16)

Earlier studies on chimpanzee knowledge of the intentions of others yielded mixed results; but those studies placed chimpanzees in very artificial surroundings, often testing whether a chimpanzee would attribute knowledge or intentions to *human* experimenters in cases requiring cooperation between chimpanzee and human. As Christophe Boesch notes:

> Until recently, all studies about theory of mind, mind reading, or the understanding of others in chimpanzees have been done with humans performing the role of the "social partner." . . . A lot of time, money, and energy have been invested in exploring chimpanzees' understanding of humans and what in the human face, eyes, attitude, and posture is most important for this ability. (2012, 211n47)

When experimenters turned to conditions in which chimpanzees were *competing* with other *chimpanzees* for desirable treats, the results were much more positive. As Brian Hare, Josep Call, and Michael Tomasello note, when testing cognitive powers it is essential to consider the settings in which those powers are likely to function best (which will of course vary from species to species):

> Evolutionary theories of primate cognition stress the fact that primates exist within a complex social field and must constantly find new ways to compete against other individuals intent on reaching their own goals. . . . It is therefore likely that primate social-cognitive abilities evolved to a large degree to allow individuals to outcompete competitors, and so it is in these kinds of settings that we are most likely to see these abilities expressed. . . . In attempting to design ecologically valid experiments of primate cognition and social cognition, therefore, researchers must always take into account not only their current behavioural skills and propensities but also the functional contexts within which their cognitive abilities have most likely evolved. (Hare, Call, and Tomasello 2001, 149–50)

The question is not whether chimpanzees practice deception: that question has long been settled. Rather, the question is whether such behavior indicates that chimpanzees have a "theory of mind." And the question is not whether it is beneficial to take an intentional and cognitive stance toward chimpanzees and their behavior: clearly it is. The question is whether chimpanzees can themselves adopt such a perspective, and that seems quite likely. That is, do chimpanzees (and some other primate species) employ a "folk psychology" similar to that used by humans, in which they base expectations concerning the behavior of others on beliefs about their intentions, what the others do or do not know, perhaps even their deceitfulness. Andrew Whiten thinks "theory of mind" sounds "rather grandiose" (Whiten 2013, 214) and suggests that "mentalism" and "natural psychology" might be less tendentious; but as he notes, "theory of mind" has become the standard phrase.

Extensive research and observation indicate that chimpanzees are quite capable of attributing intentions, knowledge, and *lack* of specific knowledge to other chimpanzees (as well as to humans), and can distinguish between intentional acts and accidental nonpurposeful behavior. In a study in which chimpanzees interacted with a human experimenter (as noted above, not the optimum experimental situation) there was evidence that chimpanzees are quite capable of understanding and interpreting intentions:

> The current study provides suggestive evidence that chimpanzees spontaneously (i.e. without training) are sensitive to others' intentions. Observing the behavior of a human not giving them food, chimpanzees demonstrated in their spontaneous behavior that they recognized a difference between cases in which he was not giving food because he was unwilling to or because, for various reasons, he was unable to. Chimpanzees thus did not just perceive others' behavior, they also interpreted it. (Call et al. 2004, 496)

A series of experiments by Brian Hare, Josep Call, Michael Tomasello, and others have shown that chimpanzees can understand what others (particularly chimpanzee competitors) know and do not know, and that they can use that knowledge to their own benefit in successfully competing for food (Hare, Call, and Tomasello 2000, 2001, 2006; Kaminski, Call, and Tomasello 2008). Others (Brauer et al. 2007) have replicated these experimental investigations with similar findings. Andrew Whiten recently described the results of this improved method of studying chimpanzee social cognition:

> In summary, the new approach of investigating such aspects of social cognition in the context of the kinds of competition between conspecifics that are likely to be more akin to the "environment of evolutionary adaptedness" that would have shaped such social cognition paid off. Chimpanzees, who had appeared

surprisingly "dumb" in not discriminating the significance of a potential human helper having a bucket over their head rather than at their side, were now experimentally confirmed as rather sophisticated in their social cognition concerning what others may be able to see and subsequently remember, consistent with the earlier evidence based on nonintervening direct observations of wild and captive primates. (Whiten 2013, 216)

UNIQUELY HUMAN FREE WILL

Why does our species have the powerful desire to believe that we are a uniquely special species? Perhaps it is related to the desire to suppose that our group—our country, our people, our team—is uniquely wonderful: that we are God's chosen people, or that God ordained us to rule the world, or that we have a right to slaughter or enslave all who are not of our ethnic group, or that our religion is the only true religion. In any case, that's a question for anthropologists; the present point is only that it *is* a strong desire, and a deep belief: Our species is the only one made in the likeness of God, our species was the one specially chosen by God to exercise dominion over all others; or in later times, our species is the pinnacle of evolution, the "highest" species, the species God guided evolution to achieve. Aristotle was too wise to claim that we are made in God's image, or that a creator god looks on us with special favor; but Aristotle nonetheless assumed that the human species is special and unique, and attempted to determine why and in what way.

Of course, humans *are* unique—like all species. But the problem with stressing human uniqueness is that the distinguishing characteristics are exaggerated, and spurious claims of additional unique characteristics are added. Though other species have impressive cognitive powers—they can make careful plans, practice purposeful deception, forge alliances, make tools, create and perpetuate cultures—humans have the most developed powers of linear reasoning. The problem is not in the claim that humans have rational powers: we do. And we have developed those powers in unique directions, enabling us to develop higher order reflection, consciously follow rules, and make remarkably extended plans. But we share most of our cognitive abilities with other species. Those shared cognitive capacities function quite well, but they do not set us radically apart; and those cognitive powers that are genuinely distinctive are quite limited, and not nearly as amazing as we like to suppose.

Even among philosophers—most of whom are atheists, almost all of whom accept evolution and acknowledge that we are closely related to other species—the commitment to the special distinctive nature of humans often survives. One clear manifestation of that commitment can be found in the philosophical devotion to human moral responsibility. Herbert Morris bases his case for moral responsibility and punishment on the importance of maintaining a special distinctive category exclusively for humans:

> When we talk of not treating a human being as a person or "showing no respect for one as a person," what we imply by our words is a contrast between the manner in which one acceptably responds to human beings and the manner in which one acceptably responds to animals and inanimate objects. (1968, 490)

In the final paragraph of *Who Knew? Responsibility Without Awareness*, George Sher defends his account of moral responsibility against the charge that it is overly complex, and his defense is based on the special distinctive nature of humans:

> What unifies the account's different elements is precisely that they *do* mirror the complexity of the beings to whom the concept of responsibility applies. Because those beings—that is, we ourselves—are at once inhabitants of the natural world and possessed of features that set them apart from it, we may naturally expect them to fall under concepts that reflect this complexity. Moreover, because the features that set us apart from (at least most of) the natural world include both our occupying a perspective from which we deliberate and our acting on the basis of reasons, it is only to be expected that some of these mixed concepts will apply to us in our capacity as agents. (Sher 2009, 154)

John Martin Fischer, in discussing his compatibilist view and why he would *not* alter his basic position if he became convinced that determinism is true, writes:

> I feel confident that this would not, nor should it, change my view of myself and others as (sometimes) free and robustly morally responsible agents—deeply different from other animals. (2007, 44)

Roy F. Baumeister has made remarkable contributions to our understanding of human behavior, including our understanding of free will (his work on ego depletion is one outstanding example). But he is deeply wedded to the belief that "free will is a distinctively human trait," and therefore "its explanation must be sought among the developments specific to human evolution" (2014, 243). Thus he focuses on the special development of complex human cultures, and the traits that enable humans to fashion such cultures and flourish in them, and particularly the distinctive rule-following and deeply deliberative processes in human behavior. Baumeister makes no secret of his underlying motives; to the contrary, he expresses them eloquently:

Being able to act in ways that transcend physical causation and natural law would undeniably violate some forms of determinism (i.e., those that insist on causation by purely physical and natural factors) and thus constitute freedom of an important sort. This is also congenial, I think, to lay conceptions of free will as freedom from the natural and animal processes of action, so that one can act as a civilized human being in the sense of being something more than an animal. The something more is the nonnatural but cultural phenomenon of culturally transmitted meaning. (Baumeister 2014, 253)

Here is the ancient desire to "transcend physical causation and natural law" and be "something more than an animal": A desire that animated the writers of the Hebrew sacred texts in which the gods shape humans as special and separate beings made in the image of God, motivated Aristotle's commitment to live a godlike life, inspired Pico della Mirandola's account of the special and unique human power of self-creation, and drove Kant to a model of ethical behavior untainted by animal emotion. But it is a motive that creates gods and miracles, distorts the powers of reason and disparages the vital elements of our social and emotional and ethical lives that we share with other species, and blocks us from understanding the deeper roots and adaptive nature of free will.

Because Baumeister focuses narrowly on what is special and unique about *human* free will, he cannot see the larger picture of free will and how human free will fits into that picture. One result of that narrowed vision can be seen in an earlier paper by Baumeister and colleagues, in which they made a claim Baumeister now acknowledges as a mistake. That paper shared the human uniqueness view that continues in Baumeister's present work: "the distinctively human traits evolved as adaptations for the uniquely human forms of social life" (Baumeister, Crescioni, and Alquist 2011, 2), and in particular for the complex life of human culture. One unfortunate effect of this narrow focus is that they could not fully appreciate the importance of variable (and apparently random) behavior in animals (including humans and white-footed mice and many other species):

Our view is that random action is the bugaboo of the free will debate. We regard it as an unfortunate and misleading case, though we cannot deny that it does correspond to some widely held perceptions of what a free action might be. Our skepticism is based on our assumptions about why free will might have evolved in the first case. (Baumeister, Crescioni, and Alquist 2011, 4)

The "assumptions about why free will might have evolved in the first case" are of course assumptions about how free will evolved *exclusively* in humans to facilitate life in complex human cultures with elaborate rules. But that assumption led Baumeister to misunderstand and fail to appreciate the benefits of variable behavior for foraging animals: benefits for humans living in complex cultures, for humans in very crude cultures, for chimpanzees in relatively simple cultures, and for many species that live without cultures. As Baumeister acknowledges:

> However, some recent works have prompted me to reconsider the notion of a random action generator. It is probably not the main form of free will and may be much older than humankind, but on biological grounds one can make a case that a bit of randomness in behavior would be adaptive. It may have been an early precursor of human free will, and there may be some remnants of that earlier structure still evident in human action. (Baumeister 2014, 246–7)

This reconsideration shows the admirable honesty of Baumeister and his willingness to change his views in light of counter evidence; but it is a rather grudging reconsideration, which refuses to reconsider the deeper problem in his overly narrow account of free will. Since this element of free will "may be much older than humankind," it cannot be "the main form of free will," but is at best "an early precursor of human free will" which leaves only inconsequential "remnants of that earlier structure still evident in human action." Thus any element of free will that is shared with animals other than humans can only be a "precursor" and not a vital element of real free will—because real free will, after all, must be exclusively human. And the special free will that is adaptive exclusively for humans is a rational rule-following free will, not one that seeks open alternatives that are often less than rationally optimum:

> What is adaptive in a cultural context is rational, meaningful action that coordinates the individual's long-term (enlightened) self-interest and current actions with the rules, values, and practices of the social group. Moral behavior is a fine example of this; random, arbitrary behavior is not. (Baumeister 2014, 246)

The variable behavior of humans, white-footed mice, and many other foraging species is neither random nor arbitrary; it is a highly adaptive trait, which adjusts to different conditions (greater variability when food resources are scarcer, for example). The importance of having choices, and control over those choices—and the opportunity to make what are sometimes apparently less than optimum choices and choices that do not "follow the rules"—is a profoundly valuable and deeply entrenched capacity, and a central element of free will for a wide variety of species. Rule-following and deliberative rationality are wonderful *enhancements* of human free will; but if we want to understand the full rich nature of free will, it is better to study the central elements of free will that made free will adaptive long before humans existed, and that human free will shares with the rich exploratory behavior of other animals. If instead the goal is to find an account of free will that makes it a special capacity of humans—a capacity that can transcend natural causes and set humans wonderfully apart from all other animals—then a much narrower and shallower focus will prove more useful. We can, if we insist, make free will something unique to humans; but in doing so we cut ourselves off from a better and larger understanding of free will and how it works and why it evolved.

THE COSTS OF TREATING FREE WILL AS UNIQUELY HUMAN

The focus on finding distinctive and unique *differences* between humans and other species has had damaging effects. First, it has made us cling more doggedly to belief in moral responsibility, as the ultimate difference maker, even as that belief becomes ever more implausible: we *know* we are morally responsible, and that is more obvious than any argument that can be brought against it. Second, it has distorted—and sometimes apotheosized—our reasoning capacities and our will power, encouraging an exaggerated view of how they work as well as of their limits and their function. And finally, because free will is the uniquely human capacity that supports uniquely human moral responsibility, our understanding of free will has been severely limited by the conviction that it must be studied only in humans. As a result, free will is not grounded in a solid empirical understanding, and that has led to implausible—and sometimes rather spectacular—free will accounts. When unrestrained by empirical connections with animal behavior, and pushed to extremes by belief in human uniqueness (which free will exemplifies) and moral responsibility (which free will must support) our accounts of free will have ranged from the inadequate to the miraculous.

What are the factors that generate these free will accounts? Human uniqueness is first and foremost, and it is based on special rational powers (though first it is justified by humans being God's favorite; only when this is no longer plausible do we find a substitute in our special power of rationality). Then at some point—when we start to ask "why do the wicked prosper?" and we assume that Job *must* have done something wrong to justify his cruel treatment by God—we get belief in a just world. Now we must *justify* punishment, and bad luck or fate is not a justification. For the Greeks, the world is *not* just, as Bernard Williams (1993) notes; the gods *are* arbitrary, injustice happens, tough luck. But it is difficult to live with that, especially with the cognitive dissonance generated when God or God's human authorities (who are obviously good and just, including ourselves) inflict punishment that is unjust and undeserved. Martin Luther's faith is strong enough to handle God's apparent injustice, but few have sufficient faith to reject their basic belief in a just world. If God is fundamentally unjust—and he certainly *appears* to be, even to Luther—we would be better off with no god at all: better disorder than a fundamentally unjust order; better chaos than a cruel and unjust tyrant with super powers. So as part of the Christian legacy—which is much less rationalistic than the Hellenistic tradition—we turn to *willpower*, and special free *choice*. Free will is not a matter of rationality, but of radical godlike choice: we are made in the image of God, and our power of free choice is a good candidate for the likeness. It is this power of free will that makes us morally responsible, and justifies punishment and reward: they are our *just* deserts. Humans are unique, we have the unique power of free will, and we are uniquely morally responsible. Out of this dual delusion—belief in human uniqueness combined with the need to fit punishment and reward into a *just* world—emerged moral responsibility, which free will was condemned to carry.

Of course most philosophers have little sympathy with the Pelagian heresy, or with the notion of free will as a special miraculous power. That is not because philosophers are concerned with a return to Christian orthodoxy, but rather because most contemporary philosophers reject miracles of all varieties, whether performed by deities or demigods or mortals. But while contemporary philosophers renounce miraculous powers, they retain belief in what the miraculous powers were designed to justify: belief in human uniqueness and uniquely human free will and exclusively human moral responsibility.

Compatibilist philosophers have made valiant efforts to provide nonmiraculous naturalistic justifications for those beliefs. Whatever one thinks of the success or failure of those efforts, it is clear that they face a remarkably difficult challenge. Start with a system built on godlike human uniqueness, a manifestly false belief in a just world, and a miracle-working power of free will; then try to make that system work in a purely naturalistic nonmiraculous world: that is a challenge indeed. Nietzsche thought we must become gods ourselves to accomplish it. That's not much of a solution, but at least Nietzsche recognized the enormity of the problem: it is difficult to sustain a system built on deities and miracles, godlike human uniqueness, and the inherent justice of the cosmos when its entire foundation is destroyed.

Humans are indeed unique: as are all distinctive species. But while it might make sense for Pico della Mirandola—centuries before Darwin—to celebrate the special uniqueness of humans that derives from being "God's favorite creation" or the only species "made in the image of God," it is strange to find scientifically knowledgeable post-Darwinian philosophers still insisting on a bright line between humans and all other species. Of course humans do have some special capacities: we have a capacity for language which (if not unique) is at least distinctly different from that found in other species; we excel at linear reasoning; we have developed cultures of enormous complexity; as E. O.

Wilson notes (2012) we are practically the only mammal—other than the naked mole rat—that is eusocial. But—setting aside claims of being God's favorite creation, or being made in God's image, or having miraculous powers of self-creation—humans are not nearly "as unique" as we have wished to suppose. Humans are unique, because we are the only species that uses tools; but other species not only use a wide variety of tools, they are also accomplished as tool makers. Humans are unique, because only humans have cultures; but we now know of a rich variety of nonhuman cultures, especially in chimpanzees. Humans are the only animals that make and carry out plans; but chimpanzees carry out quite elaborate plans. Humans are the only animals that practice self-control; but studies of effective self-control in other species are now commonplace. Only humans practice purposeful deception; but instances of purposeful deceptive behavior in other species (including purposeful deception that effectively deceives humans) are common and compelling. Perhaps moral responsibility would be good grounds for human uniqueness—but it belongs with the gods and miracles. Free will—which has long been one of the special uniquely human capacities—has been freed from theological and miraculous constraints by the splendid efforts of generations of compatibilists (aided and abetted by at least some libertarians, such as Robert Kane and David Shoemaker); but free will has remained locked in the assumptions of human uniqueness, which has limited study of free will to human behavior, and has blinded us to the rich resources for study of free will in other species.

The essential elements of free will—purposeful choice, need for open alternatives, the fundamental importance of exercising control—are found in the free will behavior of many species. As we liberate free will from the gods and miracles, and separate free will from the impossible burden of moral responsibility, and we treat free will as a fully natural and nonmiraculous and valuable element of our animal lives, then we can better understand free will writ large in the behavior of many species and in the evolutionary development of human free will; and we can better understand the special human enhancements of free will by placing them in the larger context of the basic free will we share with other animals.

Why such reluctance to study free will in other animals, and thus enhance our understanding of free will in humans? Part of the reason is the interest in maintaining a special human uniqueness. And of course humans are unique—as are chimpanzees and bonobos and white-footed mice. Furthermore, that humans have remarkable cultures and impressive cognitive capacities is not in question. Chimpanzees have not dispatched their primatologists to make a study of their human cousins; nor have they been troubled by the problem of evil, created massive cities in which strangers generally live together with some degree of cooperation, devised ways to survive and prosper in Arctic cold and Saharan heat, invented calculus, or pondered the problem of free will. Humans and human societies are different: viva la difference. But they are also similar in many ways, and sufficiently similar that behavior we would have no trouble calling acts of free will (as well as ethical or unethical acts) had they been performed by humans are also present in the behavior of other species.

We study learning in other species; we study self-control in other species; we study depression in other species; we study variable behavior in other species; we study decision making in other species; we study social relations in other species; we study need for control in other species. We study reasoning processes and problem solving by observing other species (such as crows and chimpanzees). Why would we suppose that only in the area of free will we can learn nothing from other species? If free will is the unique property of humans, then it may well be true that the study of free will must be confined to humans. But if it turns out that our understanding of free will can be enhanced by studying the behavior of other species—and that is the claim made in the following chapters—that is reason to think that free will is not exclusively human. If free will is exclusively human, then there is nothing to be learned about free will from the study of other species; but there is in fact a great deal to be learned about free will from the study of other species; therefore free will is not exclusively human. Of course one person's *modus tollens* is another person's *modus ponens*; but in this case, the *modus tollens* version has the added virtue of being sound.

Chapter 3

Uniquely Human Reason

Once the uniqueness step is taken, the next question is obvious: *What is it* that makes humans specially unique? One answer was readily available and rather pleasing, though its limits soon became clear: We are special because God chose *us*. God bestowing special favors on a particular species makes God seem rather like an eccentric uncle who plays favorites among his nieces and nephews. In any case why humans, rather than cheetahs or peacocks or nightingales or blue whales? Or perhaps beetles, the immense variety and splendor of which might well imply that beetles were among God's favorites.

Once beyond the easy but unsatisfactory answer—humans are special because God likes us best—where do we turn for a justification of special human uniqueness? Certainly not to strength, speed, or agility; size and beauty are just as implausible; on affectionate cooperativeness, we run a poor race with bonobos; on loyalty, dogs dominate. So when Aristotle seeks grounds for the view that humans are special, intelligence seems the only likely candidate. And indeed, humans do rate quite high on some important measures of intelligence. The problem is that once we make intelligence the special property that separates us from the rest of the world, our view of human intelligence becomes exaggerated and distorted: exaggerated, as human intelligence must now be radically different from the intelligence of all other animals; and distorted, as the elements of intelligence we share with other animals are ignored or disparaged.

If reason is to be the grounds of human uniqueness, human reason has to be the special deliberative power we do not share with other animals (or that we manifest in a uniquely impressive form). Humans are superb at *sequential* thinking: the important step-by-step thinking involved in developing an argument or working out a mathematical proof. We also engage in *simultaneous* thinking, which involves recognizing and integrating a wide range of simultaneous inputs. We are good at simultaneous thinking, though probably not quite as good as chimpanzees; but we have no equal in sequential thinking (though chimpanzees have substantial sequential thinking abilities). Roger Fouts, the psychologist and primatologist who was the primary sign-language teacher and care giver for Washoe, writes that:

> There is no bold line distinguishing chimpanzee intelligence from human intelligence. Each of them blends simultaneous and sequential thinking in distinctive proportions. . . . Humans and chimpanzees differ in their intelligence by degree, not in the *kind* of mental process. Chimps are not as "intelligent" as humans when it comes to sequential thinking. It is unlikely that a chimpanzee could ever use American Sign Language with the full syntax—the complex sequential patterns—of a deaf, signing human adult. But a chimpanzee can learn enough signs to communicate sequentially to a surprising degree. Similarly, we are not as "intelligent" as chimpanzees when it comes to simultaneous thinking. It is unlikely that a human could ever read nonverbal signals to the same extent as a chimpanzee. . . .
>
> Saying that human intelligence is superior to chimpanzee intelligence is like saying that our way of walking on two feet is better than their quadrupedal method. Chimpanzees spend their entire lives in small intimate groups. Their simultaneous intelligence is perfectly suited to their social environment. They don't need a heavily sequential language, much less a global electronic network. (Fouts 1997, 350–1)

Fouts' view matches the conclusion drawn by Frans de Waal on the basis of his many years of systematic observation of chimpanzees:

> Pretense during play or among political rivals [a pretense commonly practiced by chimpanzees] is one reason I have trouble with the theory of animals as blind actors. Instead of being genetically programmed when to limp or when to laugh, apes are acutely aware of the social environment. Like humans, they ponder many options in front of them and decide what to do dependent on the circumstances. In the laboratory, apes are usually tested on abstract problems, such as finding rewards pointed out by experimenters or seeing the difference among four, five, or six items (a capacity known as "numerosity"). If they fail, as they sometimes do, the conclusion is often that we're smarter than they are. In the social domain, however, in which apes deal with those they've known all their life, they give the impression of being about as intelligent as we are. (De Waal 2005, 223)

That is, when dealing with problems requiring sequential linear reasoning, most chimpanzees are not as skillful as most humans; but when simultaneous thinking is required (in small group settings), chimpanzees "give the impression of being about as intelligent as we are."

Given our superiority in sequential linear thinking, and the strong competition for leadership in simultaneous thinking, it is not surprising that humans—seeking grounds for special human uniqueness—treated sequential thinking as the most sublime power and the only form of cognition worthy of being called reason. Add to that the fact that the ones doing the ranking—such as Aristotle and Kant—are humans particularly skilled at sequential thinking, and it is not surprising that sequential thinking is treated as the glorious and distinctive capacity of the uniquely superior human species.

Since humans have particularly strong sequential reasoning powers, it must be those special rational powers that set humans apart from all other species. But the conviction that human rational powers are the distinguishing special mark of the human species leads to a special problem: it is not enough that humans be *more* rational, or *better* at sequential reasoning, than are other species; if there is to be a radical break between humans and *all* other animals, then humans must have a *monopoly* over rational powers. There is not a difference in degree between humans and other animals, but a difference in kind. Cheetahs are faster than gazelles, but gazelles are still fast; gorillas are stronger than chimpanzees, but chimpanzees are quite strong; grizzly bears have a remarkable sense of smell, but wolves are also good scent detectors. But cheetahs and gazelles, gorillas and chimpanzees, grizzlies and wolves are all grouped on the *animal* side, and differences among animals are differences in degree. Bodily, humans can be compared with other animals: we are not as fast as cheetahs, but significantly faster than armadillos; we climb better than wolves do, but not nearly so well as monkeys. But when it comes to the quality of reason—the quality that sets us *apart* from all other animals—there must be a barrier that precludes comparisons: we are not *more* rational than rats and cats and chimpanzees; rather, we are rational, and they are *not*.

Certainly there *are* reflective powers that only humans employ. Only humans read books, engage in philosophical analysis and dispute, run controlled scientific experiments, argue about the nature of free will, study calculus, and contrive cosmologies. This is obvious, but it may be helpful to ·belabor the obvious, in order to avoid confusion. Nothing in this book suggests that humans are not unique (as are all distinct species, of course); and nothing in this book claims that humans do not have some unique rational abilities. But the differences between humans and other animals should not be exaggerated, and when we make the power of reason the dividing line between humans and all other species, we both aggrandize human reason and disparage the cognitive capacities of other species; and above all, we are tempted to ignore the *common* cognitive powers shared by humans and other species.

Since the special and unique power of human reason is what distinguishes humans from the brutes, when we are seeking to understand *free will*—a power belonging, we immediately assume, uniquely and exclusively to humans—it is natural to connect uniquely human free will with our unique power of reason. That is precisely what happened; at least, that is what Michael Frede says happened in his superb study: *A Free Will: Origins of the Notion in Ancient Thought*. Frede contends that in the ancient Stoics, particularly in the work of Epictetus, "we have our first actual notion of a free will" (Frede 2011, 77). On Frede's interpretation of Epictetus and the Stoic view of free will, our free will is "of the kind that he [God] himself has" (Frede 2011, 77). For the Stoics, only the wise are free, and "freedom, like wisdom and virtue, does not admit of degrees": freedom for the Stoics is all or nothing, such that "if you admit just one inappropriate attachment, you have lost your freedom" (Frede 2011, 75). So freedom demands perfect and unfaltering rationality: true freedom requires infallible tracking of the path of wisdom, and obviously no nonhumans (and precious few humans) actually have free will.

This identification of free will with extraordinary—exclusively human, and perhaps even superhuman—rational powers has a long and impressive history, as well as some worthy contemporary champions. While few contemporary defenders of rationalist free will go quite so far as the Stoics in allowing freedom only to the flawlessly wise—Frede notes that one of the major criticisms of Stoic free will was that on their view "only one or two people have ever been wise and free" (Frede 2011, 96)—various versions of rationalist free will have been proposed by (for example) Susan Wolf (1990), Dana Nelkin (2011), Gerald Dworkin (1988), and of course by Immanuel Kant. While not all these views require super rationality there is a strong tendency to insist that only the genuinely wise and purely rational decision can be free. For example, Susan Wolf (1990) claims that one is free only when one's decisions and acts track the True and the Good, and any deviations from that straight and narrow path mean a forfeiture of freedom. Kant, of course, held that free acts must be the result of rational derivation of true principles with no influence from the emotions in either deriving or following such principles.

Linking free will with rationality runs into a number of difficulties. First and most basic, the logic of the position drives it toward a requirement of perfect rationality, as the Stoics recognized and as Susan Wolf (1980) demonstrates. To act freely is to act with understanding, with knowledge, with accurate assessment; in short, to act with genuine free will requires that we act with perfect wisdom. Thus a free act is always and only the act that follows the true path for the right reason, the act that wisely and with full understanding tracks the True and Good.

If informed rationality is to be the basis of free will, then it is difficult to stop short of perfect rationality. If we act in ignorance, or we base an act on flawed reasoning, that hardly seems like a *free* act. If during a stay at Bryce Canyon Lodge I choose to take an evening stroll—recognizing that it will improve my concentration and be good for my heart and provide innocent starlit pleasure—that is a free act; but if in my ignorance of the paths I take a wrong turn and plunge over a steep cliff while admiring the Milky Way, that is not a free act; and if I knowingly but irrationally choose to step off the cliff, believing that my arms will function as wings and allow me to soar across the canyon, that act—my last—will not be free. If I know that the right and good act is to finish the promised book review, but my obsession with video games overwhelms my reason, then I am not acting freely. Thus genuine free acts require that we act knowingly and rationally. As Susan Wolf states: "We can state the condition of freedom and responsibility more directly by referring outright to the ability to act in accordance with (and on the basis of) the True and the Good" (1990, 73). When one fails to act "in accordance with (and on the basis of) the True and the Good," that is because one is *lacking* in intelligence or willpower or understanding; that is, failure to track the True and the Good means that one is not acting freely, that one has flaws that impede or destroy genuine free will.

HUMAN RATIONALITY: NOT WHAT WE THOUGHT IT WAS

Rationalist free will carries within it a tendency toward rational perfection, as seen in the Stoics and Susan Wolf. But once we make uniquely human reason the basis for uniquely human exercise of free will, then linear sequential reason (the type of reason in which human powers are most distinctive) must dominate (rather than other cognitive processes, such as simultaneous reasoning); it must be transparent, and open to our observed decision-making; and it must be in control (rather than being under the control of nonconscious cognitive or emotional powers, or under the control of situational and environmental influences of which we are unaware). All three conditions seem to be met; in fact, none of them are.

First, our deliberative linear thinking does not dominate our cognitive processes; to the contrary, as Jonathan Haidt notes, it is generally subordinate to other cognitive processes, and that is quite beneficial:

Automatic processes run the human mind, just as they have been running animal minds for 500 million years, so they're very good at what they do, like software that has been improved through thousands of product cycles. When human beings evolved the capacity for language and reasoning at some point in the last million years, the brain did not rewire itself to hand over the reins to a new and inexperienced charioteer. Rather, the rider (language-based reasoning) evolved because it did something useful for the elephant.

The rider can do several useful things. It can see further into the future (because we can examine alternative scenarios in our heads) and therefore can help the elephant make better decisions in the present. It can learn new skills and master new technologies, which can help the elephant reach its goals and sidestep disasters. And, most important, the rider acts as the spokesman for the elephant, even though it doesn't necessarily know what the elephant is really thinking. The rider is skilled at fabricating post hoc explanations for whatever the elephant has just done, and it is good at finding reasons to justify what the elephant wants to do next. Once human beings developed language and began to use it to gossip about each other, it became extremely valuable for elephants to carry on their backs a full-time public relations firm. (2012, 45–6)

But the "full-time public relations firm" is a subordinate, rather than CEO. Our deliberative sequential thinking is rarely in charge, but instead provides rationalizations for decisions made without our conscious deliberative control. Haidt has run a series of experiments in which subjects are placed in a position in which all their good *reasons* for reaching a conclusion are no longer relevant, but the conclusion is nonetheless one to which they are deeply committed. In such cases, subjects continue to seek reasons for their conclusion, and continue to insist their conclusion is correct, even when all the reasons they could offer in its support fail. As Haidt notes, these subjects are engaged in hard linear deliberation, but the deliberation is not controlling the outcome:

These subjects were reasoning. They were working quite hard at reasoning. But it was not reasoning in search of truth; it was reasoning in support of their emotional reactions. (2012, 25)

Certainly it *seems* to us that our deliberative reasoning is not only in control, but is also completely *transparent*: we know the whole process, we are fully aware of the elements involved in our deliberative efforts. But like so many common sense beliefs—the Earth is immobile, species are fixed, air is a single substance—this obviously true belief is false. Daniel Kahneman divides cognitive processes into (what he calls) System 1 and System 2 operations. System 1 operates almost constantly, carrying out the mundane processes that make up most of our conscious life, and which—thankfully—do not require careful deliberative reflection: speaking a sentence in your native language, humming a tune, driving your car, walking to the copy machine, taking a sip of coffee. System 2 kicks in when greater attention and careful deliberation is needed. As Kahneman describes it:

Whenever you are conscious, and perhaps even when you are not, multiple computations are going on in your brain, which maintain and update current answers to some key questions: Is anything new going on? Is there a threat? Are things going well? Should my attention be redirected? Is more effort needed for this task? You can think of a cockpit, with a set of dials that indicate the current values of each of these essential variables. The assessments are carried out automatically by System 1, and one of their functions is to determine whether extra effort is required from System 2. (2011, 59)

But even when System 2 is alerted and working, System 1 processes still exert a powerful and often controlling influence, our contrary supposition notwithstanding:

In the unlikely event of this book being make into a film, System 2 would be a supporting character who believes herself to be the hero. The defining feature of System 2, in this story, is that its operations are effortful, and one of its main characteristics is laziness, a reluctance to invest more effort than is strictly necessary. As a consequence, the thought actions that System 2 believes it has chosen are often guided by the figure at the center of the story, System 1. (2011, 31)

People are often disturbed to discover that their own cognitive processes are not perfectly clear to them, but are at best "seen through a glass darkly" when they are seen at all. The "facilitator" fervently believes that he or she was guided entirely by the subtle direction of the autistic child pointing to keys on a letter board, that the poem or essay (produced by the child pointing to keys while the facilitator steadies the letter board) was the exclusive production of the child, and that the facilitator's hand on the letter board was completely controlled by the guidance of the child while the facilitator remained a passive facilitator of the child's thoughts; but in fact the poem and the essay came entirely from the facilitator, with the facilitator not recognizing that he or she was engaged in deliberative thought. When an experimenter sets up a test in which the facilitator sees a ball while the autistic child sees a dog, the facilitator uses the letter board to answer ball, certain that the answer is being given by the child, and is amazed—and sometimes still refuses to believe, no matter how many tests are done with the same result—that the answers were the facilitator's and not the child's (Smith, Haas, and Belcher 1994; Jacobson, Mulick, and Schwartz 1995; Mostert 2001).

In a study using the Iowa Gambling Task, subjects play a game with the goal of accumulating as much money as possible. There are four decks of cards, and subjects can choose from any of the four decks. For two of the decks, some cards give large gains, but there are many cards with large losses; for the other two decks, rewards are lower but the losses are also smaller. Drawing cards from the decks with the smaller rewards and smaller losses results in an overall gain, while drawing from the decks with the larger rewards and losses results in an overall loss. Subjects begin to choose cards advantageously—from the low reward and low risk decks—before consciously recognizing that this is an advantageous strategy, and they generate anticipatory skin conductance responses before choosing cards from the disadvantaged decks prior to conscious recognition that choosing from those decks is disadvantageous (Bechara, Damasio, Tranel, and Damasio 1997). Even subjects who *never* reach conscious knowledge of the optimum playing pattern nonetheless make advantageous choices while playing. Knowledge of advantages and disadvantages can be acquired without that knowledge reaching consciousness.

An experimental subject finds a dime in a phone booth, and moments later stops to help a stranger who dropped a set of papers. Obviously finding a dime had no influence on one's deliberative decision to stop and help, or so we all suppose; but in the experiment, almost everyone who found the dime stopped to help, while few of those who left the phone booth dimeless stopped to give assistance (Isen and Levin 1972). A powerful influence on our decision to stop and help is entirely absent from our conscious deliberative process. Similar results are found in priming studies, in which words or images significantly increase the likelihood of specific behavior patterns: a learning exercise involving money primes—words associated with money—resulted in increased selfishness in a subsequent game (Vohs 2006). Kahneman notes that people are strongly disinclined to believe that such subtle influences—of which they are not consciously aware—can have a substantial impact on their behavior:

> When I describe the priming studies to audiences, the reaction is often disbelief. This is not a surprise: System 2 believes that it is in charge and that it knows the reasons for its choices. . . . You do not believe that these results apply to you because they correspond to nothing in your subjective experience. But your subjective experience consists largely of the story that System 2 tells itself about what is going on. Priming phenomena arise in System 1, and you have no conscious access to them. (2011, 56–7)

Our careful System 2 deliberative sequential thought is rare and wonderful, but it is not what we readily suppose it to be: it is not transparent, but instead operates in ways and under subtle influences of which we are generally unaware; and it is not typically the director of operations, but rather a rationalizing subordinate.

These are the fundamental factors that challenge our belief in the special and unique power of deliberative reasoning; but that deep belief has caused us to distort our view of deliberative reason in other important ways. In particular, being largely unaware of the many nondeliberative factors that shape and control our deliberative results, we exaggerate our conscious deliberative System 2 powers. The most common exaggeration—and the one to which philosophers are particularly vulnerable—is the exaggeration of our capacity for easily switching into System 2 deliberation, and of the fortitude with which we engage in deliberation. Philosophers are especially prone to such exaggeration, because philosophers are classic *chronic cognizers*, and we live in the midst of chronic cognizers.

Chronic cognizers (Cacioppo and Petty 1982; Cacioppo et al. 1996) occupy one extreme on the *need for cognition* scale. Those who are high in need for cognition (the chronic cognizers) find deliberative System 2 thinking more appealing, are more likely to engage in deliberation and continue it longer (Osberg 1987), and typically have greater confidence in their ability to carry out deliberative tasks. In contrast, cognitive misers—at the other end of the need for cognition spectrum—are more reluctant to engage in deliberative thought and they deliberate for a shorter time. Most people, of course, fall somewhere between those extremes. Most of those in academia—and thus most of those with whom philosophers daily associate—tend to be chronic cognizers; and philosophers are probably toward the high end of the need for cognition scale among academics (not that philosophers are necessarily *better* at deliberative cognizing; we just enjoy it more). We shouldn't exaggerate this philosophical tendency toward chronic cognizing: we are in many circumstances as likely to muddle along in System 1—when it would behoove us to exert System 2 energies—as are butchers and bakers and candlestick makers; and even when we do engage in effortful System 2 deliberation, it is often a process of performing rationalizations in the service of our System 1 managing director (who lurks unnoticed behind the conscious scenes). But the fact that we are often in the midst of chronic cognizers may lead us to overestimate the general tendency toward chronic cognizing and the facility with which people switch into System 2 thinking.

Philosophers are high in need for cognition, but probably higher still in cognitive self-efficacy. Self-efficacy (Bandura 1977 and 1997) concerns the confidence one has in one's ability to successfully carry out some project or act. Being strong in self-efficacy means that one generally is confident of one's abilities to succeed, but most self-efficacy studies are more localized. Self-efficacy powers are not a unified whole, but tend to vary for different tasks. Obviously one can have a very strong sense of self-efficacy when it comes to mastering a foreign language, and be weakly self-efficacious when confronted with a problem in math. Though there is a connection between self-efficacy and actual competency—my continued inability to hit a curve ball eventually eroded my earlier strong sense of baseball self-efficacy—strong self-efficacy does not always correlate with actual ability: most of us have encountered philosophy graduate students who maintain a sturdy conviction of their logical brilliance in the face of powerful contrary evidence; and some students become so convinced that they "just can't do math" that their actual abilities never manifest themselves. Those who are particularly weak in self-efficacy are often the most frustrating students, who "won't even try"; they may need the most help, but they are the least likely to receive it.

On the important dimension of *cognitive* self-efficacy, philosophers are blessed with abundance. That does not imply that philosophers are smarter than most people, but only that they generally *believe* themselves to be. That is hardly surprising. Philosophers are often drawn to philosophy by profound interest in difficult and sometimes ancient philosophical quandaries ("What is the nature of time?" "Is the world one or many?" "Is there a proof for the existence of God?") and by their confidence that they can find the answer that has eluded—perhaps for centuries—everyone else. So just as we are tempted to suppose that everyone is a chronic cognizer, we are also inclined to suppose that almost all are blessed with strong cognitive self-efficacy.

Philosophers may be especially inclined to exaggerate the confidence in and the inclination to deliberative activity, because philosophers tend to be high in cognitive self-efficacy and at the far end of the scale in chronic cognizing. But there is another exaggeration of deliberative powers that is widely shared: the belief that there is almost no limit on the power to *sustain* System 2 rigorous deliberation. This belief may be a legacy of the traditional split between the physical body and the nonphysical mind: hard physical labor reaches a point of physical exhaustion, but hard mental labor has no such limits; run a long series of sprints and the last will be a relatively poor showing, but following a long series of System 2 deliberative efforts the next deliberative episode can be just as good as the first. But that is false; and in the absence of mind-body dualism, that should not be surprising. Extensive research on "ego depletion" (Baumeister et al. 1998; Danziger, Levav, and Avnaim-Pesso 2011) shows that after a lengthy period of deliberative effort, we are less likely to switch into rigorous System 2 thought in response to a situation that calls for such efforts, and when we do make the switch our deliberative efforts are shorter and weaker.

The frustrated math teacher exclaims in exasperation to the failing student she is sincerely trying to help: "Look, even if you aren't the best math student in the world, at least you can *try*. Think *hard* about this problem; maybe you can't get the right solution, but you *can* make a strong *effort* at the problem. I can't help you if you won't even try." But this frustrating and frustrated student has made a series of failed efforts, and is now in a state of extremely low mathematical self-efficacy, compounded by severe ego depletion, and he *cannot* think long and hard about this problem. And it is difficult for his math teacher—strong in mathematical self-efficacy and a long-time chronic cognizer—to recognize the special difficulty.

It is not surprising that to philosophers—chronic cognizers powerful in cognitive self-efficacy—it seems obvious that no matter what *other* limitations we may confront, we can always *think harder*. Charles Taylor—an insightful chronic cognizer whose many philosophical insights and cognitive successes have shaped a person of powerful cognitive self-efficacy—postulates a universal power of effortful deep deliberation that seems plausible to Taylor and others with his exceptional cognitive abilities:

> Because this self-resolution [deep self-evaluation] is something we do, when we do it, we can be called responsible for ourselves; and because it is within limits always up to us to do it, even when we don't—indeed, the nature of our deepest evaluations constantly raises the question of whether we have them right—we can be called responsible in another sense for ourselves whether we undertake this radical evaluation or not. (1976, 299)

And Dan Dennett, another chronic cognizer but one who also is extremely knowledgeable concerning contemporary psychological research, makes a similar assumption in one of his earlier accounts of free will:

> the model I propose points to the multiplicity of decisions that encircle our moral decisions and suggests that in many cases our ultimate decision as to which way to act is less important phenomenologically as a contributor to our sense of free will than the prior decisions affecting our deliberation process itself: the decision, for instance, not to consider any further, to terminate deliberation; or the decision to ignore certain lines of inquiry.
>
> These prior and subsidiary decisions contribute, I think, to our sense of ourselves as responsible free agents, roughly in the following way: I am faced with an important decision to make, and after a certain amount of deliberation I say to myself: "That's enough. I've considered this matter enough and now I'm going to act," in the full knowledge that I could have considered further, in the full knowledge that the eventualities may prove that I decided in error, but with the acceptance of responsibility in any case. (1978, 297)

It does seem obvious that "I could have considered further"; but like much that seems obvious, it is false. Our cosmos is not at all what we imagined it to be: the Earth is not stationary, the Sun and the planets do not orbit the Earth, the stars are not fixed on a rotating spherical surface at no great distance from Earth, and our Milky Way galaxy is not the limit of the cosmos but instead only one among billions of galaxies. Likewise, our human cognitive powers are very different from what we imagined them to be; and many of our cognitive operations are as invisible to our introspection as distant galaxies were invisible to Ptolemy. The bulk of our cognitive processing is invisible to our consciousness; our deliberative efforts are more likely to be rationalizations of System 1 decisions than genuine deliberative processes aimed at finding the right answer; the influence of situations and primes is much greater than we imagined; the capacity for switching into and sustaining System 2 deliberation is greatly influenced by large differences in need for cognition and cognitive self-efficacy; the general capacity for sustained deliberative reflection is quite limited. From ancient to contemporary models, rationalist accounts of special and unique human free will are based on a model of human rationality that is approximately as accurate as Aristotle's account of biology. It is hard to relinquish our cherished view of our own rational powers; but the Earth is not stationary, species are not fixed, and human reason is quite different from what we had supposed it to be.

REASON AND SITUATIONS

There is much concern over situationism, with all sorts of philosophers (and others) challenging the results of that extensive area of social science research (Athanassoulis 2000; Sreenivasan 2002; Montmarquet 2003; Kametekar 2004). Of course there are also philosophical champions of situationist research, particularly John Doris (2002) and Gilbert Harman (1999). Even tough-minded Patricia Churchland, who could never be accused of a romanticized or exaggerated perspective on the brain and its powers, challenges the research on situationism (Suhler and Churchland 2009), insisting that it doesn't show as much as researchers suppose. Perhaps situationists have sometimes overstated the importance of situational factors, but on the other hand it is clear that situational influences play a much larger role in our behavior than is generally recognized. But it seems curious that there would be such concern over situationism. After all, the situationist research primarily shows that our capacity to detect and respond to environmental cues is quite sensitive, and working well; and our nonconscious detection of subtle environmental stimuli is functioning effectively, without the need for engaging System 2 deliberation. Of course that capacity is not working *perfectly*, but no product of evolution ever does. As evolutionary anthropologist Brian Hare points out:

> Evolution does not lead to perfection. Evolution tinkers—leading to organisms adapted to survive and reproduce more skillfully than competitors. Like any other species, humans are just good enough to win the race, but far from perfect, thanks to our long evolutionary history. (2014, 366)

We pick up cues—which may never reach the level of conscious deliberation—about our social roles: as prison guards (Zimbardo 1974) and as dedicated assistants to a powerful authority (Milgram 1963); cues concerning need to focus exclusively on a task (Darley and Batson 1973); cues about responding to the receipt of benefits (Isen and Levin 1972). Sometimes these powerful cues have unfortunate effects, and prevent us from shifting into careful consideration of our behavior. The Stanford students—as well as the Abu Ghraib guards—who adopted roles as brutal guards, the theology students who rushed past the apparently suffering person, the "teachers" who continued to deliver (what they believed were) powerful or even lethal shocks: all of them wish they had ignored the strong situational cues and instead reflected carefully on the wrongness of their behavior. But a system that constantly prompted us to stop and carefully deliberate would be of no use to active animals in a rapidly changing world (however useful it might be to Aristotle's God).

System 1—by responding to situational cues without requiring the direction of careful deliberation—generally works very well. If you had to stop and deliberate before speaking a sentence in your native language, before making the correct turn in your daily commute to work, while operating your fork to propel food into your mouth, or to direct the placement of each foot as you walk a familiar path, you would be unable to function at all. System 1 alerts System 2's careful consideration when construction blocks your standard commuting path or the green leafy vegetable on your fork suddenly begins to crawl; and generally it does a good job of calling problems to System 2 active attentiveness. But not always, as the Stanford prison guards and Princeton theological students will attest. So System 1 and System 2 cognitive operations do not function perfectly. But that does not mean that they are hopelessly flawed, or that we are invariably the pawns of situational cues, or that we never exercise effective control. It means, rather, that our cognitive processes—even when they are generally well-functioning—are not perfect: that we are not, and—in order to have System 1 do its essential work at an optimum or even minimal level—*cannot* be perfectly rational. Aspiring to a goal of perfect rationality would mean aspiring to become beings that have no use for System 1 operations; it is, in short, an aspiration to be gods, not animals; and that lofty aspiration has a long and depressing history.

Our well-functioning System 1 response to changing situations works quickly and alertly. It doesn't always get things exactly right, but it is a very useful system nonetheless: evolution did not aim at perfection. When System 1 responds rapidly to environmental cues, then it is working well: our options are enlarged and informed by environmental features, which is precisely what we want (not absolute options unrelated to the environment). And generally it is working without our conscious awareness, and that also means it is functioning well (again, not perfectly). After all, there is no reason for System 2 to kick in when we stop to help someone pick up papers, or pass by. But why suppose that only when System 2 is activated do we get real free will? Is it because we somehow think—not clearly—that somewhere deep in that special rational process we must find (or there must be lurking, or hiding) the special power, the miracle, that we require for moral responsibility? There is an indication of that when people do *not* want the whys of reason probed too carefully: why does one think longer, more deeply, more accurately than another? If we look for causes we find crucial factors that we did not control and that were matters of luck—luck in our early nurturing, or luck in our immediate environmental influences (Levy 2011)—and that is disturbing to many people (particularly those who cherish moral responsibility). If we don't like looking for deeper causes, is that because of the assumption that there must be something going on in the reasoning process that lifts it above causes, something *causa sui*, something miraculous?

VALUABLE HEURISTICS

The capacity of animals—including human animals—to respond swiftly and often nonconsciously to situational stimuli is a valuable capacity. Our System 1 responses are not perfect, but they are of great benefit. Not only do they prevent System 2 deliberative resources from being overburdened and exhausted, but they also enable us to respond swiftly and smoothly (rather than through the slower process of System 2 reflection). And the responses generated by System 1 are often superior to those reached as a result of deliberation. This is not surprising: System 1 has had a much longer period to refine its operations and eliminate many of the problems, while System 2 is a newer process. As noted earlier, Jonathan Haidt recognizes the polished and valuable nature of System 1 cognitive processes: "Automatic processes run the human mind, just as they have been running animal minds for 500 million years, so they're very good at what they do, like software that has been improved through thousands of product cycles." And System 1 is not only good at swift (and generally effective) responses to situational cues; it also runs a great many very useful "heuristics" that guide our behavior—again not perfectly, but generally quite well—in both ordinary circumstances and when confronting new challenges. These heuristics might be thought of as useful "apps" that enhance the functioning of our System 1 cognitive processes.

Our heuristic processes are not infallible, and a number of excellent researchers have uncovered the fascinating variety of errors that sometimes occur when employing such heuristic devices. System 1 thinking takes the limited information it has, constructs a coherent picture on the basis of that limited information, and draws a conclusion; as Kahneman points out: "When information is scarce, which is a common occurrence, System 1 operates as a machine for jumping to conclusions" (2011, 85). Often it jumps to the right conclusion, and usually to a conclusion that is at least workable, and that makes it valuable for human animals who must constantly make decisions and cannot devote exhaustive research to each of them; but its very functioning as a swift decision maker—that leaps before it exhaustively looks—insures that it will sometimes jump into errors.

One useful (but imperfect) heuristic device is substituting an easier somewhat similar question when confronted with a difficult quandary (Kahneman 2011, 97ff.).[1] Another—extensively researched—heuristic is the use of "anchors" to make judgments in conditions of uncertainty. Like other heuristics, this one is beneficial: it is often useful to have a workable starting point or "anchor" when making quantitative estimates. But it can lead us astray, even when we have considerable experience in a given area, and this potential for error becomes obvious through the manipulations of creative researchers. Professional real estate agents visited a house that was on the market and read information on the house, including a listing price. Half the agents saw a very high listing price, and the other half saw a very low listing price. They were then asked to name a reasonable asking price for the house, as well as the lowest price at which they would sell the house if they owned it. Both groups denied that the listing price had any effect on their judgment; but the differences in listing prices seen by the two groups was the only difference in their experience of the house, and those who saw the high listing price set a price 12% above the actual listing price, while those who saw the low listing price set a price 12% below that actual listing price (Northcraft and Neale 1987). More remarkable still are experiments showing that even when the "anchor" number is recognized as random and in no way related to the decision, it still exerts a powerful effect. In an experiment with German judges, each judge was given the same scenario involving a woman who was caught shoplifting; each judge then rolled a pair of dice (loaded dice, so that they always landed on 3 or 9), and then asked what sentence they would give the shoplifter. The judges that rolled 9 gave an average sentence of 8 months; those who rolled a 3 gave an average sentence of 5 months (Englich, Mussweiler, and Strack 2006). Like the other heuristics that generally serve us well, or well enough, in our cognitive processes—heuristics without which our cognitive processes would grind to a slow and ineffective crawl—heuristic anchors do not match the model of sublime rationality.

Human rationality is not perfect; and that is not a plausible goal—much less a plausible model—for human cognitive processes. That does not mean that we should not discover and seek ways of avoiding some of the errors that our useful heuristic devices generate. For example, Daniel Kahneman writes of finding a way to counteract the "halo effect" (the tendency of initial judgments of liking or disliking to influence later judgments) when grading exams (a good or bad grade on the first question influenced how subsequent questions were graded), resulting in a more accurate grading process:

I adopted a new procedure. Instead of reading the booklets in sequence, I read and scored all the students' answers to the first question, then went on to the next one. I made sure to write all the scores on the inside back page of the booklet so that I would not be biased (even unconsciously) when I read the second essay. (2011, 83)

But that is very different from supposing that "human rationality" can constantly rise above such "sources of error," since those "sources of error" are often vitally important to our effective functioning in a changing world.

While there is naturally a tendency to emphasize the ways these heuristic processes may lead us astray, that should not blind us to the fact that the heuristic devices are generally very effective, and certainly valuable—indeed, for human animals (as opposed to perfectly rational and untiring gods) they are essential. Kahneman notes that even with a lifetime of effort—an effort facilitated by his profound understanding of the processes—he has not freed himself from errors generated by heuristics:

As I know from experience, System 1 is not readily educable. Except for some effects that I attribute mostly to age, my intuitive thinking is just as prone to overconfidence, extreme predictions, and the planning fallacy as it was before I made a study of these issues. I have improved only in my ability to recognize situations in which errors are likely. . . . And I have made much more progress in recognizing the errors of others than my own. (2011, 417)

Certainly it is good to learn how to recognize and not be misled by some of these errors; but the dream of *eliminating* the occasional errors that are the inevitable accompaniment of such heuristic processes is not an appropriate goal for human animals. As Kahneman states:

The definition of rationality as coherence is impossibly restrictive; it demands adherence to rules of logic that a finite mind is not able to implement. . . . I often cringe when my work with Amos is credited with demonstrating that human choices are irrational, when in fact our research only showed that humans are not well-described by the rational-agent model. (2011, 411)

Like our heuristics, our emotions sometimes lead us astray (as we all recognize to our sorrow); and certainly there are those emotion-based beliefs (such as racism) that we should make great efforts to eliminate if possible and severely constrain if not; but without our emotions—as Damasio (1994) notes—we would be much worse off as ethical beings, and indeed as free animals. Emotions fuel our ethical judgments and ethical behavior, and without emotions—imperfect though they be—the result is not Kantian rational moral perfection, but instead an apathetic indifference to the needs and interests of others, and a general failure of empathy-driven ethical behavior. The same applies to our heuristics, that lead us occasionally into temptation, but more often deliver us from evil.

In sum, heuristics are valuable for human animals like ourselves with limited reasoning capacities and a need for smoothly operating and efficient behavior. They would be an impediment to gods, but for us they are useful, though imperfect. Human cognitive processes—like the cognitive processes of related species—are good, but not infallible. That is important to remember, especially when we are tempted to make reason something so special that it sets us distinctly apart and justifies claims and ascriptions of moral responsibility.

NOTE

1. Waller 2015, chapter 2, discusses the impact of this heuristic on philosophical models of moral responsibility.

Chapter 4

Will Power in a Just World

Reason is marvelous: God forbid that a philosopher should disparage the glories of reason. But when reason is pressed into service to carry the heavy weight of special human uniqueness along with a free will that can justify moral responsibility, reason is being asked to carry a burden it cannot bear. The resulting problems have led many philosophers and most of the folk to very different grounds for free will and moral responsibility: the special— even miraculous—power of human will.

The special godlike power of human will is a remarkable power: so remarkable that it prompts the question of what motivated us to claim such a special power for our species. The deep belief in human uniqueness is obviously one part of the story—but only part. Another key element was the need to justify claims and assumptions of moral responsibility. But then the question arises: why this strong push to justify moral responsibility? What is behind this deep need to believe in moral responsibility: a need so strong that it generates belief in a remarkable—and remarkably implausible—power of human will? The answer to that question requires examining another deep belief: belief in a just world.

BELIEF IN A JUST WORLD

The world is not just. That will hardly come as a shock to most people, though many philosophers and even more theologians find it difficult to accept. That is, for most people it will not come as a shock when we consider it carefully and consciously, using our deliberative System 2 powers. But our belief in a just world does not often come to consciousness (unless we are trying to solve the problem of evil or asking if virtuous living promotes true happiness).

But that belief plays a major motivational role in our deeper cognitive functioning. We go to great trouble—sometimes to remarkable extremes—trying to preserve and protect belief in a just world against powerful evidence to the contrary.

Before examining how our deep belief in a just world has twisted and distorted our conception of free will, it is important to be clear on exactly what the belief in a just world is. It has been the subject of extensive psychological research, and the basic idea is summarized by one of the leading contemporary researchers on belief in a just world (BJW), Adrian Furnham: "The BJW asserts that, quite justly, good things happen to good people and bad things to bad people despite the fact that this is patently not the case" (2003, 795). Melvin Lerner was one of the pioneers in research on belief in a just world, and on the negative effects of that belief. But belief in a just world is deep and widespread, and it would have been unlikely to become so well entrenched had it not also had considerable benefits. Lerner and Miller note that belief in a just world is important for promoting a sense of order and a confident belief that things work out for the best for those who act well, and thus promotes effort and prevents a sense of futility:

> Individuals have a need to believe that they live in a world where people generally get what they deserve. The belief that the world is just enables the individual to confront his physical and social environments as though they were stable and orderly. Without such a belief it would be difficult for the individual to commit himself to the pursuit of long range goals or even to the socially regulated behaviour of day to day life. . . . Since the belief that the world is just serves such an important adaptive function for the individual, people are very reluctant to give up this belief, and they can be greatly troubled if they encounter evidence that suggests that the world is not really just or orderly after all. (1978, 1030–1)

For most of us, belief in a just world is neither consciously held nor reflectively approved. When we consider it carefully, it is painfully obvious that the world is *not* just, nor anywhere near just. Innocent people spend their lives under the cruel tyranny of a brutal ruler, while the ruler lives in luxury and dies amidst all the glory and honor his government—and perhaps the governments of many other countries—can offer. Generations live and die under the oppression of slavery, while rich plantation owners revel in "gracious living" and are treated as the most honorable and respected people of their region. Good hard-working people perish under drought conditions, drown in tsunamis, are buried under earthquakes. Innocent children suffer and die from terrible widespread diseases. Horrific genocidal policies are aimed at African tribal groups, at European Jews, at the natives of the "new" world, at tribal and ethnic groups around the globe. Yet this overwhelming reflectively acknowledged evidence against our belief in a just world has little effect on that deeply held *non*conscious belief; to the contrary, our conscious deliberative resources are often deployed to protect that deep belief through ready rationalizations.

An old friend fervently believed that there *must* be an eternal afterlife for those who have suffered unjustly in this life (he had lost many family members in the Holocaust), because only by an eternity of bliss could the terrible suffering endured by those victims be canceled out: only from the perspective of *eternity* can such suffering become comparatively insignificant. This was not a deduction drawn from the initial premise that the world is just; rather, it was a way of preserving a deep and very important but largely nonconscious belief that the world *must* be just. In this case, the deep belief in a just world may have provided valuable psychological comfort; in other cases, the nonconscious belief in a just world is not so benign.

The most notorious result of belief in a just world is its effect on how we judge those who suffer misfortune. Since the world is just, those who suffer must justly deserve their suffering. The people suffering from a prolonged drought did not take proper precautions to plan for such perils; those suffering from disease must have done something to expose themselves to infection, or neglected to take proper steps to promote their own health; the person who is homeless and impoverished must be lazy. One of the most disturbing and extensively studied manifestations of this "blame the victim" phenomenon—promoted by belief in a just world—is the treatment of rape victims. Rape is a brutal, traumatizing crime, which often results in both physical and psychological damage. Though women are the most common victims, men (especially those in prison or military settings) are also victims of rape and other forms of sexual abuse, and men are less likely to report the crime and seek help. The terrible vulnerability to this awful crime heightens the fear of the crime, both for potential victims and for those who love them. Thus there is a particularly strong desire to be reassured that this will not happen to me or to my loved ones. The deep largely nonconscious belief in a just world provides that assurance: Such terrible things only happen to those who somehow deserve them, so I am safe. But that assurance is bought at a terrible price: the rape victim must have done something to bring this on herself. She "led him on," was not properly cautious, dressed provocatively; in some manner she *must* have deserved what happened to her.

Even after we had discovered some degree of order in our world—the planets follow their epicycle-aided regular orbits, the seasons take their turns, the moon follows its phases—we still did not live in a world that was *justly* ordered. The wicked sometimes prosper, the virtuous suffer cruel fates, and bad things happen to good people. As Bernard Williams makes clear in his brilliant study (1993), the Greek dramatists did not believe this was a just world. Plato, of course, insisted that it must be. Williams claims that we live in a world more like that of the Greek dramatists than that of Plato. In our conscious reflective moments, perhaps we do. But in our deeper nonconscious beliefs, we embrace the Platonic and Christian belief: this *must* be a just world, whether governed by a just god or natural forces. We know it's false when we consciously deliberate about it; but that does not lessen the power of that belief within our systemic cognitive nonconscious operations.

The ancient Hebraic tradition had few illusions about the world being just. The God of the Israelites fought for Israel; the question of whether the war was just was not an issue. It is striking that in all the multitude of wars and massacres described in the bloody pages of the Hebrew Bible, there is little if any question of whether the wars are just. God kills the first born, and punishes even unto the third and fourth generation, and demands the slaughter of entire nations who happen to be in the path of the children of Abraham. Job is a righteous and upright man; but that does not prevent his family from being killed, his property destroyed, and his body covered with painful bleeding sores from the crown of his head to the soles of his feet. And when he presumes to ask God for an explanation, God quickly puts Job in his place: "Then the Lord answered Job out of the whirlwind, and said, Who is this that darkeneth counsel by words without knowledge? . . . Where wast thou when I laid the foundations of the earth?" (Job 38:1-4). In short, I have the power, you are my creation, I will do with you as I wish, and questions of justice do not arise. Certainly *some* questions of justice can arise: the Prophet Nathan condemns King David for his unjust treatment of Bathsheba's husband. But one can hardly expect the *world* to be just, when governed by a rather capricious god who plays favorites and often changes his mind.

When Jesus of Nazareth taught his followers, he taught them to love one another and practice charity and treat one another with kindness, but he did not teach that the world itself is just. To the contrary, God "maketh his sun to rise on the evil and the good, and sendeth rain on the just and on the unjust" (Matt. 5:45). Rather than the world being just, Jesus taught that injustice is deeply entrenched. Contemporary Christians—viewing the teachings through the lens of belief in a just world—twist his words to imply that the world *is* just. Consider the famous parable (told in slightly different versions in the Gospels of Matthew and Luke) of the talents. A man is going to a far country, and he calls three servants to him, giving each one talents (or measures) of gold to keep until his return. One servant received five talents, and he "went and traded with the same, and made them other five talents" (Matt. 25:16). A second servant received two talents, and he also doubled his master's money. The third servant received one talent, and he "went and digged in the earth, and hid his lord's money" (Matt. 25:18). When the master returns, he praises and rewards the two servants who had doubled his money, making each a "ruler over many things." But the servant who simply returns what he had been given is condemned:

Then he which had received the one talent came and said, Lord, I knew thee that thou art an hard man, reaping where thou hast not sown, and gathering where thou hast not strawed: And I was afraid, and went and hid thy talent in the earth: lo, there thou hast that is thine.

His lord answered and said unto him, Thou wicked and slothful servant, thou knewest that I reap where I sowed not, and gather where I have not strawed: Thou oughtest therefore to have put my money to the exchangers, and then at my coming I should have received mine own with usury. Take therefore the talent from him, and give it unto him which hath ten talents. For unto every one that hath shall be given, and he shall have abundance: but from him that hath not shall be taken away even that which he hath. (Matt. 25:24-29)

What is the moral of the parable? Ask almost any contemporary Christian (or consult almost any Christian website or Bible commentary) and you get the same answer: Work hard and you will be rewarded, and the lazy also get what they justly deserve; a just God rewards us for using our abilities well, and justly punishes anyone who is indolent by taking "even that which he hath." In short, the world is just, and both the prosperous and the impoverished are getting their just deserts. That is appealing to those who believe in a just world (particularly those who are prospering in that just world), but it is precisely the opposite of what the parable actually teaches. The "lord" or master in this story does *not* represent a just god; to the contrary, this master is a very hard man, who seems to take pride in the fact that "I reap where I sowed not, and gather where I have not strawed." This is also a man who is eager to profit from usury (from loaning out money at a high interest rate); and making money by usury is regarded as vile behavior under traditional Jewish law, and would certainly have been seen as such by those Jesus is teaching. So the moral hero in this story is not the hard avaricious master who reaps where he does not sow and is greedy for money from usury; nor is it the two servants who are rewarded for increasing their master's ill-gotten gains: those servants do their master's bidding, follow his methods, and satisfy their master's greed at the expense of those who suffer by that greed. Rather, the hero is the man who is condemned by this avaricious and unprincipled master for returning to the master that—and only that—which is rightly his, and refusing to follow the master's greedy wishes. But this hero is *not* rewarded for his virtue; to the contrary, the rewards of this world go to those who already have, and whose unscrupulous behavior provides them abundance far beyond their needs; while the person who follows the path of virtue and rejects greed does not prosper, but instead loses "even that which he hath."[1] Jesus (in the parable) was teaching a painful lesson for believers in a just world: the world is *not* just; the wicked prosper; and if we wrongly suppose the world is just, we will call the poor wicked and the rich righteous, when the contrary is more likely to be the case.

No one is likely to confuse Sophocles with Jesus of Nazareth, but they had one thing in common: they dramatized the view that we do not live in a just world. In contrast to the Greek dramatists, Plato and Aristotle devoted heroic efforts to arguing that the world *is* just (with Plato's *Republic* story of the ring of Gyges the centerpiece of this effort). Perhaps Plato was so concerned with this question because the dominant view of his contemporaries was precisely the opposite, as shown in the great works by Sophocles. Oedipus devotes all his virtuous efforts to avoiding the awful crimes—murdering his father and marrying his mother—that are his prophesied destiny, but those efforts are in vain. In Aeschylus's story of *Agamemnon*, he is compelled to choose between two profoundly wrong acts: the world (as directed by the gods) is such that Agamemnon *cannot* act justly (Williams 1993, 132–3). There is, of course, substantial order in this world: the stars follow their courses, the seasons pass at their times; but that order is not a moral order, and this world is not just.

One would hardly expect the world of the ancient Greeks to be a just world, governed as it is by powers who seem to take a perverse delight in placing humans in dreadful moral predicaments. The same applies to the ancient Hebrew people, whose god was a local and provincial deity so narcissistic that he is obsessed with finding a people who would worship only him. This god punishes not only those who offend him but also their innocent children "unto the third and fourth generation" (Exodus 20:5). He certainly felt no obligation of justice to poor Job, much less to the many innocent cities and nations the Hebrew people encountered and conquered on their way to the Promised Land: he orders that every man, woman, and child of those groups be put to the sword.

But as the world becomes more understandable and orderly, there is a desire that the order of the world become not only understandable but also just; and as the Judeo-Christian god matures from a small-time deity who "fights for Israel" into omnipotent and omniscient God—a deity who, incidentally, metes out horrific punishments which *must* be just—and who is obviously in control of the cosmos, there is a need for the world governed by this just god to be a just world. If we are to be justly punished and rewarded—particularly if the reward is eternal bliss and the punishment eternal torture—then we must be getting our *just deserts*, and so we must have moral responsibility. Since moral responsibility is unique to humans, the best candidate to prop up moral responsibility is uniquely human free will.

FREE *WILL* POWER

If free will is based in special unique powers of human *reason*, difficulties soon develop. If moral responsibility requires free will, and free will requires perfect rationality, then very few people will have free will and so very few will be morally responsible and therefore eligible for just rewards or just punishments. But we do not want to confine moral responsibility to only a few; after all, we want to justify punishment and reward (including the punishments and rewards of a just god) for *all* humans, and certainly it is not the case that all humans have this remarkable power of perfect rationality. Instead, few if any humans have the extraordinary rational powers that would enable them to consistently and perfectly track the True and the Good. Some of us may occasionally get on track, but we frequently lose the scent. A free will available only to the sublimely enlightened will be of little value to the rest of us: who make up, after all, the vast *un*enlightened majority, muddling along with imperfect and easily distracted reason. Furthermore, Christianity is not a religion of sophisticated reason, but instead a religion of simple faith: the kingdom of heaven is more accessible to little children than to brilliant thinkers. You can't *reason* your way into the Christian heaven; rather, it requires that you set aside critical reason and rely entirely on faith. St. Paul recognized that Christian belief is not arrived at by means of reason: "For the Jews require a sign, and the Greeks seek after wisdom: But we preach Christ crucified, unto the Jews a stumbling block, and unto the Greeks foolishness" (First Corinthians 1:22-23). Martin Luther went further, despising reason as "the Devil's greatest whore."

The Hebraic-Christian God is not a god of reason. He changes his mind— "And the Lord said, I will destroy man whom I have created from the face of the Earth . . . for it repenteth me that I have made them" (Genesis 6:6); "And the Lord repented of the evil which he thought to do unto his people" (Exodus 32:14)—on numerous occasions; indeed, God changes his mind so often that he seems arbitrary. He creates humans, and repents of having done so: you get the feeling he wishes he had stopped with the fowl of the air. He resolves to destroy all humans, then decides to save a few. He becomes intensely angry and wrathful, and his wrath seems to overwhelm his reason. He becomes so obsessed with the disrespect shown him by his human creatures that only a blood sacrifice—a sacrifice, indeed, of his own son to be put to death by torture—will satisfy his desire to punish the beings of his own creation.

If humans wish to be godlike—and the model of God is this rather capricious deity who has a powerful will but a reason that seems often confused and always inconstant—then the power of will, rather than reason, is the feature that shows humans to be made in the image of God. Thus the dominant element of free will becomes the power of *free choice*, the power to choose (or reject) repentance and salvation, the power to make a leap of faith: a leap that seems foolish to cautious judicious reason. According to Descartes, it is our *will*—not our reason—that makes us godlike:

There is only volition alone, or the liberty of the free will, which I experience
to be so great in myself that I cannot conceive the idea of any other more ample
and extended, so that this is what principally indicates to me that I am made in
the image and likeness of God. (1641/1960, Fourth Meditation)

Nietzsche, when he celebrated the murder of God and the necessity for
humans to now become gods, saw the power of *will*—or the *will* to power—
rather than intellect as the feature that gives us the right to be replacements
for the old dead gods.

This power of free choice is not without its problems for the Christian
faithful. After all, this grown-up Christian God is now *omni*potent, so it is
hard to imagine any power of choice that humans could have independently
of God. St. Augustine struggles long and hard with the problem, but—as
Eleonore Stump (2006) notes—never resolves it. The canonical letters of St.
Paul make it clear that "it is not of him [humans] that willeth, nor of him that
runneth, but of God that showeth mercy" (Romans 9:16). Both Lorenzo Valla
and Martin Luther demonstrate the overwhelming difficulties of squaring a
power of human free choice with God's awesome monopoly on power. Valla
(1443/1948) concludes that the whole problem is beyond human understanding; and Luther, like Valla, is certain that the ways of God must be just, but
clearly God's ways are beyond our understanding and the justice of God must
be accepted on faith rather than understood by reason:

> This is the highest degree of faith—to believe that He is merciful, who saves so
> few and damns so many; to believe Him just, who according to His own will
> makes us necessarily damnable. . . . If, therefore, I could by any means compre-
> hend how that same God can be merciful and just who carries the appearance
> of so much wrath and iniquity, there would be no need of faith. But now, since
> that cannot be comprehended, there is room for exercising faith. . . . (1525/1823,
> section 24)

For Luther there can be no question of whether and how God can be just.
There is no justice other than what God commands, for if there were it would
place a standard of justice above God, and require that God—as a just God—
must follow the principles of justice. For Luther, whatever God commands *is*
just; it is just simply because God commands it, rather than God commanding
it because it is just. When God issues a commandment not to murder, murder
becomes wrong; but if and when God commands to murder—"But of the cities of these people, which the Lord thy God doth give thee for an inheritance,
thou shalt save alive nothing that breatheth" (Deuteronomy 20:16)—then
murder is right. The will of God is not bound by the demands of transcendent
values, the constraints of reason, or considerations of consistency. When
God sends vast multitudes to eternal torture, with no possibility for avoiding

their God-ordained destiny—"I will have mercy on whom I will have mercy, and I will have compassion on whom I will have compassion" (Romans 10:15)—that is necessarily just. We must accept it by faith, for certainly we cannot understand it by reason. To the contrary, it seems flatly contradictory to any reasonable view, and thus we understand that reason is the enemy of Christian faith.

Few people can muster sufficient faith to believe a doctrine that seems flatly contrary to reason, especially when that doctrine implies that they are likely to burn eternally in a lake of fire with nothing whatsoever they could do to avoid that horrific outcome. So most Christians eventually moved in a different direction: a direction contrary to Scripture but consistent with a deep belief in a just world. Humans have a godlike first cause power of free *choice* to opt for either salvation or damnation, a power to *make ourselves* by our own absolutely free choices.

Why does God justly punish? Because (the objections of Paul and Luther notwithstanding) by our own special power of *free will* and *free choice* we choose evil rather than good, and thus we are morally responsible and justly deserve punishment. Why does God justly reward? Because we freely *choose* to take the leap of faith and repentance, and thus we are morally responsible for choosing the path of salvation.

This power of will takes on a life of its own, to such a degree that it can be totally divorced from rationality and even operate dead contrary to rationality. The best example is Dostoyevsky's underground man, who sees free will as a power of radical choice that is not constrained by rationality:

> So one's own free, unrestrained choice, one's own whim, be it the wildest, one's own fancy, sometimes worked up to a frenzy—that is the most advantageous advantage that cannot be fitted into any table or scale and that causes every system and every theory to crumble into dust on contact. And where did these sages pick up the notion that man must have something that they feel is a normal and virtuous set of wishes; what makes them think that man's will must be reasonable and in accordance with his own interests? All man actually needs is independent will, at all costs and whatever the consequences. (Dostoyevsky 1864/1961, 110)

When the power of free choice becomes the grounds for free will, there is a problem: of course humans make choices, but so do many other species. The fox chooses one path rather than another for its foraging; the increasingly powerful and aggressive young chimpanzee chooses to challenge the older alpha male rather than show submissiveness; the young male elk chooses discretion rather than valor in considering whether to challenge the older male for his harem; the white-footed mouse usually takes the path to a ripened berry patch, but today chooses a different destination. So if making choices qualifies one for free will, then free will is not the exclusive property of humans. There are two distinctly different ways of dealing with this problem and keeping free will a uniquely human capacity. One is the path taken by Harry Frankfurt: the essential free *will* choices made by humans involve special higher-order reflection (of which only humans are capable). The second is the path preferred by libertarians such as C. A. Campbell: make *human* free will choices special (godlike) contra-causal choices, which C. A. Campbell describes as a *"creative activity*, in which . . . nothing determines the act save the agent's doing of it" (1957, 177).

Theologians might worry about how humans can have this special *power* of free choice when God is *omni*potent, but once the uniquely human power of free will became associated with the power of free choice, it was too attractive an idea for most to resist. After all, the limits on our powers of rationality seem painfully clear; but (as Descartes notes) the power to will a free choice seems a power we can exercise to the full. Human free will as a power to exercise will and freely choose among alternative paths and open possibilities was an appealing idea indeed, and it was cast into a variety of charming shapes. Pico della Mirandola openly embraced the notion of a god-given human power of miraculous free will to make ourselves according to our own choices, describing it from the perspective of the god who created humans as his favorites: "We have made thee neither of heaven nor of earth, neither mortal nor immortal, so that with freedom of choice and with honor, as though the maker and molder of thyself, thou mayest fashion thyself in whatever shape thou shalt prefer" (1486/1948, 225). Though Pico's miracle-working will was proposed more than half a millennium ago, the tradition of ascribing miraculous or semi-miraculous powers to human will continues to the present. C. A. Campbell (1957) maintains that humans have a special *first cause* contra-causal power of choosing among alternatives, and he insists that belief in this super free will power must be maintained even if it conflicts with our scientific understanding of the natural world. Richard Taylor claims that his favored account of human *agency* must be true, though he acknowledges it is so extraordinary that: "one can hardly affirm such a theory of agency with complete comfort, however, and wholly without embarrassment, for the conception of men and their powers which is involved in it is strange indeed, if not positively mysterious" (1963, 52). A similar idea was suggested by Nietzsche: we have killed god, and broken free of any prescribed destiny; and so we must ourselves become gods, and create our own chosen destiny in the form of the Overman. Sartre concluded that we are a special unique substance, being-for-itself, which has the special power of self-making with no limits or restrictions. Roderick Chisholm posited a godlike first cause power that constitutes human free will and supports our moral responsibility:

If we are responsible, and if what I have been trying to say is true, then we have a prerogative which some would attribute only to God: each of us, when we really act, is a prime mover unmoved. In doing what we do, we cause certain events to happen, and nothing and no one, except we ourselves, causes us to cause those events to happen. (1982, 32)

Few contemporary philosophers worry about how the human power of miracle-working free will can be consistent with belief in an *omni*potent God. But they do worry about squaring free will with naturalism, and giving an account of free will that avoids mysteries and miracles. What sort of choice is this free will choice, this act of will that supports claims and ascriptions of moral responsibility? If it is not a miraculous first-cause choice, whatever that might be, and is a sufficiently rich choice to be something that only humans can do and that will bear the weight of moral responsibility, it must be special—but not so special that it transcends natural causes and events. This is the challenge faced by contemporary defenders of a uniquely human free will that can support moral responsibility: contriving a plausible account of this quite remarkable free will that stays strictly within the limits of naturalism and makes no appeal to mysteries or miracles.

FREE WILL WITHOUT MIRACLES

Our basic belief in *uniquely* human free will—a free will that can justify claims and ascriptions of moral responsibility—developed within a world view that was radically different from contemporary naturalism. In that world view humans were the specially crafted favorites of God rather than products of natural selection, there were few limits on our rational powers, and a miraculous human power of free will seemed altogether plausible. The challenge for contemporary naturalist philosophers—philosophers who reject miracles, refuse to rely on mysteries, and recognize that our evolutionary history only recently diverged from that of other closely related animals—is to transplant uniquely human free will into our contemporary world view, and have it make sense on a purely naturalistic basis. The profound commitment that most have to this extraordinary moral-responsibility-supporting human free will obscures the magnitude of the challenge. Most are inclined to agree with Peter van Inwagen (1983): we *know* we are morally responsible, so we *must* have a free will that supports moral responsibility, and it is merely a matter of discovering the workable account of free will that we know must exist. Since we know that such free will exists in our natural world, how hard can it be to give an account of it?

Certainly a miracle-working account of human free will—the power to be a prime mover unmoved, the power to make choices between duty and desire with no causal antecedents for our choices—keeps free will the exclusive property of humans. But if we have doubts about the perfect rationality of humans, then basing human free will on the godlike first cause miracle-working power of will is even more problematic. In Pico's world of gods and souls and miracles, such a will might seem plausible—particularly as a special gift from God to his last and favorite creation. But in a world without gods and miracles, in which humans evolved like other animals and were not specially crafted by God—that is, in our natural nonmiraculous world—that account of free will is a nonstarter.

If humans have neither perfect reason nor miraculous powers of will, what foundation can there be for a uniquely human free will that supports uniquely human moral responsibility? Harry Frankfurt proposed a remarkable solution, which solved all the philosophical problems. Employing higher-order and uniquely human powers of reflection (but avoiding claims of perfect rationality) together with a power of willing (but *not* a godlike first cause power of miraculous choice among open alternatives), Frankfurt gives an account of reflective uniquely human free will unencumbered by miraculous powers of either reason or will. This is an account of a free will that is uniquely human, employs the uniquely human higher reflective powers of human reason but avoids implausible perfect rationality, and eliminates the need for open alternatives and thus requires no godlike powers of self-caused choice. Small wonder that Frankfurt's model has become a pivot point in the contemporary discussion of free will.

Frankfurt is deeply concerned with human uniqueness, and his account of free will is explicitly designed to establish an "essential difference between persons and other creatures":

> We do in fact assume . . . that no member of another species is a person. Accordingly, there is a presumption that what is essential to persons is a set of characteristics that we generally suppose—whether rightly or wrongly—to be uniquely human.
>
> It is my view that one essential difference between persons and other creatures is to be found in the structure of a person's will. Human beings are not alone in having desires and motives, or in making choices. They share these things with the members of certain other species, some of whom even appear to engage in deliberation and to make decisions based upon prior thought. It seems to be peculiarly characteristic of humans, however, that they are able to form what I shall call "second-order desires" or "desires of the second order." (Frankfurt 1971, 6)

On Frankfurt's account of free will, so long as one has "the will one wants to have," then one has free will; and if one can also act in accordance with that will, one has freedom of action; and if one has both freedom of action and freedom of the will, then one may not have everything, but certainly one has all that one could wish for in the way of free will: "there is nothing in the way of freedom that he lacks" (Frankfurt 1971, 17).

Frankfurt's dramatic and counterintuitive example of a person who enjoys free will is a drug addict: an individual often offered as a prime example of someone who does *not* have free will. But this is not an ordinary drug addict; rather, he is a *willing* drug addict who reflects on his addictive state, deeply approves of his addiction, and is delighted that he is an addict:

> He is a willing addict, who would not have things any other way. If the grip of his addiction should somehow weaken, he would do whatever he could to reinstate it; if his desire for the drug should begin to fade, he would take steps to renew its intensity.
>
> The willing addict's will is not free, for his desire to take the drug will be effective regardless of whether or not he wants this desire to constitute his will. But when the takes the drug, he takes it freely and of his own free will. I am inclined to understand his situation as involving the overdetermination of his first-order desire to take the drug. This desire is his effective desire because he is physiologically addicted. But it is his effective desire also because he wants it to be. His will is outside his control, but, by his second-order desire that his desire for the drug should be effective, he has made this will his own. Given that it is therefore not only because of his addiction that his desire for the drug is effective, he may be morally responsible for taking the drug. (Frankfurt 1971, 19–20)

Frankfurt's "willing addict" is a famous and fascinating philosophical case. But this is not a counterintuitive case that reveals the strength and ingenuity of Frankfurt's model; rather, it is a case that—on careful examination— reveals the deep problems with treating higher-order reflection as the essence of free will, rather than a special enhancement of free will that is sometimes (but not invariably) useful to human animals. Instead of the abstract blood- less philosophical example of a willing addict, consider the actual history and circumstances of such an individual. The willing addict does not awaken one morning from a pleasant and fulfilling life as a philosopher or physician or artist, and decide—after careful reflection—that he or she deeply approves of the life of a drug addict. Certainly it is possible for an addict to reflectively approve and genuinely prefer a life of addiction, but that will be a special— and specially depressing—case. We are not speaking here of someone who enjoys recreational drugs and has slipped over the line into addiction and is trying to escape. This is not a drug addict who is struggling to overcome his addiction, but an addict who embraces and reflectively approves of addiction.

Neither the willing addict nor the unwilling addict starts out with a desire to be a drug addict. Instead, the addict starts experimenting with drugs, con- vinced that he "has it under control" and is only using drugs for an occasional high or a special boost or a pleasant recreational interlude. But the drug dalliance evolves into drug addiction, and the user finds that he cannot stop, even when he desperately wants to stop. The drug use is alienating him from his friends, destroying his career, wrecking his family, and undercutting his self-respect along with his sense of self-control. This is now an *un*willing addict, who has been trapped by an addiction he despises, and who deeply regrets the losses—family, friends, fortune, self-respect—he is suffering. This addict lacks free will, as Frankfurt acknowledges.

As the addict finally loses friends, career, hopes, and self-esteem he clings desperately to the only thing left: his narcotics addiction. The addict who recognizes and *reflectively approves* his enslavement to drugs is an addict who has lost all hope of freedom, and who clings to drug addiction as the only straw in his sea of desperate suffering. For this *willing* addict, who *embraces* enslavement to drugs, all other paths are empty or blocked. Clearly the person who struggles against her addiction is not free; but the person who has given up the struggle, and clings desperately to addiction as the only source of even minimal satisfaction, has not become free. Instead he suffers the ultimate loss of freedom, when one is no longer capable of *wishing* to be free. Abandoning all hope of gaining freedom does not make him free.

A still uglier example of unfree reflectively willed acquiescence—one that was cruel reality rather than philosophical fantasy—can be found in the history of slavery. Consider the horrific system of slavery in the eighteenth- and nineteenth-century United States (as well as in places like Haiti and Brazil). This was such a vile and brutal system—and so fundamentally inconsistent with the principles of liberty that the U.S. pretended to honor—that it is almost impossible for many Americans to face, then or now: the cognitive dissonance is too profound and painful. Instead they cultivated images of slaves toiling contentedly under the benevolent supervision of enlightened slave owners and their overseers. Whites happily sang songs about "old Black Joe," about the "gaiety" of the slaves at my "old Kentucky home," and about the profound grief of the slaves at the death of "Massa" who was so kind that he "made the slaves love him" and who now was in "the cold cold ground": the slave in the song states that he "cannot go to work tomorrow, for the teardrops flow; got to drive away my sorrow, strumming on the old banjo" (as if slaves, whenever they wished, could devote a leisurely day to banjo strumming). It was not only such notorious films as *The Birth of a Nation* that perpetuated such myths, but also widely acclaimed popular films like *Gone with the Wind*. The reality was savage brutality, horrific torture with whip and branding iron, mutilations, men and women worked literally to death in the heat and humidity of Louisiana sugar cane fields and Mississippi cotton plantations and North Carolina tobacco farms and South American mines, women repeatedly raped and their children sold away from them. Some never gave in, and died under the lash. A slave who struggles for her freedom, who fights against her bonds, who courageously rejects the demeaning role of slave, who seeks every means of resistance and escape: this is an unwilling slave, who is certainly not free (as Frankfurt would acknowledge). But others were finally broken by this unrelenting and inescapable cruel treatment, and ultimately lost any hope or even desire for freedom. They became "happy slaves," or rather slaves who accepted their enslavement and no longer had the capacity to seek freedom.

Under such nightmare conditions of hopelessness and helplessness, almost everyone "learns" that resistance is futile, and that—although conditions are always painful—they are slightly less painful when one gives up all resistance and acquiesces to those conditions. Every effort at escape and resistance not only fails, but brings brutal punishment. As resistance efforts weaken, the shackles are reduced and meager comforts—slightly better food, a blanket against the chill—are provided. Other slaves who had kept a careful distance (lest they also suffer the sadistic overseer's well-known cruelties) offer some degree of comfort and companionship. Eventually the painful futility of resistance wears away all hope and desire of liberation, and the slave accepts and even embraces and reflectively approves her enslaved status, teaching her children the "virtue" of meek acquiescence and their "proper place" as loyal slaves. The slave who is no longer capable of seeking freedom may—in this horrible system—be a happier slave than the slave who sustains fierce and futile efforts at resistance; but this willing slave is at an even greater distance from freedom and free will. The slave who struggles courageously against her chains is not free; but the slave who embraces enslavement is even further removed from freedom. When all hope of making free choices and controlling her own life has been destroyed, and she becomes so powerless and hopeless as to embrace the forces that destroy all hope of self governance, the result is not free will. Under sustained cruel conditions, the slave may accept demeaning servitude, and even *reflectively* embrace slavery; but only deep reluctance to look closely at the conditions that shape acquiescent slaves and willing addicts can make it seem plausible that they have free will and are morally responsible for their profound enslavement.

Willing addiction and reflectively satisfied slavery are not marks of free will, but of the most extreme deprivation of free will. This is not obvious, because in most cases higher-order reflection enhances human free will; and Frankfurt does significant philosophical service in making clear the nature and typical advantages of such higher-order reflection. But higher-order reflection can also be an impediment to free will; and some who are striking examples of the most dedicated and reflectively approved paths—the cult member, the willing addict, the satisfied slave—are also sad examples of the ultimate loss of free will.

Higher-order reflection is often an enhancement of human free will, but it is neither a necessary nor sufficient condition for free will. After struggling with his affection for his friend (the escaped slave, Jim) and his sense of moral duty (his moral obligation to return the slave "property" to its "rightful owners"), Huck Finn decides that the struggle—the struggle involving higher-order reflection on whether he wishes his will to be guided by affection or duty—is just not worth it. Huck resolves to abandon such efforts, and in the future he "wouldn't bother no more about it, but after this always do whichever come handiest at the time." At that point Huck becomes (what Frankfurt famously christens) a "wanton": "I shall use the term "wanton" to refer to agents who have first-order desires but who are not persons because, whether or not they have desires of the second order, they have no second-order volitions" (Frankfurt 1971, 11). Huck, who in future will do "whichever comes handiest at the time" may be a wanton; but Huck is not deprived of free will. In contrast, the willing addict and acquiescent slave—who reflectively approve their respective enslavements—are certainly not wantons, but they have little if any free will. Huck, wanton that he is, has deprived himself of one of the important ways of *enhancing* his own free will through careful higher-order reflection; but he nonetheless has rich resources of free will, and considerably more free will than that enjoyed by the reflective willing addict.

Frankfurt's model emphasizes something valuable for humans and many other animals: the commitment that keeps paths open when they might otherwise be abandoned. Higher-order reflective processes afford humans a special and useful means of preserving commitments, thereby keeping valuable options available. The poet who is profoundly committed to her poetry—who delights in writing poetry, and is reflectively *glad* that she loves poetry—may hit a rough patch: several of her submissions are rejected, an eagerly anticipated reading is canceled, she is stuck in a metrical rut while her muse seems to be off on holiday, and her rhyming dictionary is stolen. This steady flow of disappointments begins to erode her deep love of poetry, and she finds herself watching more television and writing less poetry. Because of her profound higher-order commitment to poetry, she may take steps to preserve and rejuvenate her poetic passion: she reads some of her favorite poems, looks again at some of the best poetry she has written, seeks out friends who have great enthusiasm for her poetry, perhaps takes a trip to a new setting that might inspire a new style of verse. By these purposeful efforts, she may effectively restore and preserve the poetic path that might otherwise have been lost. But such commitment enhancement is not an essential mark of free will, nor does it make free will exclusively human. In struggling to keep free will the exclusive property of humans, Frankfurt underestimates the importance of the elements of free will that are shared by humans and many other animals, and treats human *enhancements* of free will as the essence of free will.

VALUABLE SELF-CONTROL

The ability to will and choose and exercise self-control is of great importance for free will; but if it is to be the basis for a uniquely human free will (and one that will support moral responsibility), we must either make it miraculous or ignore the actual limited nature of that will and the causes for stronger and weaker powers of will. Perhaps gods can always try harder; human animals cannot. If we examine natural powers of will, including deferred gratification, it is not uniquely human; and if we look carefully at the forces that shape such varying degrees of will, it will not support moral responsibility. Descartes regards the human power of will as a godlike capacity, with no apparent limits. Kant agrees: it is the power of the will alone—with no aid whatsoever from the emotions—that enables us to follow the moral law. But this is the stuff of philosophical and theological fantasy. Careful examination reveals that the power of will is not uniquely human, and it is not without limits.

There are many factors that influence our "will power" in any given situation. The debilitating experience of learned helplessness—studied by Seligman (1975) in dogs, but well-established in studies of humans as well—can leave one devoid of will power. At a less extreme level, one's sense of self-efficacy (which can vary greatly from task to task) is also a pivotal factor in the degree of effort and will one can exert (Bandura 1997): those strong in self-efficacy persevere when facing difficult challenges (Bandura and Cervone 1983), while those with a weak sense of self-efficacy give up more quickly (Bandura and Schunk 1981; Schunk 1981; Weinberg, Gould, Yukelson, and Jackson 1981). And those with a strong sense of internal locus-of-control generally have greater resources of will than those who have an external locus-of-control (Rotter 1966, 1975, 1979, 1990). The power to sustain careful System 2 deliberative efforts and make meticulously examined decisions is not an unlimited power: Recent cognitive demands result in ego-depletion (Baumeister et al.1998), that leaves few resources for rigorously reflective choice-making. And *situations* can have an enormous impact on how vigorously and effectively will power is employed, and in many cases whether it is employed at all. No doubt many participants in the Milgram (1963) experiment—many of whom delivered (what they believed to be) severe or even fatal shocks to another experimental subject—looked back on their participation, and with sad amazement questioned *why* they had not exerted the will power to stand up against the experimenter and insist that the shocks be stopped. In another situation, most of the participants who (so they believed) meted out severe punitive shocks to an innocent fellow subject would have exerted strong efforts of will power to avoid such behavior: they would have resisted the temptation of monetary reward, and perhaps would have suffered severe shocks themselves rather than apply them to another.

But for most of the participants in that notorious experimental situation, the will power resources required to resist the experimenter's commands were never activated.

One of the most important elements of free will is the capacity of self-control, and a vital element of self-control is the capacity for deferred gratification: the ability to forgo an immediate pleasure in order to gain greater benefits at a later time. One of the most interesting and well-known experiments on deferred gratification was carried out by Walter Mischel and his colleagues (1970, 1972). Children (aged 4–6) selected a treat (such as a cookie or marshmallow). The treat was placed on a table, and the child was told that he or she could eat the treat now, or wait 15 minutes at which time the child would receive a second treat. Then the researchers left the room, observing through a one-way mirror. Approximately one-third of the children waited 15 minutes for the second treat (often employing a variety of techniques to distract themselves from the immediately available treat). Perhaps the most interesting aspect of the experiment was a follow-up study (Mischel, Shoda, and Peake 1988) showing that the children who at this early age had better self-control (deferred-gratification) capacities were more likely to have higher SAT scores many years later.

Self-control is obviously a vital element of free will: if I really want to stop eating so many sweets (or stop smoking, or exercise more, or drink less), but I lack sufficient powers of self-control to resist the immediate desire for sweets, then my free will is seriously impaired. But self-control is by no means the exclusive property of humans. Mischel and his colleagues observed that children who successfully exercised self-control were those who found ways of distracting themselves from the immediate temptation; in a study of chimpanzee self-control, the chimpanzees used the same method: they focused on playing with toys to distract themselves from the immediately available and very desirable candy. As the experimenters noted, the chimpanzees "were not passively distracted by the presence of the toys but were actively engaged in toy manipulation to divert their attention from the accumulating candies" (Evans and Beran 2007, 601). Successful methods of self-control in chimpanzees run parallel to successful methods employed by humans, and evidence for the powers of deferred gratification in nonhuman primates and monkeys is varied and extensive (Tobin, Logue, Chelonis, Ackermann, and May 1996; Beran and Evans 2012; Beran et al. 2014; Evans et al. 2014; Parrish et al. 2014).

By studying self-control in other animals, we observe things about self-control that are too easily neglected, especially by those who believe in moral responsibility. We say that either one has or lacks "will power" and that's just the way it is; or that everyone *has* will power and the power of self-control and deferred gratification, but some choose to use it and others do not: everyone has the power, and it's your own fault and your own moral responsibility if you fail to employ that power. But not only is the power of self-control something we tend to acquire (or not) at a tender age, but also it is deeply influenced by environmental factors. That should be obvious to us; but only when we see it in other animals does it really become so. A child who grows up in poverty has few chances to develop strong resources of self-control. In an environment of desperation, exchanging a smaller immediate benefit for a larger benefit at a later time is likely to be a bad strategy: the later larger benefit that was hoped for is not likely to materialize; and failing to grab the immediately available benefit likely means that it will be lost to hungry people who are unlikely to leave scarce benefits unappropriated. An animal that hunts individually—such as a sea lion (Genty and Roeder 2006)—is likely to have different needs for deferred gratification than do animals that hunt in groups. Crows are very good at deferred gratification, if the deferring will lead to a more desirable treat; but they have little interest in deferring gratification to gain more of the same treat (Hillemann et al. 2014). That makes sense when we think about it, since the crow cannot carry four or five different similar items in its beak, but may well find it useful to pass up a desirable food source in favor of a significantly more desirable one. There would be little or no selective advantage to deferring an immediate treat in favor of waiting for more of the same treat (when more of that treat is generally of no use).

The experimental evidence makes clear that several species, in addition to humans, have the capacity to exercise self-control (deferred gratification). As Beran and Evans (2006) conclude on the basis of their studies:

> Chimpanzees will wait and inhibit the impulse to consume highly preferred food items if that means more of those items can be obtained in the future. This is true both when the items yet to be presented are visible and when they are not visible and the chimpanzees must infer that additional accumulation of food is possible. As such, this behavior reflects a level of self-control that is perhaps linked to planning behavior in the sense of making decisions based not solely on immediately available outcomes but also on outcomes available only in the future. (2006, 323)

The findings of Alexandra Rosati and her fellow researchers are even more striking, demonstrating that when humans and chimpanzees are tested for powers of deferred gratification for securing food treats, "chimpanzees were actually more patient than humans when compared on similar temporal tasks" (Rosati et al. 2007, 1666). In reviewing a range of such results, Hayden and Platt state:

These observations suggest that self-control may not be uniquely human and may have evolved in primates sometime before the divergence of humans and other apes some five to eight million years ago. More generally, these results suggest that patience itself is not a single biological trait, like running speed— nor is it a virtue. The capacity for self-control may instead be viewed as a cognitive adaptation that evolves in response to selective pressures favoring delayed gratification and may be differentially deployed in distinct behavioral contexts. (2007, 923)

Human culture affords more opportunities for greatly extended processes of delayed gratification: through savings accounts, for example, in which the gratifications may be delayed for decades (though the accumulating savings balance may serve as a more immediate secondary reinforcer, and there may be the short-term gratification of a greater sense of security). But recent research indicates that if chimpanzees had retirement plans, some chimpanzees would likely reach retirement with more substantial savings than would some humans.

Chimpanzees and humans are rather good at self-control, and that impressive capacity is an important enhancement of their powers of free will. But self-control *enhances* free will; it is not an essential condition for free will. An individual who invariably grabs at the first item that catches its fancy may be disqualified from free will; but that is not an accurate description of animals that are weak in deferred gratification, whether that animal is human or chimpanzee or rat or pigeon. Many of those not blessed with great powers of self-control—or high powers of deliberation, for that matter—can still make intelligent choices and exercise effective control and value choices. And for some species, strong powers of deferred gratification may be undesirable and maladaptive. As Tobin and Logue (1994) note:

It has been hypothesized that greater impulsiveness is adaptive when an organism is at risk of dying if it does not receive a certain amount of food within a short period of time. . . . For example, a bird, foraging in an inconstant environment at dusk, which has not yet consumed enough food to allow it to last through the night, may be more likely to survive by taking smaller, more immediately available prey items than by waiting for larger, riskier prey items. Given that organisms with higher metabolic rates are more likely to die if they do not obtain food at regular, short intervals, the degree of self-control shown by an organism may be expected to correlate negatively with metabolic rate. (Tobin and Logue 1994, 127; see also Logue 1988)

Thus studying self-control in other species may help us understand the adaptive nature of human self-control.

It is true that some humans become quite good at deferred gratification, and most humans are significantly better at it than are most nonhumans; but that does not change the fact that many species other than humans can practice at least modest self-control in the form of deferred gratification. Of course we could exclude modest powers of self-control—whether in humans or nonhumans—from the category of self-control, counting only the most exemplary levels of exclusively human self-control as *real* self-control. As Frans de Waal notes concerning nonhuman examples of culture, we can arbitrarily exclude such cases if we set the bar high enough:

> It is not hard to come up with a definition of culture that rules out all species except our own. Even tools can be defined in such a way that they are found only in our species—for example, by requiring that they fit a symbolic context. Such exclusive definitions tend to focus on the highest human achievements associated with a process, declaring these absolutely essential. (2001, 25–6)

But such exclusive definitions cripple our efforts to understand how powers of self-control might have evolved, and how self-control functions in larger contexts.

Some humans are not very good at self-control—their capacity for deferred gratification is in the same range as that of chimpanzees, or somewhat worse—and they have less self-control and less freedom than you have; but though the free will they enjoy is somewhat less robust, it still exists. We can acknowledge that humans with strong self-control capacities have stronger free will than do humans (and chimpanzees and bonobos) with weaker capacity for self-control; but those humans and chimpanzees and bonobos have weaker free will, rather than no free will.

Will is an important element of free will: to suffer from learned helplessness is to suffer the loss of free will. The capacity for higher-order reflection is an important and probably species-specific enhancement of human free will; but it is neither necessary nor sufficient for free will. When we study the *will* element of free will, as it is writ large in the behavior of many species, we gain a better understanding of free will generally and of human free will particularly.

NOTE

1. For detailed interpretation of the parable, see Herzog (1994).

Chapter 5

The Burden of Moral Responsibility

We understand free will better when we cease trying to restrict it to humans, and instead look at free will from a longer and broader perspective. But there appears to be an insurmountable problem with the possibility of nonhuman animals having free will: If other animals have free will, then they can also behave morally and immorally; and if they behave morally and immorally, they can justly deserve moral praise and moral blame, and justly deserve punishment; and that lands us back in the manifest absurdity of ascribing moral responsibility to lions and tigers and bears, and carrying out the executions of pigs and elephants and other animals for committing crimes. We read of earlier times when pigs and horses and even elephants were executed for killing humans (never for killing other elephants or members of any species other than humans); and we marvel at the primitive impulses fueling such proceedings. Obviously we do not want to return to such procedures: they are ludicrous as well as repugnant. Therefore extending free will to nonhuman animals results in a clear *reductio ad absurdum*.

Mark Rowlands is a powerful advocate of counting other animals as moral *subjects*, and thus capable of a substantive range of ethical behavior. He offers a version of this *reductio* argument to insist that while animals are indeed moral subjects, it is a mistake to suppose that animals are full moral *agents*:

> The claim that animals can be moral agents is, I shall argue, deeply problematic—and I suspect that proponents of this view have failed to appreciate just how problematic. First of all, the concept of agency is inseparable from that of responsibility, and hence from the concept of praise and blame. If animals are moral agents, it follows that they must be responsible for what they do. But if they are responsible for what they do, then, it seems, they can be held

71

accountable for what they do. At one time, courts of law—both nonsecular and secular—set up to try (and subsequently execute) animals for perceived crimes were not uncommon. I assume that few would wish to recommend a return to this practice. (2012, 83)

The final step in this *reductio* argument is a powerful one: applying the judicial machinery of execution to nonhuman animals is absurd, and disgusting. And the first step in the argument is also legitimate: if animals other than humans can have free will, then at least some animals other than humans can behave morally and immorally (perhaps not animals that have only the most rudimentary elements of free will, such as fruit flies; but certainly nonhuman animals such as other primates). The linchpin in this argument is the claim that "the concept of agency is inseparable from that of responsibility." But from the fact that animals other than human animals behave morally and immorally, and are genuine moral agents (just as humans are) it does not follow that they are morally responsible for their behavior; and therefore it does not follow that they justly deserve punishment and reward for their immoral and moral behavior. Robert Harris, a brutal murderer, acted from his own free will. He acted purposefully, and he intentionally caused terrible harms, and he may have engaged in some modest degree of reflection in which he gave his stamp of approval to his life of cruel brutality: I chose the road to hell, that made me what I am, and I have no wish whatsoever to lose my desire and capacity for brutality. But—as argued in Chapter 6 (see also Waller 2011)—it does not follow that either Harris (or his virtuous counterpart) is morally responsible for his vicious and morally egregious behavior and the character from which it flows. If we find it impossible to avoid applying some punitive measures to Robert Harris (such as isolating him) it does not follow that he *justly deserves* such punishment, and the punishment should be the least possible punishment consistent with protection of others.

THE LINK

That any adequate account of free will *must* support moral responsibility is an article of faith among contemporary philosophers. There are those who reject free will but maintain that moral responsibility can survive *without* free will: John Martin Fischer's semicompatibilism is based on that claim, and recently Michael Gazzaniga (2014) has championed the view that moral responsibility does not *require* free will. And of course several philosophers—such as Derk Pereboom, Galen Strawson, and Gregg Caruso—deny that we have free will, and on that basis also deny that we have moral responsibility. But there seems to be almost universal agreement that whatever free will turns out to be (if it exists at all) it must support moral responsibility.[1]

The unbreakable link between free will and moral responsibility is a powerful philosophical conviction (at least in the West). Any account of free will that fails to support moral responsibility is a nonstarter. Susan Wolf insists on this point:

> it seems to me that the philosophical problem of free will is and has been fundamentally connected to the question of whether and how the distinctive set of attitudes and the practices that constitute my kind of blame [what Wolf calls "angry blame" involving attitudes such as "resentment, indignation, guilt, and righteous anger"] can be justifiable and appropriate. We cannot understand the history of the free will debate without making reference to this set of attitudes and practices, nor can we do justice to the continued discussion of the problem if we fail to recognize that the intelligibility and legitimacy of this set of attitudes and practices in particular is at least part of what is at stake. (2011, 335)

Susan Wolf is in good company. In Michael McKenna's view, "Free will is just the capacity that gives persons the relevant sort of control required for morally responsible agency" (2008,187–8). Eddy Nahmias insists that "we should be concerned primarily with free will understood as the set of powers or abilities required to be morally responsible—that is, potentially to deserve blame or praise, punishment or reward" (Nahmias 2014b, 43). C. A. Campbell claims that it is the deep connection with moral responsibility that makes the free will question so important:

> It is not seriously disputable that the kind of freedom in question is the freedom which is commonly recognised to be in some sense a precondition of moral responsibility. Clearly, it is on account of this integral connection with moral responsibility that such exceptional importance has always been felt to attach to the Free Will problem. (1957, 159)

But free will is not only a necessary condition for moral responsibility; according to Willard Gaylin it is also a sufficient condition: "Freedom demands responsibility; autonomy demands culpability" (1982, 338). Putting these together, Walter Glannon concludes that free will is both necessary *and* sufficient for moral responsibility, and you can't have one without the other: "Autonomy and responsibility are mutually entailing notions" (1998, 45).

Taking moral responsibility as given, some now use the assumed link between moral responsibility and free will to make moral responsibility support free will. This is explicit in Van Inwagen:

> If we do know that moral responsibility exists, then we should have no doubt about whether we have good reason to believe we have free will. . . . [I]t is as adequate a defence of the free-will thesis as has ever been given for any philosophical

position to say, "Without free will, we should never be morally responsible for anything; and we are sometimes morally responsible." (1983, 209)

Taking moral responsibility as given, and free will as the inseparable and essential foundation of moral responsibility, we need no longer worry that there is not an adequate account of free will that can support moral responsibility. Since we know that moral responsibility exists, and free will is essential for moral responsibility, it follows that whatever account of free will is best *must* be sufficient for the support of moral responsibility. Adina L. Roskies counsels precisely that approach:

> We ought to explore the possibility that freedom is a concept derivative on more robust intuitions about responsibility rather than vice versa. I favor a compatibilist view of responsibility, which has several advantages over incompatibilist views. It provides an account of responsibility that is not hostage to the outcome of the determinism/indeterminism debate, which, as I've argued, does not hold much promise for progress. Doing so preserves perhaps the most vivid of our intuitions about human behavior: that, given certain circumstances, we are responsible for our choices and actions. (Roskies 2014, 121)

Daniel Dennett (2003, 297) proposes a similar approach: rather than obsessing over what sort of metaphysical foundation is required to justify blame and punishment and moral responsibility, count free will (and "could have done otherwise") as *whatever* model of free will provides the best grounds for moral responsibility. Since we know that moral responsibility is justified, whatever working model is providing that justification must be doing its job well.

Cory J. Clark, Peter H. Ditto, Azim F. Shariff, Jamie B. Luguri, Joshua Knobe, and Roy F. Baumeister (2014) recently published a remarkable set of studies on the sources as well as the effects of belief in moral responsibility. They open their account with a quote from Nietzsche:

> Today we no longer have any pity for the concept of "free will": we know only too well what it really is—the foulest of all theologians' artifices, aimed at making mankind "responsible" in their sense. . . . Wherever responsibilities are sought, it is usually the instinct of wanting to judge and punish which is at work. (Nietzsche 1889/1954, 499)

The studies that they ran (particularly the first and second experiments) found a powerful desire to justify the punishment of harmful immoral behavior; which led to belief in moral responsibility (and belief in a free will power that can support moral responsibility). As the authors describe the results of their first experiment: "Reactions to misdeeds by others seemed to cause mental shifts that went beyond the specific incident to invoke broad assumptions about human nature and responsible action in general" (Clark et al. 2014, 504). And similar results were obtained in the second experiment, under the assumption that free will beliefs are used to support belief in moral responsibility: "It demonstrated that a heightened desire to punish accounts for the heightened levels of both specific free will attributions and general free will belief" (2014, 504). That is, the results from both experiments showed that the desire to punish—and particularly to *justify* punishment (in order to preserve belief in a just world)—resulted in *distorted* beliefs concerning the amount of control persons have: the control that both specific wrongdoers and ultimately everyone has over their behavior. So moral responsibility rests on a false belief in a just world and a desperate desire to *preserve* that false belief by providing a just deserts "justification" for punishment. That belief in moral responsibility results in two major distortions: first, a widely held belief in a miracle-working power of free will; and second, beliefs—both specific and general—about the powers of control exercised by those who behave badly. The challenge these studies pose for belief in moral responsibility is summarized in their conclusion:

> We tested an idea dating back to Nietzsche (1889/1954): the idea that free will is embraced, at least partly, in order to justify holding others morally responsible for their wrongful behaviors. Our investigation has supported Nietzsche's hypothesis with multiple findings, diverse methods, and different populations. (2014, 510)

The thought process revealed by the experiment appears to be something like this (with vital elements functioning nonconsciously): We must mete out punishment; because we live in a just world, any punishment we are required to inflict must be just; punishment is just only if it is justly deserved; an act justly deserves punishment only if one is morally responsible for that act; therefore, people are sometimes morally responsible for their acts; and there-fore—since we can only be morally responsible for an act if we acted from free will—we must have a robust free will that supports moral responsibility.

In sum, belief in moral responsibility starts from a false belief in a just world, and then protects that belief by generating a false conception of free will together with false beliefs about the causes of behavior. The thesis of this book is that we can have a valuable account of free will if we *restore* free will to its natural state as a vital element of animal behavior, and we liberate animal free will from the impossible task of supporting moral responsibility. The moral of the study by Clark and his fellow researchers is clear, though they seem reluctant to draw it: belief in moral responsibility is based on a false assumption of a just world and requires a range of false beliefs and false conclusions in order to prop up that implausible belief; and moral responsibility—and any free will account that purports to justify moral responsibility—rests on a false foundation. The *reductio* argument examined at the beginning of this chapter concludes that it is manifestly absurd to hold nonhuman animals morally responsible and subject them to execution or other punitive "just deserts." But that manifest absurdity is just absurdity writ large, so that it is easier to see than the absurdity of applying moral responsibility to human animals.

THE FORCES INFLUENCING PHILOSOPHICAL MODELS OF FREE WILL

Several factors work together to twist our concept of free will into strange and even miraculous forms. Insisting on human uniqueness is bad enough; but when we add a just world and moral responsibility, free will bends beneath its burden. As Bernard Williams notes:

> the traditional metaphysical problem of the freedom of the will . . . exists only for those who have metaphysical expectations. Just as there is a "problem of evil" only for those who expect the world to be good, there is a problem of free will only for those who think that the notion of the voluntary can be metaphysically deepened. In truth, though it may be extended or contracted in various ways, it can hardly be deepened at all. What threatens it is the attempt to make it profound, and the effect of trying to deepen it is to put it beyond all recognition. (1993, 68)

When we try to devise a free will that can carry the weight of a just world and moral responsibility, then the illegitimate "deepening" of free will twists free will into impossible form: human will becomes miraculous, human reason becomes super, and free will is removed from its natural setting in the natural world. At that point we are no longer giving an account of free will to make sense of free will; we are giving an account of free will to make sense of moral responsibility.

In one respect, the passage quoted earlier from Susan Wolf is right: we cannot understand our notion of free will and the debate over free will without understanding the role it has played in supporting moral responsibility:

> It seems to me that the philosophical problem of free will is and has been fundamentally connected to the question of whether and how the distinctive set of attitudes and the practices that constitute my kind of blame [a robust "angry blame"] can be justifiable and appropriate. We cannot understand the history

of the free will debate without making reference to this set of attitudes and practices. . . . (2011, 335)

But it is precisely that role of propping up moral responsibility that takes free will out of the animal realm and obscures its natural function. Like many other animals, humans have the valuable capacity for exercising free will. It is highly adaptive for foraging animals, and it evolved in a variety of animals in a variety of forms to fulfill the same basic function—but the function free will serves and evolved to perform is not the function of supporting moral responsibility.

How did free will become so rigidly linked with moral responsibility? That linkage seems obvious to many, philosopher and folk alike; but there is no reason why free will should be the inseparable companion of moral responsibility. Our capacity for free will—even if you confine that capacity to humans—did not evolve in order to support moral responsibility. Belief in moral responsibility was a late cultural development: harsh punishments were meted out—by both gods and humans—without any regard for just deserts. Deities often punished the sins of the fathers by harsh treatment of their children and grandchildren; and in honor societies (Sommers 2012) a wrong committed by Alfred could be avenged on Alfred's innocent brothers and children—indeed, if Alfred died before vengeance could be exacted, the honor morality *demanded* the killing of some worthy but innocent close relative or friend. The powerful desire to "strike-back" (Kawamura 1967; Potegal 1994; Virgin and Sapolsky 1997; Barash 2005; Barash and Lipton 2011) existed prior to belief in moral responsibility; and free will existed—in humans and other animals—long before anyone contrived the notion of moral responsibility. The earliest stoical conceptions of free will—involving remarkable powers of rationality (Frede 2011)—had little if any relation to moral responsibility. (Moral responsibility is centrally concerned with the just desert of punishment; and on early rationalist views, only those with perfect rationality have free will; and those who are perfectly rational never commit wrongs that deserve punishment.)

When the fates are no longer tricksters and the gods no longer arbitrary, then we start to look for ways to justify God's ways to man and to justify our punitive treatment of our fellow humans. The world must be not only orderly but also *just*. Punishment, which was always necessary, must now also be morally justified: the wicked must *justly deserve* the punishment they receive, while the righteous justly deserve their rewards. Belief in a just world required belief in moral responsibility; and free will—being uniquely human—was the best candidate to support uniquely human moral responsibility.

Free will of the rationalist variety would not answer the needs of moral responsibility, for two main reasons. First, only a very few very special persons achieved the superior and sustained level of reason required for free will. Second, and even more problematically, those we most want to punish—who commit vile deeds—are certainly not those with the super levels of rationality requisite for free will. That is a problem Susan Wolf (1980) made clear for the contemporary discussion of free will and moral responsibility: The only real freedom is in following the True and Good because one has knowledge of the True and Good; anyone who deviates from that path must be acting in ignorance, and thus is not acting freely; so those who commit bad acts are not free, and thus not morally responsible, and not justly deserving of punishment for their misdeeds. But obviously we are more concerned about finding a justification for punishment than for reward. In fact, recent research has shown exactly that (Clark et al. 2014): when we offer identical scenarios in which person A does something wrong and person B does something virtuous, subjects are more likely to attribute free will to the person who did wrong (in order to hold that person morally responsible and legitimize justly punishing the person).

Since rationalist free will does not provide a basis for just punishment of malefactors, a more vigorous version of free will was required. Pico della Mirandola was happy to provide it. In Pico's account, God assigns all the other creatures specific abilities; but to humans—God's last and favorite creation—God assigns a very special capacity: the capacity to make oneself in whatever form one chooses. This worked fine, with humans as God's special creation made in God's image and granted the special godlike power to make themselves from scratch as uncaused causes. Since each person chooses good or evil, godliness or beastliness, and no earlier or more basic causes play any role, the punishment (or reward) they receive is justly deserved: each person ultimately chooses it for himself or herself, and could have chosen otherwise.

The human godlike power of *causa sui* free will worked fine as a basis for moral responsibility and just deserts (miracles are just the thing for moral responsibility); but as gods and miracles were forced into smaller and smaller corners, and finally swept away by the naturalistic scientific world view, problems arose. We wanted to keep the just world and special free will and moral responsibility, but get rid of gods (who made the world just) and miraculous free will (on which moral responsibility and just deserts were built). We hung on to our belief in a just world: that belief had become so deep as to be nonconscious, so we didn't really need to find a godless justification for it; and we found a substitute compatibilist free will that did not require miracles. And because free will had been chained to moral responsibility it was easy to suppose that this natural free will—this *compatibilist* free will—would support moral responsibility. Nietzsche was wrong about a lot, but he was right about this: when you kill God and deny miracles, things change; we can't just go on as we did, having destroyed the foundation of our moral responsibility/just world system.

Understanding the connection between belief in moral responsibility and belief in a just world requires only a couple of steps. First, it is a sad but undeniable fact that punitive measures are sometimes required. At the very least, sometimes we must isolate violent offenders. When we place someone in mandatory isolation from society, without their permission and almost always in direct opposition to their own preferences, then we are imposing upon them a form of punishment, which may be quite unpleasant and is certainly disruptive of their life plans and counter to their deep desire for freedom and control. We do it for the protection of ourselves and others and our society, and we believe it is necessary and unavoidable; but it is still punishment. So we cannot—at the present time or the foreseeable future—eliminate punishment from our world. But if we believe that our world is *just*, then we must believe that when someone suffers the pains of punishment, the suffering must be *just*; and that is particularly true when we (or our representatives) are required to carry out the punitive measures ourselves: in a just world, it cannot be possible that we *must* act unjustly; if we *ought* not inflict unjustified suffering, then surely we *can* avoid doing so. At this perilous point moral responsibility rides in to save the day, and preserve our comforting belief in a just world: the punishment imposed is *justly deserved* because the malefactor is *morally responsible* for his misdeeds and thus justly deserves to suffer censure and even punishment, including punitive confinement. When punishment is required, moral responsibility is our way of protecting our deep belief in a just world from the threat of severe cognitive dissonance. The same motive operates in our system of criminal justice, as Michele Cotton notes:

> If free will is real, then people could at least be called upon to assert their will and obey [the law], whatever other factors were operating. . . . Legal endorsement of free will [a free will that supports moral responsibility] may therefore be wishful thinking that prefers the account that at least makes it theoretically possible for all people to obey under all circumstances. However, a naive illusion would not be a good basis for supporting a free will assumption. (Cotton 2005, 42)

MORAL RESPONSIBILITY IN A JUST WORLD

Moral responsibility is the powerful buffer that protects our belief in a just world. That is one of the main reasons we are so reluctant to give it up, its profound implausibility—in a world without miracles—notwithstanding. Belief in a just world is almost immune to challenge because it operates as an invisible nonconscious principle. But to the degree that we recognize that this is *not* a just world, we can also recognize that moral responsibility is a desperately contrived coping device. We are better off facing squarely the injustice of our world, and the part we must sometimes play in such injustice.

As noted in the previous chapter, our belief in a just world runs very deep. As Adrian Furnham describes that basic and widespread and largely non-conscious belief in a just world (BJW): "The BJW asserts that, quite justly, good things tend to happen to good people and bad things to bad people despite the fact that this is patently not the case" (2003, 795). When we look at it consciously and deliberately we know quite well that we do *not* live in a just world. The evidence that our world is not just is clear, massive, and profoundly depressing. Why do the wicked prosper? That query presupposes that there *must* be some answer that will make moral sense of it all. We can suppose that "we will understand it better by and by," and that in the afterlife all wrong will be requited and unjust suffering somehow nullified by eternal bliss. But in the absence of such faith—and in the presence of our naturalistic world view—there is no way to consciously convince ourselves that the world is just. But belief in a just world rarely comes to consciousness, unless we are making some heroic effort to "justify God's ways to man" and seeking some way of dealing with the painful problem of evil. But its status as a deep nonconscious belief does not hobble its effectiveness; to the contrary, it enhances its power and scope.

Psychologists have made extensive studies of our nonconscious belief in a just world, and the influence it wields. Part of that influence is positive: belief in a just world motivates us to try and to keep trying, believing that our good efforts will be rewarded. But belief in a just world also causes harm, and the harm often exacerbates injustice. Because people find it difficult to relinquish belief in a just world (Lerner and Miller 1978), they seek ways of preserving the belief. When terrible harm befalls an innocent person, our belief in a just world is threatened; and one of the most convenient and widespread methods of sustaining that belief in the face of strong contradictory evidence is to reinterpret the event: the person who was harmed—such as the victim of rape—was not so innocent after all, and probably brought the harm upon herself or himself (and thus the world remains just, and *true* innocents—such as ourselves and our loved ones—need not fear unjust harm).

The widespread blaming of victims is demonstrated by a variety of studies, particularly studies demonstrating the positive correlation between stronger belief in a just world and increased likelihood of blaming victims for their unfortunate fates (Wagstaff 1983; Furnham and Gunter 1984; Harper and Manasse 1992; Dalbert and Yamauchi 1994; Montada 1998). The just world belief is so strong and resilient that innocent victims often blame themselves for their misfortune rather than relinquish their belief in a just world (Lerner 1980, 123–5).

We can find indirect evidence of belief in a just world even among psychologically astute, fervently naturalistic and deeply insightful philosophers such as Daniel Dennett and George Sher. In *Elbow Room*, Dennett argues that (with rare exceptions) we are morally responsible for what we are and what we do: true, we have uneven early starts, but "racing luck" over the marathon course of our lives evens out the initial differences: "After all, luck averages out in the long run" (1984, 95). Dennett knows full well that luck does not "average out in the long run," but that instead the early advantages tend to build even larger later advantages. The initially lucky child who is born into a loving and affluent extended family has enormous early advantages over the child born into a poor and dysfunctional family. (It may be tempting to suppose that the child of a poor family will get more love and attention and encouragement, while the material benefits available to the child of the affluent family are balanced out because the child of the wealthier family receives less affection in this colder and more distant family setting; but that is just another instance of the deep just world belief: the world is just because the poor have less money but more love, fewer material advantages are balanced—in our just world—by greater affection and happiness.) Is the initial disadvantage of a poor learning start likely to be balanced later by special attention and encouragement in school? More likely the contrary. The child who has been encouraged and is eager to learn gains more attention than the lethargic child who "won't even try." The academically advanced child is placed in honors courses, with smaller classes and more interesting projects and the advantage of being around other children who are also interested and eager. Add to that the benefits of expensive prep schools or the best suburban schools, advanced placement courses, strong school and family encouragement to prepare for the SAT, and—along with all the other cumulative advantages—a family legacy advantage when applying to the most selective universities, which leads to better graduate schools and better opportunities for securing the best job offers. Early disadvantages may—on rare occasions—be offset by later racing luck, but the smart money is on the early leaders.

George Sher offers an argument along the same lines as Dennett's:

> Even if M is initially stronger or more intelligent than N, this difference will only entail that M does not deserve what he has achieved relative to N if the difference between them has made it impossible for N to achieve as much as M. However, differences in strength, intelligence, and other native gifts are rarely so pronounced as to have this effect. The far more common effect of such differences is merely to make it more *difficult* for the less talented person to reach a given level of attainment. He must work harder, husband his resources more carefully, plan more shrewdly, and so on. (1987, 31–2)

That is an appealing story, that fits well with our belief in a just world: the fortitude of the tortoise offsets the speed of the hare, the agile David defeats the mighty Goliath, the hard-training athlete overcomes the superior athleticism of her rival. It makes for great children's books and inspiring myths, but it fails as an account of the nonjust reality. Positive character traits and abilities are not distributed in an even manner. The youthful advantage in athleticism results in greater initial success and thus more playing time, which also contributes to greater fortitude and more athletic self-confidence; the young person who is initially more skillful at challenging cognitive tasks develops a greater sense of cognitive self-efficacy (Bandura 1997) and is also more likely to become a chronic cognizer (Cacioppo and Petty 1982), while her less cognitively talented friend experiences more cognitive frustration and becomes a cognitive miser who spends less time in careful deliberation, develops little confidence in her cognitive capacities, and thus develops less cognitive fortitude. Fortitude and self-confidence and skill are more likely to group together rather than balance out evenly.

The "natural lottery" is not fair, the world is not just, "luck" does not even out, and attempts to justify moral responsibility on the basis of everyone having a roughly equal fair chance gain their appeal not from accurate observation of our actual world but instead from nonconscious commitment to a just world. When scientific naturalism eliminates the space for a just god it also eliminates the plausibility of a just world. The increased scientific understanding of the deeper and more subtle causes of our behavior poses increasing challenges for belief in moral responsibility; but that very advance in our psychological understanding motivates increasingly desperate efforts to save moral responsibility: the more we fear that punitive measures might be unjust (though unavoidable) the more desperate we become to save moral responsibility and preserve belief in a just world.

We do not live in a just world; luck plays an enormous and pivotal role in every part of our lives. That is not to suggest, of course, that the splendid and genuine philosophical accomplishments of Dennett and Sher and many others are "merely a matter of luck," like my severely hooked but lucky golf shot that ricocheted off a tree, bounced hard on the cart path and dropped sweetly into the cup for par. But it was their good luck to have fortunate genetic makeups (none were so unlucky as to have been born with genes that destined them for death from Tay-Sachs at a very tender age), and to have been nurtured in a supportive early life (we take almost for granted the remarkable love and support and encouragement and care given liberally to our children and grandchildren by their families and their extended families, and it is easy to forget the enormous contrast between that safe, secure, and supportive environment and the early childhood and youth of children who are ignored, neglected, or even abused). They were lucky to have developed strong resources of self-control and deferred gratification (capacities that research indicates are well-established—or not—by age 5 or 6), and to have lived in an environment that encouraged education and made good educational resources readily available (rather than growing up in a culture or subculture in which a good education is not valued or is even forbidden as contrary to faith).

Both Dennett and Sher have accomplished wonderful things, and they can and should find great satisfaction in those genuine accomplishments. Dan Dennett's brilliant ideas and delightful writing and remarkably broad knowledge are a great joy to him (and to his friends and colleagues and to the philosophical community), and certainly there is no suggestion that fairness requires we deprive him of those attributes (through some ghastly process of brain surgery "leveling" until his impressive intellectual capacities are brought down to the lowest common denominator). Dennett is lucky to be brilliant. He has certainly exerted enormous efforts, but his impressive capacity to exert sustained vigorous intellectual effort is ultimately the product of his good fortune: he did not initially exert tremendous effort in order to gain the capacity to exert tremendous effort. None of that means that we should fail to appreciate Dennett's remarkable abilities, and certainly he should be in a position that will enable him to utilize those genuine abilities most productively. So Dennett enjoys the fascinating thoughts and ideas and projects that enrich his intellectual life (and benefit the academic community), while others find themselves enmeshed in drudgery and mental and physical torpor. Neither Dennett nor his opposite justly deserve their situations in life, and it is well worth remembering that: it will prevent us from treating the latter cruelly, and it will perhaps motivate us to make the life of the latter as comfortable and interesting as we can manage. We cannot make their lives equal in satisfaction (the person mired in mental torpor will never experience the joys that Dennett experiences in discovering a brilliant insight or working out a fascinating connection); but we should face that fact honestly, rather than taking refuge in the deep assumption that the world is fair and just, and everyone justly deserves what they get.

Recognizing that our world is *not* just becomes even more important when we consider the painful subject of punishment. No one justly deserves punishment. It does not follow that we can or should or must eliminate punishment from our world. The world in which we live is unjust. We have an obligation to promote justice and stop injustice to the degree possible in our inherently unjust world. But we are better off recognizing that we live in an unjust world, and that in our unjust world we sometimes cannot avoid punishing people (in some cases failure to punish would cause even greater injustice), but that in carrying out the unavoidable punishment we are *not* promoting just deserts but instead participating in an *in*justice. It is hard to acknowledge this; it goes against a deep belief in a just world, and it goes against a deep aversion to recognizing that we are sometimes caught up in committing acts that are both wrong and unavoidable, and that in some cases we *cannot* do what we *ought* to do. But recognizing that uncomfortable fact will go a long way toward improving the way we treat those whom we must punish, and in promoting efforts to change environments so that we prevent the need for punishment: we will look more willingly and carefully at the causes, and try to fix them.

THE LIMITS OF COMPATIBILIST FREE WILL

That free will could support moral responsibility seemed easy enough; but that was under the assumption that free will included miracle-working powers, and with miracles you can support anything. Compatibilists have given insightful and instructive accounts of free will, but compatibilist justifications of *moral responsibility* are another matter. Understanding the *authenticity* of our choices and behavior is an important contribution to understanding a special element of human free will; but those benefits notwithstanding, authenticity is not a justification of moral responsibility.

Authenticity is a vital element of animal free will, and it serves an important role. Frankfurt and Fischer have elaborated and elucidated it (while also perhaps exaggerating it), and it is not surprising that the genuinely valuable authenticity aspect of free will should be thought to suffice for moral responsibility. It does not. While the advocates of authenticity—advocates of the *deep* or *authentic* self view of free will—have given us a clearer picture of this element of free will, the focus on the deep authentic self contributes nothing to the support of moral responsibility. If an act comes from my *own* character which I fully endorse and reflectively approve, then the act is my *own* act. But whether I am morally responsible for that act, or for the character from which it flows, is a different question altogether. The "happy slave" may fully and reflectively endorse his defeated acquiescent character, but that does not make this profoundly brutalized person morally responsible for his servile character and servile behavior. This was recognized many centuries ago by Lorenzo Valla, who—with his example of Sextus Tarquinius, who was made by omnipotent God to be vicious and arrogant and to fully endorse that character as his own—noted that when we are clear about the deeply vicious character of Sextus, that is where the question of Sextus' *moral responsibility* for that character starts, rather than where it ends (Valla 1443/1948). It was emphasized by Susan Wolf much more recently:

A satisfactory theory of (deep) responsibility must not only be able to identify which agents are responsible, and for what—it must be able to explain why they are responsible, and ultimately, why the idea of responsibility makes any sense at all. In the absence of such an explanation, the view that responsibility is equivalent to attributability to an agent's real self cannot even be regarded as a candidate for a satisfactory theory of responsibility. (1990, 45)

There are of course a multitude of efforts to find an account of free will that eliminates miracles—both miraculous powers of reason and miraculous powers of will—yet supports moral responsibility, and this chapter examines only a small sample of important and insightful and influential efforts. One of the most important proposals is by John Fischer, and it falls on the minimal-ist side of the spectrum of contemporary free will accounts. Fischer requires only "guidance" control rather than the much stronger "regulative" control; and rather than perfect rationality, his account makes do with a modest level of reasons-responsiveness. This is the veggie burger version of moral respon-sibility: it may be lower in fat, and it has some attractive qualities, but it's not the real thing. The substitutes are marvelous, so long as we make clear that they do not justify blame and punishment; but those who propose the substitutes insist they do, and that's the problem: when we look carefully at the ingredients, they do not. Fischer has proposed a modest but creative and insightful account: a combination of minimal (or more recently, *moder-ate*) reasons-responsiveness with guidance (rather than regulative) control. Furthermore, it is an account that is fully compatible with naturalism—it contains not a hint of miracles or mysteries—and is also a good match with the way our system of moral responsibility (and our system of justice) treats the conditions for moral responsibility. That is, Fischer provides an excellent account of our common conditions for holding people morally responsible; but there remains a question of whether his account can *justify* holding people morally responsible.

The key elements of Fischer's subtle account are *guidance* control and *moderate* reasons-responsiveness; thus Fischer deftly avoids the major temp-tations of miraculous perfect rationality and super powers of choice. But does this modest account have sufficient strength to support moral responsibility? Consider the first element of Fischer's free will account: *guidance* control (as distinguished from *regulative* control). Fischer here draws a fascinating and valuable distinction. Regulative control requires the freedom to take genu-inely alternative paths. Are such choices among open alternatives compatible with determinism? Would the exercise of such regulative control require some special libertarian power that can blast a gap in the world's causal pattern? The verdict on those questions is not a major concern for Fischer: it is not *regulative* control that is required for moral responsibility, but *guid-ance* control. Guidance control does not require open alternatives; rather, it requires only that one exerts control, even if that control allows no deviation from the fixed track. Fischer offers the example of driving a car (a natural enough illustration for a long-time resident of California). Under guidance control, I am driving the car, even if—given all the factors operating on me—I could not drive the car in any direction other than the one I am now following. At the conclusion of his 1994 *Metaphysics of Free Will*, Fischer gave this marvelous—even inspiring—account of guidance control:

> even if there is just one available path into the future—I may be held account-able for *how I walk down this path*. I can be blamed for taking the path of cruelty, negligence, or cowardice. And I can be praised for walking with sensitivity, attentiveness, and courage. Even if I somehow discovered there is but one path into the future, I would still care deeply how I walk down this path. I would aspire to walk with grace and dignity. I would want to have a sense of humor. Most of all, I would want to do it my way. (1994, 216)

Fischer's account of guidance control is somewhat similar to a passage from the great Stoic philosopher, Epictetus:

> Remember that you are an actor in a drama of such sort as the Author chooses—if short, then in a short one; if long, then in a long one. If it be his pleasure that you should enact a poor man, see that you act it well; or a cripple, or a ruler, or a private citizen. For this is your business, to act well the given part; but to choose it, belongs to another. (107/1865)

It's an inspiring idea: Whether your job is big or small, whether your work is famous or obscure, always do it the very best you can. You don't always get to decide what you will do, but whatever you do, do it well. But what makes for inspiring advice does not always make for plausible philosophical analysis.

This view might well make sense given the world view of Epictetus. Epictetus seemed to believe that the major events and forces in your life are controlled by the fates, and you cannot influence or modify them (whether you are slave or ruler, rich or poor, live a long or short life—all of this is controlled by fate); but the details of *how* you live that fated life are up to you. If it is your destiny to be a peasant, then a peasant you shall be; but you can be a kind or cruel peasant, a cheerful or a grumpy peasant, a diligent or a dilatory peasant: the way you live your fated life—within the parameters of your fate—is up to you, and you have options. But contemporary determinists aren't fatalists, and they do not believe that the fates control your life and that your efforts avail nothing. You may not control the hour of your death; but that hour is not written in the book of fate, and by driving carefully, getting some exercise, and watching your diet you can have a significant influence on your longevity. As Al Mele argues (2006, chapter 7) and Eddy Nahmias (2011) insists, there is nothing in determinism or naturalism implying that the major causal factors in your life *bypass* you. Even more important, it might make sense for Epictetus that the details are under your free control while the larger picture is not, but that makes no sense in our contemporary naturalistic world view: whether you live a grumpy or graceful life, whether you are optimistic or pessimistic, a chronic cognizer or a cognitive miser, all of these are the crucially important details of your life and character that are shaped by the genetic and environmental forces operating on you, and that in turn have a great impact on whether your larger life story is one of success or failure. Those who embrace naturalism believe that *everything* is shaped by natural forces, and those forces apply just as much to the tiny details as to the most significant events in our lives. In fact, it is the details that are likely to have a powerful impact on the larger result: the chronic cognizer who has a strong sense of self-efficacy and pursues her life's work with optimism and pleasure and confidence is likely to experience greater success than the pessimistic cognitive miser who is short on self-confidence.

But on closer inspection, Fischer's view has less in common with Epictetus than might appear. Michael Zimmerman notes that Fischer's writings are open to misinterpretation—the *mis*interpretation that the overall direction of your life is set, but you have open alternatives for the *manner* in which you live—and suggests a modification:

> To say that, even if there is just one path available into the future, that I may be accountable for how I walk down this path, suggests (to me, at least) that I have alternative ways of walking down the path open to me. One wonders, then, whether we should be talking of one path or two; even if we stick to talking of just one path, that there are alternative ways of walking down it is something that the semicompatibilist must declare unnecessary. What I think Fischer should have said is this: even if there is just one available path into the future and just one available way of walking down it, I may be held accountable for walking down it in that way. (1966, 344)

And in response, Fischer states that: "I gladly accept the interpretation of my rather florid prose offered by Michael Zimmerman" (2006, 28). Fischer's prose is elegant and delightful, never florid; but leaving that aside, consider the account of moral responsibility that remains under this interpretation: Not only are there no alternative paths, but under *guidance* control there is only one way one can walk down that path. Fischer aspires to walk down his path (as noted earlier) "with grace and dignity" and "a sense of humor," and he does indeed saunter along his path in that manner. He could take no other path, and he could travel it in no other style. Still, he is walking in *his way*, he "does it my way," he strongly and positively identifies with his path and his manner of traversing it, and *that* is sufficient for guidance control, which in turn (combined with moderate reasons-responsiveness) is sufficient for moral responsibility.

But Robert Harris—the brutal murderer described so insightfully by Gary Watson (1987)—also "does it my way": "I chose the road to hell," he insisted, and he went down that road his own way with his own approval; but no one who makes even a cursory examination of the horrific conditions in which Robert grew up can feel *confident* that Robert is morally responsible. It is his own life, and he identifies with it as his own; but that does not make him morally responsible. I cannot take any other path, nor follow it in any other manner; but I identify with the path and the way I am following it, I embrace it as my own. This is a healthy attitude, surely; much better than a life lived in envy of others, or a life—like that of Edward Arlington's Miniver Cheevy— who was "born too late," and who "loved the days of old When swords were bright and steeds were prancing," and who in a life of deep reflective regret "called it fate, And kept on drinking." But it doesn't make the acquiescent slave or the willing addict or Robert Harris or—on the positive and admirable side of the ledger—John Martin Fischer morally responsible for his life or his manner of living it.

Fischer's account of free will involves guidance control, and it also emphasizes reason: but (like guidance control rather than the more robust regulative control) Fischer's reason requirement (which Fischer regards as an element of guidance control) is also quite modest. Rather than a Kantian or Platonic or Susan Wolf super reason that is always ready to exert the most strenuous and profound efforts and that never deviates from the True and the Good, the reason proposed by Fischer is not *strong* reasons-responsiveness but instead a much weaker and more plausible level of reasons-responsiveness. A morally responsible agent need not *always* recognize relevant reasons, nor need the agent respond correctly or appropriately or wisely to those reasons; it is sufficient that in *most* circumstances the agent will recognize and respond to the relevant reasons.

This moderate reasons-responsiveness is a much more plausible capacity than the strong reasons-responsiveness that traditional Western philosophy—from Plato to Kant and beyond—has treated as the special capacity of rational human animals. After all, it is painfully obvious to most of us that while we may count as rational beings, there are many occasions when we fail to recognize and appropriately respond to important reasons. Joe saw the construction signs, and typically in such cases Joe recognizes that there are good reasons to proceed cautiously and he acts accordingly; but this time Joe didn't pay sufficient attention and did not respond to reasons that should have guided his behavior. Joe is not blind to either construction signs or reasons, and so Joe qualifies as moderately reasons-responsive, and therefore Joe is morally responsible for causing an accident by his negligent recklessness on this occasion. Fischer's goal is to provide an account that fits well with our actual practice of holding people morally responsible, and he succeeds splendidly. The driver is not demented, not coerced, not under the control of alien mind manipulators; he has often responded appropriately to the warnings of this dangerous situation, and so he is obviously capable of doing so; thus when he acted carelessly on this occasion, it is legitimate to hold him morally responsible for his failure and punish him appropriately. That's the way both common sense and the criminal justice system would deal with Joe's act of criminal negligence (when his carelessness and thoughtlessness causes serious injury to a construction worker).

But consider more carefully the moderately reasons-responsive capacities of Joe: capacities that vary with every individual and every circumstance. Joe is a cognitive miser, who strongly resists switching into careful deliberation (though he occasionally does so). On this occasion, Joe was in a state of severe ego-depletion. What Joe can manage—in terms of reasons-responsiveness—when his reflective resources are fully charged is quite different from what Joe is capable of when in a state of deep ego-depletion. The rechargeable flashlight that has beamed for several straight hours now is incapable of shining a bright light; and to suppose that it is always capable of doing so because under other circumstances it shown brightly is not a good way of understanding flashlights. It is also not a good way of understanding Joe. We could go on. When Joe is under the influence of strong alertness primes, he is capable of careful watchfulness. When Joe is in a situation that prompts a narrower focus on his destination (Joe has been encouraged by his wife to hurry home so that he will not miss his daughter's ballet recital), then—like the participants in the Princeton Seminary study (Darley and Batson 1973) who were told to hurry to the next building and failed to be reasons-responsive to the needs of someone slumped on the ground—Joe is not as mindful of relevant factors in his immediate environment. When Joe is in a weakened state of cognitive self-efficacy, he is much less likely to carefully consider potential dangers than when he is more confident in his ability to effectively deliberate. The fact that in some circumstances and some situations and at some times Joe can and does recognize and respond appropriately to reasons—Joe is moderately reasons-responsive—does not mean that in other circumstances at other times Joe can recognize and respond effectively to relevant reasons. What Joe can and does do at time X does not establish what he can do at time Y. The difference is in the details, but the details are critical.

THE PLATEAU OF MORAL RESPONSIBILITY
AND LIMITS ON INQUIRY

Currently popular plateau models of free will are another effort to avoid miracles and super rational powers while protecting and preserving belief in moral responsibility. Looking at the details, looking deeply into the full range of causal factors, is fatal for a free will model that attempts to support moral responsibility. Philosophers have worked for centuries to find ways—ranging from the miraculous to the mundane—to preserve moral responsibility from the perils of deeper causal inquiries. With the advances in scientific understanding of the causes of behavior, those perils have become ever more threatening. It is not surprising, then, that free will accounts—accounts that attempt to preserve moral responsibility—turn to a *plateau* model that marks these deeper causal inquiries as off-limits and irrelevant to questions of free will and moral responsibility. That the plateau model is a perfect partner to contemporary standards for criminal justice procedure makes the plateau model even more appealing; indeed, it makes it sound like good old common sense, in stark contrast to the wild and crazy and *perilous* efforts to look deeper into the causes and details that threaten belief in moral responsibility and the special free will that supports it.

The plateau model of moral responsibility (sometimes called the threshold model) is currently a very popular proposal for understanding moral responsibility (Dworkin 1988, 31; Metz 2006; Smith 2008). Dennett was one of the first to explicitly propose the plateau model, and he describes it with characteristic clarity and verve:

> moral development is not a race at all, with a single winner and everyone else ranked behind, but a process that apparently brings people sooner or later to a sort of plateau of development—not unlike the process of learning your native language, for instance. Some people reach the plateau swiftly and easily, while others need compensatory effort to overcome initial disadvantages in one way or another.
>
> But everyone comes out more or less in the same league. When people are deemed "good enough" their moral education is over, and except for those who are singled out as defective . . . the citizenry is held to be composed of individuals of roughly equivalent talents, insofar as the demands of such citizenship are concerned. (1984, 96)

Thus we can acknowledge that there are significant differences in backgrounds and histories, while insisting that so long as one reaches a plateau or threshold of competence, those differences in history can be safely ignored:

> It is . . . not in any way your own doing that you were born into a specific milieu, rich or poor, pampered or abused, given a head start or held back at the starting line. And these differences, which are striking, are also diverse in their effects—some inevitable and some evitable, some leaving life-long scars and others evanescent in effect. Many of the differences that survive are, in any

event, of negligible importance to what concerns us here: a second threshold, the threshold of moral responsibility—as contrasted, say, with artistic genius. (Dennett 2003, 274)

Like the plateau model, other contemporary accounts of moral responsibility function by blocking deeper inquiry into the details of our causal histories and our current circumstances. Angela Smith insists that we keep a narrow focus on one's *current* meeting of the minimal standard for moral responsibility and not worry about the history of how one's capacities developed to differing degrees nor about the remaining differences among those who qualify as meeting minimal competence standards:

> I think we would do well to distinguish two different questions: the question of one's responsibility for becoming a certain sort of person, and the question of one's responsibility for the judgments expressed in one's actions and attitudes. It will be a complex story, for each and every one of us, how we became the sorts of people we are, with the particular values, interests, cares and concerns that we hold; and very few, if any, of us can plausibly claim to bear full or even substantial responsibility for how we became the particular people we are. Even so, I submit, we cannot help but regard ourselves as responsible and answerable for the particular judgments expressed in our actions and attitudes, regardless of what circumstances may have shaped these assessments. (2008, 389)

Harry Frankfurt's model of hierarchical reflective free will is a landmark in the free will and moral responsibility debate, and it is rightly celebrated as one of the most creative and stimulating contributions to that debate. But one of the reasons why it is so attractive—at this time of moral responsibility plateaus that reject deeper inquiry—is that Frankfurt's model limits the moral responsibility question in such a manner that it can be adjudicated without any knowledge of individual history; the only question is whether this person at *this moment* can and does *reflectively approve* of his or her character or choice. It matters not how the willing addict became a willing addict, how the willing slave became a willing slave; it is irrelevant that the willing slave has suffered such extensive abuse that he or she no longer has the strength to seek or even desire liberty; so long as at the *present* moment the acquiescent slave *reflectively affirms* his or her enslavement, the willing slave is morally responsible and "has all the free will anyone could wish to have."

Among those who propose a *pragmatic* justification for holding people morally responsible and imposing punishment, the focus remains on the *present*, and deeper searches into the past avail us nothing. For example, consider Moritz Schlick's classic justification for moral responsibility (which he claims is derived from David Hume):

The question regarding responsibility is the question: Who, in a given case, is to be punished? Who is to be considered the true wrongdoer? The problem is not identical with that regarding the original instigator of the act; for the great-grandparents of the man, from whom he inherited his character, might in the end be the cause, or the statesmen who are responsible for his social milieu, and so forth. But the "doer" is the *one upon whom the motive must have acted* in order, with certainty, to have prevented the act (or called it forth, as the case may be). Consideration of remote causes is of no help here, for in the first place their actual contribution cannot be determined, and in the second place they are generally out of reach. Rather, we must find the person in whom the decisive junction of causes lies. The question of who is responsible is the question concerning the *correct point of application of the motive.* (Schlick 1939, 152–3)

There is a common thread in all of the remarkably inventive and instructive and insightful accounts of moral responsibility-bearing free will: all of them insist that at some point we must stop looking further or deeper. With Pico we find naturally inexplicable godly miracles; with Chisholm, literally a godlike *first cause* or *causa sui*, which leaves no deeper level to explore; C. A. Campbell relies on "contra-causal" definitive choice, and there are no deeper causes to examine because such a free choice is a "*creative activity*, in which . . . nothing determines the act save the agent's doing of it (Campbell 1957, 177); with Kane, we find quantum indeterminacy and chaos blocking deeper inquiry; with Frankfurt, a reflective choice that settles the question without further inquiry; with Dennett and Angela Smith, a plateau of competence that makes all deeper questions irrelevant; with Susan Wolf, a level of intellectual insight into the True and the Good which limits inquiry to studies of why some *fail* to have free will and moral responsibility. It may be difficult to imagine Pico della Mirandola, Daniel Dennett, Robert Kane, and Susan Wolf having any philosophical principles in common, but in fact they share an important one: moral responsibility requires that we *stop looking deeper*, either because there is nothing there to find or because such deeper inquiries are irrelevant.

Not only are deeper inquiries into causes and details irrelevant; they are also perilous to your philosophical mental health and even to your very being. Dennett warns that the temptation to pursue deeper inquiry into *why* one person chooses virtue and another opts for vice is symptomatic of a longing for metaphysical absolutism:

Skepticism about the very possibility of culpability arises from a misplaced reverence for an absolutist ideal: the concept of total, before-the-eyes-of-God Guilt. The fact that *that* condition is never to be met in this world should not mislead us into skepticism about the integrity of our institution of moral responsibility. (1984, 165)

John Martin Fischer counsels a good moderate "middle way" path that avoids the "metaphysical megalomania" that drives moral responsibility skeptics to make mad causal quests "excessively far into the past":

> certain approaches to moral responsibility require us to trace back excessively far into the past; this is, as I have argued, a case of "metaphysical megalomania." . . . Galen Strawson and Robert Kane both—in different ways—put forward exceedingly stringent sourcehood requirements. Although I am inclined to agree that an agent must be the source of his behavior, in order to be morally responsible for it, I do not conclude from this intuitive point that such an agent must be the "ultimate source," in a sense that requires causal indeterminism (or certainly a sense that requires a kind of impossible self-creation). I believe that our moral responsibility requires that we play the cards that are dealt us (in a certain way—a way that crucially involves guidance control); but surely this does not require that we deal ourselves the cards, or that we own the factory that makes the cards (as well as all of the inputs into the manufacturing process), and so forth. (2012, 21)

But on this point, Fischer and Dennett have things precisely backward. Demanding that we inquire *deeper* into the detailed causes of behavior is not a demand for metaphysical absolutes or godlike understanding or miraculous powers. To the contrary, recognizing that human animals do not have such miraculous first cause powers is what opens the way to deeper scrutiny of the causes of human behavior. Sandra and Tamara are firmly stationed on the plateau of competence: both can reason, both are moderately reasons-responsive, both can and do make choices, both can consider alternatives, neither is delusional. Both have the opportunity to launch a pyramid scheme that will enrich them, but at the cost of harming many others. Both of them deliberate and consider reasons, and Sandra eagerly launches the scheme while Tamara firmly rejects this path. *Why* did they choose so differently? For those who embrace the plateau model, the answer is: Don't ask! Any deeper inquiries are irrelevant, and certainly fruitless, and they run the risk of metaphysical megalomania. But why are such questions irrelevant and fruitless? When we suppose that we have reached a point at which no further questions are worthwhile, it is because we have reached some final point of first cause, where deeper causal questions are impossible. If we have reached a point at which all that is left is quantum indeterminacy (as in Kane's model), then indeed it is difficult to imagine how to go further. If we have reached Chisholm's *causa sui*, or C. A. Campbell's contra-causal free will, or Sartre's equally mysterious "being-for-itself," then no deeper inquiry is possible. If we have reached a point of godlike perfect reason—as championed by Aristotle, Kant, and Susan Wolf—then inquiry has reached an end point. But for compatibilist naturalists, no such limits to inquiry are plausible.

If the perils of metaphysical megalomania are not sufficient to deter you from deeper inquiries, Dennett warns of an even graver peril: Push those deep causal questions to greater depths and you run the danger of becoming so small that you externalize everything and simply *disappear*, and you are not the cause of anything; instead, things happen to you, but you vanish from the causal process. In commenting on the case of a young father who negligently causes the death of his child, Dennett notes precisely this possibility:

> We can note that if he makes himself really small, he can externalize this whole episode in his life, almost turning it into a bad dream, a thing that happened to him, not something he did. (2003, 302)

But even if I know in deep detail the causes of my character and the behavior that flows from it, that does not make the character any less mine or my acts any less my own. To the contrary, as we better understand the causes that shape our character and influence our behavior, we can take better steps to improve character and behavior: our own and others. But that same valuable understanding—when pushed unchecked into the vital causal details that separate the virtuous from the vicious—does raise serious questions about whether I justly deserve blame or credit for causes (including the causes of my character) that I did not choose or control.

What champions of moral responsibility nonconsciously fear is what our system of justice explicitly recognizes: you must find some way to block deeper inquiry, or moral responsibility and just deserts don't work. The moral responsibility model of free will must find some way of halting inquiry—with miracles or quantum indeterminacy or plateau myopia. But blocking inquiry is rarely an advantageous way of understanding or improving, and that applies to our understanding and enhancement of free will just as it does to any other area of inquiry.

It is quite remarkable that philosophers should take up the criminal justice model of moral responsibility, as if that provides a justification. That model is appealing because it fits the way the moral responsibility system and the U.S. justice system work, and thus it seems a reasonable common sense method of establishing moral responsibility. But the criminal justice system merely formalizes a process; it does not *justify* that process. Justifying that system and its moral responsibility foundation was a task left for philosophers. Now philosophers, having found the task impossible, are pretending that the system itself provides its own justification. We set a standard or *threshold* for moral responsibility, and count all those who meet that standard as morally responsible. This *plateau* model of moral responsibility sets a minimal competence standard for moral responsibility and then holds everyone who meets that standard morally responsible. On this approach to moral responsibility everyone is treated as *equal* so long as they meet the minimum competence standard. For those who are rated competent—those who qualify for admission to the plateau of moral responsibility—any differences in intelligence, history, self-confidence, education, self-control, and situations are irrelevant.

Tamara—who rejects the pyramid scheme—is a careful and judicious thinker, a chronic cognizer who enjoys deep deliberation, a person of very high cognitive self-efficacy who is sublimely confident in her own capacities for effective thought, a person with a strong internal locus-of-control who believes that the major events in her life are under her own effective control; and she is cognitively well-rested and well-equipped to think energetically and assiduously. Sandra is competent, but she is a cognitive miser, she has little confidence in her capacity for effective cognitive efforts, she does not believe that her own efforts make much difference in the outcome anyway (she has an external locus-of-control), and she is currently in a state of ego-depletion. The justice system treats Tamara and Sandra as completely equal in ability to avoid criminal behavior, but that is acknowledged to be a "legal fiction." Philosophers, unfortunately, treat the assumption of "equal capacities" as a literal truth that must not be scrutinized: Tamara and Sandra both are "competent" and thus there is no real difference between them and both *could* have done the right thing (if Tamara could find and follow the right path using her cognitive abilities, then Sandra also could have done so, since both are on the plateau). But obviously the "plateau" of moral responsibility has major differences in elevation. If we stand far enough away, the "plateau" may look roughly even; but closer scrutiny shows enormous differences. That is precisely what our system of criminal justice does: if you are judged competent, then no mitigation based on your history or your abilities is allowed; everyone who is minimally competent is regarded as *equally* competent, and that is a good description of the criminal justice system as well as the "common sense" standard for moral responsibility. That *describes* the system, but does nothing to justify it. But it does do something to prevent us from looking closely at the process, and to prevent us from recognizing the deep problems in supposing that everyone who is "minimally competent" is thus even roughly equal. Robert Harris was minimally competent: he had the intelligence to plan, and he acknowledged his own values and reflectively approved of them. But Harris labored under a burden most of us—thankfully—can hardly imagine: a visceral hatred of the world that had treated him so callously and brutally throughout his entire life. Most of us carry less visible weights, and often we do not even know we are carrying them; but that doesn't change the influence of the burdens.

What do we believe happens when Sandra and Tamara make different choices? Both are certainly on the plateau of competence, both are intelligent and capable of reflective thought, both have some degree of self-control; but in the same situation, they act very differently. If we don't think it was a miracle, we must believe there were causes. Both reasoned; but why did they reason differently? Reason is important, but it is not miraculous. If Sandra reasons more briefly, or is more subject to error, then why? Or if Sandra's careful System 2 deliberation never activates, while Tamara's does, then why? If we look deeper, we find causes that undermine belief in moral responsibility. That may require looking beyond the most obvious factors. We won't always find the blatantly obvious causes that corrupted the unfortunate Robert Harris; but unless we believe in miracles, we will find causes that the person did not control. Even if those causes do not bypass, and they flow through our conscious deliberation, they are still there (unless conscious deliberation is a form of godly transcendence). The likelihood that our conscious deliberation is a cause in anything like the way we imagine is remote; but even if it is, it will not support moral responsibility. The conscious deliberation does not spring out of nothing, but is instead shaped by forces we did not control.

The plateau approach doesn't justify moral responsibility; rather, it describes how the moral responsibility system works: Don't look deeper. If we look closely, we find causes that invalidate claims of moral responsibility; which is why systems that endeavor to sustain belief in moral responsibility must find ways of blocking or severely limiting such inquiries. That's what criminal justice does; that's what common sense does; that's what the plateau of moral responsibility does.

When free will is liberated from the burden of justifying moral responsibility, then we can appreciate the genuine insights of both compatibilists and libertarians and their essential contributions to our understanding of natural free will. When we strip away the moral responsibility accretions we not only have free will, but a richer and deeper understanding of free will—or at least, that is the claim made in the account of restorative free will (Chapter 8). We can have an account of free will that supports moral responsibility, or we can have an account of free will that is plausible in the natural world devoid of gods, miracles, and superhuman powers. We cannot have both.

NOTE

1. Derk Pereboom (2014) has recently argued that we can have a substantial and emotionally satisfying free will that is divorced from moral responsibility "in the basic desert sense."

Chapter 6

Free Will and Criminal Justice

Philosophers deploy creative efforts to block deeper inquiry and preserve belief in moral responsibility; but the struggle occurs on a larger scale in the criminal justice system, which fights a constant and desperate struggle to block deeper detailed examination of the causes and circumstances of criminal behavior. This is not surprising; after all, the criminal justice system uses the same "plateau of competence" to block deeper inquiries into the causes of criminal behavior: inquiries that undercut belief in the basic fairness of the criminal justice system, just as the same inquiries call into question philosophical accounts of moral responsibility. They both depend on a "normal humans have powers that make deeper inquiry irrelevant" perspective. David L. Bazelon—a former Justice on the District of Columbia Court of Appeals—wrote that:

> Although it has been asserted repeatedly that only a free choice to do wrong will be punished, in practice the law presumes, almost irrebuttably, that proscribed behavior is the product of [quoting Roscoe Pound] "a free agent confronted with a choice between doing right and doing wrong and choosing freely to do wrong." (Bazelon 1987, 90)

This assumption that the defendant acted with all the special powers of a "free agent" applies almost universally, with only two exceptions. First, the defendant may be ruled insane; but following the Hinckley verdict of not guilty by reason of insanity (and even before), that hardly ever happens, even in extreme cases (some states have abolished the insanity defense altogether). Second, the defendant can offer a special excuse (such as coercion or self-defense) which counts as an "affirmative defense" and shifts the burden of proof to the defendant. Otherwise, the accused is counted as having the full power of free will, such that using one's powers of reason and will one could literally make an undetermined choice between the open options of right and wrong.

Because these powers are (barring insanity or special affirmative exceptions) capable of overriding any causal factors in one's history or present situation, it follows that evidence of severe childhood abuse, traumatic recent events, and powerful contemporary situational factors are irrelevant. One young man suffered a severely abusive childhood and youth, has been traumatized and brutalized repeatedly, and is now in a situation (he is taunted and demeaned) that threatens his last vestiges of personal dignity. A second young man grew up in a loving and supportive environment in which powers of deferred gratification (self-control) were promoted, strong cognitive self-efficacy and a strong sense of internal locus-of-control were shaped, chronic cognizing was strongly encouraged, and a sense of personal dignity and worth were deeply ingrained. The criminal justice system treats them as having exactly the same resources for "choosing freely" between right and wrong. Neither is insane, neither was coerced, and so they are fully equal in capacity to avoid criminal behavior.

That principled blindness to important differences in the histories and capacities of various individuals—all of whom pass some minimum competence standard for sanity—is essential for our system of justice as it presently functions. Deeper examination of the actual causes of criminal behavior would quickly expose the notion of "choosing freely to do wrong" as a pernicious myth. Of course people do indeed choose to do wrong (and also choose to do right), but when we look closely at the causes for such behavior, that deeper examination soon destroys any sense that it is *fair* to punish those shaped for criminal behavior. As Neil Levy (2011, 196) phrases it, when we punish those who choose the wrong path, then they are *doubly* disadvantaged: disadvantaged first by the conditions that shaped their criminal behavior, and then disadvantaged by the penalties we impose on that behavior.

The young man who reacts violently to a perceived slight—a taunt, or a relatively mild case of "disrespect"—is not insane, he knew what he was doing, he chose to commit a violent crime, and he justly deserves punishment. You and I would have ignored the taunt, and certainly would not have reacted violently to a small act of disrespect (which, after all, most of us are subjected to daily by students, colleagues, and deans). But we also have a vast reservoir of successes—from elementary school on—that resulted in a powerful sense of self-worth that is not easily diminished by a few minor challenges; and we have powerful resources of self-control (shaped at an early age) in contrast to the violent young man's sense of near-helplessness (from repeated inescapable childhood and adolescent abuse).

FREE WILL AS THE FOUNDATION FOR CRIMINAL JUSTICE

Those most dedicated to preserving the retributive foundation of the American criminal justice system are typically most dedicated to the belief in a special—even a miraculous or God-given—power to make free choices independent of all causal history, choices that make examination of histories and causes and situations irrelevant. One of the most resolute defenders of that view is Supreme Court Justice Antonin Scalia, who acknowledges his own Christian inspired devotion to the special power of free will while despising the "post-Freudian secularists" who insist on looking for deeper causes:

> The doctrine of free will—the ability of man to resist temptations to evil, which God will not permit beyond man's capacity to resist—is central to the Christian doctrine of salvation and damnation, heaven and hell. The post-Freudian secularist, on the other hand, is more inclined to think that people are what their history and circumstances have made them, and there is little sense in assigning blame. (2002, 19)

Scalia makes manifest the miracle-working God-bestowed view of free will that "justifies" the criminal justice system: God grants to each person a free will with the power to resist wrongdoing, and "God will not permit [temptations] beyond man's capacity to resist," and thus anyone who does wrong does so of his own free will and could have done otherwise and justly deserves the full weight of the law's punitive force. This holy trinity of uniquely human godlike powers, a just world guaranteed by God, and complete individual moral responsibility is the solid rock that supports severe punishment for wrongdoers while shielding the privileged who sit in judgment from doubts and dissonance.

Although not everyone couches it in overtly theological language, a similar view of a special libertarian "first cause" free will is a common belief in the criminal justice system, stretching back hundreds of years and continuing to the present. In 1769, William Blackstone—in his famous commentaries on the law—stated that "Punishments are . . . only inflicted for abuse of that free will, which God has given to man" (Blackstone 1769/1992). And belief in the special power of human free will as the foundation of criminal justice has been repeatedly acknowledged by the Supreme Court. In 1937, Justice Cardozo stated that "the law has been guided by a robust common sense which assumes the freedom of the will as a working hypothesis in the solution of its problems" (*Steward Machine Company v. Davis*, 301 U.S. 548, 590; 1937). In 1952 (*Morisette v. United States*, 342 U.S. 246, 250; 1952). the Court insisted that "belief in freedom of the human will and a consequent ability and duty of the normal individual to choose between good and evil" is a basic and universal element of the criminal law; and in 1978, in *United States v. Grayson* (438 U.S. 41, 52; 1978), the Court stated that a determinist view is "inconsistent with the underlying precepts of our justice system" (found in Kirchmeier 2004). No one has stated this position more clearly and unequivocally—in words that echo C. A. Campbell's commitment to the special human power of contra-causal free will—than Sanford Kadish, a leading legal scholar who served as dean of the University of California Law School:

> While events in the physical world are governed by laws of nature that imply the existence of necessary and sufficient conditions, voluntary decisions are not. They are controlled by the choice of the actor, a "wild card," for whose action no set of conditions is sufficient and no condition is necessary, save the condition of a free act of will. Therefore, though it may be in any particular case that the principal would not have chosen to act without the influence of the accomplice, it is never so as a matter of necessity, since the principal could have chosen otherwise. (Kadish 1987, 198)

The problem is that when one works every day in a world in which causes of problems are obvious, and the very limited capacities of some persons to overcome those problems is painfully clear, it is difficult to continue believing in this mysterious power of free will. Perhaps if one lives in the insulated chambers of the Supreme Court, and constantly wears the blinders provided by one's religious doctrines, it is possible not to lose one's faith in such special cause-transcending powers. After all, if one can believe in miracles—the Nile turns into blood, the Sun stands still in the sky so the Israelites can complete the slaughter of their enemies, a virgin gives birth, water becomes wine, and the dead return to life—then belief in a miraculous power of human free will poses no problems. But for those who deal more directly with the real world—and daily life in the criminal court system offers it up in graphic colors and detail—such beliefs are difficult to sustain.

The criminal courts constantly face powerful and painful evidence that people do *not* have the special power of free will endorsed by the traditions of the Anglo-American criminal justice system and by Scalia's version of Christianity (though not endorsed by either Catholic or Protestant orthodoxy). Therefore the criminal justice community and its legal theorists have proposed a variety of ways to cope with the challenge. It is not surprising that many of those methods mirror the efforts made by the philosophical community to sustain belief in a free will that can support moral responsibility; it is even less surprising when we consider that some of the most dedicated and insightful efforts from the legal community are made by people like Stephen Morse and Michael S. Moore, who hold joint law school and philosophy appointments. Perhaps philosophers have devoted more time and effort to struggling with this issue; but those in the criminal justice system have more direct and painful dealings with the details of the problem: it is no accident

that some of the most important and influential examples in the philosophical discussion—such as Gary Watson's (1987) account of the brutal and
remorseless murders performed by Robert Harris, and the details of Harris's
horrific childhood—are drawn from the criminal courts.

PROTECTING JUDICIAL BELIEF IN MORAL RESPONSIBILITY

One way of attempting to preserve a free will that can support robust moral
responsibility is by insisting that we simply *must* sustain our system of
criminal justice. Michael S. Moore argues that allowing detailed evidence
concerning what *caused* a competent person to make a criminal choice
would lead to an absurd conclusion: no one is ever morally responsible, no
one ever justly deserves punishment (1985, 1112–13). Moore develops his
argument carefully, and he gives excellent reasons why deeper scrutiny of the
causal processes that shaped us all—including the full set of causal factors
that shaped criminals and resulted in their criminal behavior—would reveal
sufficient causes for both virtuous and vicious human behavior. This is an
insightful argument, and Moore sees clearly the result: once we allow such
causal evidence, there is no stopping point. We would be driven to saying
people are excused for causes we *know* but not for causes we do *not* know but
which we believe—if we are determinists, as Moore is (1985, 1112)—*must*
have been present:

> It may well be that the factors social scientists cite as the causes of crime are not
> sufficient conditions: they only make bad behavior probable, not inevitable. Yet
> this lack of sufficient conditions may only reflect our ignorance of factors that
> inevitably produce the criminal behavior. (1985, 1117)

Moore then acknowledges that it is not legitimate to base claims of responsibility on our present ignorance of the full range of causes for that behavior:

> It is inconsistent with our basic moral beliefs to attribute responsibility accord-
> ing to our present, completely fortuitous, state of knowledge. If we truly believe
> that all behavior is fully determined and that fully determined behavior is not the
> actor's responsibility, it would be immoral to hold people responsible because
> *we* were ignorant of what caused them to act. To say otherwise would be tanta-
> mount to excusing those who have some particular excuse about which we have
> knowledge, but holding all others responsible because we are ignorant of what
> excuse they have—even though we believe that all of those others have some
> valid excuse. If causation by external factors excuses, it excuses everyone on
> determinist assumptions. Who is excused cannot be based on such a fortuity as
> how much of the causal story we happen to know at any particular time. (1985,
> 1119)

Of course there is a long—and ongoing—debate about whether determinism (or as it is usually now discussed, *naturalism*) is compatible with free will and moral responsibility; and Moore is aware of that controversy. Ultimately Moore is arguing that even if we had full knowledge of all the determining factors that caused criminal behavior, that would not be grounds for rejecting moral responsibility; indeed, determinist that he is, he nonetheless regards the denial of moral responsibility as blatantly absurd.

Moore's solution to the problem is to insist that even if there are, and we *know* there are, complete causes for our behavior, it may still be the case that the behavior is our *own*, and that we act freely, and that we are morally responsible for our acts. In support of his claim, Moore offers the case of Patty Hearst, who was kidnapped by a radical group and "brainwashed" into becoming an enthusiastic and dedicated member of that group, and who then willingly participated in armed robberies:

> Consider our difficulties with the borderline defense of brainwashing. In the most famous recent example, the Patty Hearst case, we were certain of a causal connection between the conditioning Hearst received and her criminal behavior. That certainty, however, was irrelevant to the issue of whether her behavior was an action. She robbed the bank; it was her act, whether or not a situation that was not of her making implanted in her the beliefs that caused her to act. (1985, 1136)

Certainly Moore is right: Patty Hearst did act, and she acted from her own desires with which she strongly identified. But there remains the question of whether she is morally responsible—deserves blame and punishment—for acting from desires and values she could not avoid, did not choose, and did not control. Moore is aware of that possible response to his claim, and he takes it seriously:

> Even after the conceptual confusions are cleared away, the causal theorist has a moral argument: if a person could not help doing what he did, he is not morally responsible for it. This is true even if his behavior was an action, and an action not covered by the conventional moral excuses. (1985, 1141)

In answering that argument, Michael Moore turns to an analysis of moral responsibility developed by G. E. Moore (1912, 84–95). According to G. E. Moore, it is true that moral responsibility requires that one "could have acted otherwise"; but the phrase "could have acted otherwise" should not be understood as implying a break from determinism; rather, it means only that one "could have acted otherwise" *if* one had *chosen* to act otherwise. That is, even if Patty Hearst was brainwashed into a profound and unquestioning commitment to the goals and activities of her group, when she participated in the armed robbery she acted freely and was morally responsible for her act because *if* she had chosen otherwise she could had acted otherwise. But of course if determinism is true (as Michael Moore believes) then when we choose it is not true that we could have chosen otherwise. If Robert Harris makes a violent choice that is the product of his own violent and frustrated and deeply abused character, and given the forces that shaped him he lacks any capacity for careful reflection and sympathetic feelings that would have led him to choose otherwise, he is morally responsible: because *if* he had chosen otherwise (which was not possible) he could have done otherwise. If Patty Hearst had been a different person with different goals and different values, nothing would have prevented this imaginary Patty Hearst from choosing in accordance with those values. That rickety hypothetical is supposed to bear the weight of moral responsibility.

At this point, Michael Moore seeks a means of supporting that hypothetical grounds for moral responsibility, and he concludes that the hypothetical interpretation is supported by "the totality of our moral experience involving praise and blame" (1985, 1144). As he writes:

To justify any moral proposition is to show that it is a part of the most coherent account of our moral experience, considered as a whole. That is exactly what I claim about the Moorean interpretation of the principle of responsibility. Our practices of assessing merit and responsibility are consistent with the proposition that persons are responsible for their (determined) choices, inconsistent with its negation. (1985, 1144)

But this has carried us in a large circle back to our starting point. The question is whether careful detailed study of the causes of our behavior will challenge our traditional belief in moral responsibility. It turns out that it does, of course; but we can dismiss that challenge, because it conflicts with "our practices of assessing merit and responsibility" based on the "proposition that persons are responsible for their (determined) choices." It is certainly true that if we remain true to the principles of moral responsibility underlying our criminal justice system, then the rejection of those principles is impossible, even absurd. But that does nothing to prove that we should remain true to those principles.

THE IDEAL OF MORAL RESPONSIBILITY

A second way that the criminal justice community has tried to save moral responsibility is by insisting on the importance of moral responsibility as an ideal: an ethical belief so basic that abandoning it would have terrible ethical consequences. In particular, loss of the special free will that supports moral responsibility would undercut our belief in human dignity, with incalculable costs to both our ethical system and the judicial system which rests on that ethical foundation. Stephen Morse (1996) appeals to the importance of "preserving human dignity" as his grounds for insisting that the criminal justice system must preserve belief in just deserts and moral responsibility, and this is a view shared by Michael S. Moore (1985 and 1997), Herbert Packer (1968), Sanford Kadish (1968 and 1987), Herbert Morris (1968), and C. S. Lewis (1970). Legal theorist Herbert Packer states unequivocally the principled value element in this approach:

> The idea of free will in relation to conduct is not, in the legal system, a statement of fact, but rather a value preference having very little to do with the metaphysics of determinism or free will. . . . Very simply, the law treats man's conduct as autonomous and willed, not because it is, but because it is desirable to proceed as if it were. (1968, 74–5)

Sanford Kadish presents the "preserve dignity" view with passion and eloquence:

> Much of our commitment to democratic values, to human dignity and self-determination, to the value of the individual, turns on the pivot of a view of man as a responsible agent entitled to be praised or blamed depending upon his free choice of conduct. . . . The ancient notion of free will may be a myth. But even a convinced determinist should reject a governmental regime which is founded on anything less in its system of authoritative disposition of citizens. Whether the concept of man as responsible agent is fact or fancy is a very different question from whether we ought to insist that the government in its coercive dealings with individuals must act on that premise. (1968, 287)

Appeals to "preserving human dignity" are the death rattle of argument. Whenever there are severe threats to a cherished belief about humans, the threat is rejected as false because believing it would "undermine human dignity." If we are not made by God in God's image, then there is no basis for our special human dignity; if we are not placed at the immovable center of the universe, with everything else revolving around us, then we lose our special dignity; if we evolved like other animals from common ancestors, then our dignity is destroyed; if the mind is just the physical brain, then we are merely machines with no dignity; if our behavior can be conditioned in the same manner as a dog's behavior, then we do not have godlike dignity; if we are not first causes with free will that can transcend all mechanical causes, then humans have no dignity. In short, when humans and human behavior become subjects for scientific explanation, our special dignity is destroyed.

If humans require mysteries and miracles and special uniqueness and exemption from scientific understanding in order to retain human dignity, then human dignity is on shaky ground. But looking carefully into the causes of bad (and good) behavior and trying to understand and improve that behavior does not threaten human dignity. In any case, this claim of "commitment to preserving human dignity" rings hollow (Waller 2015, chapter 11). Placing prisoners in Supermax isolation, in conditions that threaten their sanity, is not a way of promoting individual dignity. Convicting defendants using the well-known lies of "jailhouse informants" and false "forensic evidence" is not defending dignity. Subjecting children to the dangers of lead exposure— which reduces their intelligence and undercuts their powers of self-control— and placing them in substandard schools and ignoring the fact that they are in abusive situations and refusing to provide them with health care, and then blaming them when they commit crimes (because they "freely chose" a life of crime, and it's all their fault) is not respecting dignity. It would hardly be surprising if the prisoner whose dignity is preserved in the isolation of a Supermax prison cell echoed the plaint of Cool Hand Luke, when told that his heavy chains are really for his own good: "Wish you'd stop bein' so good to me, cap'n." As Judge Bazelon once noted:

> We cannot produce a class of desperate and angry citizens by closing off, for many years, all means of economic advancement and personal fulfillment for a sizeable part of the population, and thereafter expect a crime-free society. (1976, 402)

Jeffrey L. Kirchmeier claims that if we took seriously the deeper causes of criminal behavior and explored them carefully, then: "Ultimately, these inquiries would force society to address crime in other ways besides incarceration and to directly attack the causes of crime, such as poverty" (2004, 646). That would show a genuine concern for the dignity of those whose opportunities are denied and development is skewed by the terrible conditions in which our wealthy society forces them to grow up; but that sort of concern for individual dignity would take great effort and cost considerable resources and demand substantial changes in the structure of society. It is cheaper and easier to show "respect for dignity" by blaming persons for conditions beyond their control and then locking them in cages when this treatment results in criminal behavior.

THE PLATEAU ARGUMENT FOR MORAL RESPONSIBILITY

The third means of preserving belief in moral responsibility—and a free will that supports it—is very familiar to contemporary philosophers: Place all who qualify as minimally competent on a moral responsibility plateau, and refuse to look deeper at the detailed causes of their radically divergent behavioral results. A particularly interesting version of the "plateau" argument for criminal responsibility is developed by Stephen Morse:

> Analysis of responsibility usually begins by asking about all the difficulties, burdens, problems, and misfortunes suffered by the perpetrators, all the criminogenic reasons why obeying the law seemed so hard, why offending seemed so inevitable. But suppose we start with a different question: How hard is it not to offend the law? How hard is it not to kill, burgle, rob, rape, and steal? The ability to resist the temptation to violate the law is not akin to the ability required to be a fine athlete, artist, plumber, or doctor. The person is not being asked to exercise a difficult skill; rather, he or she is being asked simply to refrain from engaging in antisocial conduct. Think, too, of all the factors mitigating against such behavior: parental, religious, and school training; peer pressure and cultural expectations; internalized standards ("superego"); fear of capture and punishment; fear of shame; and a host of others. Not all such factors operate on all actors or with great strength: there will be wide individual differences based on life experiences and, perhaps, biological factors. Nonetheless, for all persons there are enormous forces arrayed against lawbreaking. It is one thing to yield to a desire to engage in undesirable conduct such as to gossip, brag, or treat one's fellows unfairly; it is another to give in to a desire to engage in qualitatively more harmful conduct such as to kill, rape, burgle, rob, or burn. (1984, 30–1)

So we can ignore all the miscellaneous "difficulties, burdens, problems, and misfortunes suffered by the perpetrators," since those on the plateau find it so easy to obey the law that such "difficulties" are irrelevant. If you were trying to solve a challenging problem in modal logic, the fact that you are tired, distracted by a noisy environment, and currently low in self-confidence would be important factors in explaining why you failed; but if instead you are working out the sum of 7 plus 2, the task is so easy that such factors can be considered irrelevant. So it is with the plateau of moral responsibility: All of us competent actors find following the law so simple that the details of our differing capacities and situations and histories are rendered irrelevant.

Certainly it is no challenge for Stephen Morse—and for other philosophers and law professors—to resist the temptation to "kill, burgle, rob, rape, and steal"; but to suppose that everyone on the "plateau" (everyone who meets minimal competence standards) has roughly equal talents and capacities for such resistance manifests a striking failure of imagination and inquiry. In fact, "all the factors mitigating against such behavior"—in the case of you and me and Stephen Morse—often function as factors *promoting* such behavior in those who commit crimes. Those whose parents were themselves criminals, or whose parents engaged in violent abusive acts toward their children, provided important early training in favor of (rather than against) criminal behavior; Stephen Morse had school training that shaped respect for the law as well as self-respect—but many children have school experiences that are very different; "fear of shame" may motivate both Morse and the offender, but the sources of shame may be very different (for the criminal offender, failing to strike back at any insult or show of disrespect may be a greater source of shame than a criminal conviction); and as Morse himself acknowledges in a footnote, "peer pressure or subcultural expectations might be criminogenic rather than inhibitory in some cases," though he apparently regards that possibility with some skepticism. And that does not even scratch the surface of enormous differences between Stephen Morse and violent criminals in such critical factors as self-control, need for cognition, sense of self-efficacy, and internal locus-of-control. For example, a person dealing with substance addiction or having certain forms of brain damage may be normal with respect to intellect, memory processes, and other cognitive processes—and be judged competent, and admitted to the plateau of moral responsibility—though his or her capacity for resisting immediate temptations (and capacity for impulse control) is severely compromised. As Kelly Burns and Antoine Bechara note:

> Our research has demonstrated that individuals who are substance dependent, or those who have suffered bilateral damage to the ventromedial prefrontal cortex, show similar behavior patterns related to dysfunction of the reflective system. . . . First, both groups are in denial or unaware that they have any problem. Second, individuals in both groups tend to act in such a way that brings about immediate reward, even when that comes at the risk of incurring extremely negative future consequences, which may include loss of job, home, important life relationships, and reputation, and often troubles with the law. Such individuals act seemingly in ignorance of this risk. (Burns and Bechara 2007, 270)

The self-control of substance dependent subjects may also be compromised by the brain's exaggeration of the intensity of reward:

> It is also possible for the impulsive system to exaggerate the somatic response of reward stimuli, resulting in it becoming exceedingly difficult for even a well functioning reflective system to generate somatic responses that bias the person toward inhibiting action, or executing will. We might conceptualize this as a "hijacking" of the execution of willpower by an overactive impulsive system, where will becomes guided by the amygdala rather than the prefrontal cortex. Research using varieties of the Iowa Gambling Task has shown exactly this hypersensitivity to reward in substance dependent subjects. (Burns and Bechara 2007, 271; see also Bechara, Dolan, and Hindes 2002)

It is precisely those vital differences in details that the plateau is designed to hide. Russell Stetler paints a clear picture of the important differences that the plateau model and Stephen Morse prefer to ignore:

> The diverse frailties bestow the kinship of humanity. We all have them, to varying degrees, but, for most of us, the protective supports of family and society along with our individual strengths offset those frailties. For many capital clients, the frailties are overwhelming, and the supports are absent. (2007, 241)

Morse makes it quite clear that his model of criminal justice is a close partner to the plateau model of moral responsibility:

> So little self-control and rationality are necessary to obey the law, that when all the elements of a prima facie case are present, the person should be held fully legally culpable. The culpability of those who satisfy the prima facie case is fundamentally equivalent, although there may be differences in their characters or psychologies. (1984, 32)

This model may seem plausible if we consider each factor in isolation. True, growing up in a violent and dysfunctional family is a disadvantage; but there are lots of people who suffered such early disadvantages and managed to overcome them and live good decent law-abiding lives. But no one suggests that childhood abuse is a perfect predictor of adult crime; rather, it is one factor that causes crime. In like manner, smoking cigarettes is a cause of lung cancer; but obviously not every smoker will develop lung cancer. If you add some genetic propensities for developing cancer, and other environmental factors (such as exposure to high levels of air pollution, or exposure to asbestos), then eventually we get a full causal account of an individual's lung cancer. When one chain smoker develops lung cancer at age 50, while another chain smoker lives to age 75 and never develops lung cancer, we do not conclude that smoking is not a cause of lung cancer; still less do we suppose that there is *not* a full causal explanation for why the 50-year-old developed cancer, even though we will probably know only a fraction of the causal factors. In like manner, when we track the lives of two brothers from the same violent and abusive home, and we find that one became a violent criminal while the other lived a peaceful and productive life, we do not suppose that childhood abuse is not an important cause of violent criminal behavior; rather, we believe that there *are* causes for why one succumbed to violent crime while the other avoided it, but those causes are extraordinarily complex, involving some possible genetic factors but certainly a great variety of other social factors. Perhaps the peaceful brother developed a relationship with a woman who had a stabilizing effect upon his rather impetuous character, and then they had a child, which also can provide greater stability. Or he enjoyed some success in school—a special elementary school teacher praised and encouraged his writing, and strengthened his sense of self-efficacy as well as his sense that he could exert control over the events in his life. Or the violent brother had more intensive exposure to lead poisoning (the family moved out of an apartment building with heavy coats of leaded paint just before the younger peaceful brother was born). Or the older brother was at a particularly vulnerable age when his mother suffered deep depression and felt no affection or concern for him.

Unless we believe that the brothers enjoyed first cause miraculous powers, we believe that there were causal factors resulting in their different paths, and those crucial causal factors were not under their control. *Of course* the younger brother's resolve to "escape the cycle" and "not follow his father's path" and "make a success of his life" was a very important factor in his avoidance of violent crime and his successful life. But if we ask why he had such resolve when his older brother did not, we soon find causes that were not of their making and not under their control, and those factors challenge our easy belief that both of them are morally responsible for their very different lives. The two brothers are not "puppets," and neither are we. We do make our own choices, but the motives and capacities behind our own choices are the product of causes we did not control. Principled refusal to look closely at those causes is one way of preserving moral and criminal responsibility from inquiries that call them into serious question. If we don't look closely, it may appear that there were no important differences between the brothers, both of whom occupy the "plateau of competence"; when we look closely, we see differences in the details that are of vital importance, and only by neglecting them can we be comfortable in believing that both brothers are morally responsible.

Morse also throws in a "dignity" point in favor of treating all minimally competent criminals as equal (no matter what their differences in abilities or backgrounds or problems):

> The differences that exist between offenders convicted of the same crime are morally insignificant compared to the similarities. The great value of this position, placing the burden of persuasion on those who believe it is hard to obey the law, is that it treats people with greater respect and dignity than the opposing view, which treats them as helpless puppets buffeted by forces that rob them of responsibility for their deeds. (1984, 31–2)

But this adds a strawman to the dignity claim. Those who insist on looking at the detailed differences among people—including the detailed differences between those who conform to the law's requirements and those who fail to do so—do not regard either offenders or upstanding citizens as "helpless puppets." There is no invidious distinction between those who do and do not commit criminal acts (Waller 2011, 206–20): the criminals are not "robbed of responsibility," because *no one* is morally responsible.

ISOLATING THE THREATS TO CRIMINAL RESPONSIBILITY

The fourth way to preserve belief in moral responsibility and just deserts—in the face of the powerful challenges faced in the criminal justice system—is by bracketing questions of moral responsibility, thereby confining them to a small sphere where they can be isolated and controlled to prevent the challenges from contaminating the whole system. Deeper causal inquiry will be allowed, but only for narrowly defined issues. That is what we do with capital punishment, when the deeper causal problems become too severe to ignore.

It is obvious that there are profound differences among those who are counted as competent. Consider a person who grew up in an abusive and violent home, and who was the object of sustained and inescapable abusive cruelty (and developed as a result a high level of helplessness) instead of loving care and encouragement; who suffered lead poisoning, which reduced the person's intellectual capacities as well as capacity for self-control; whose environment neither encouraged nor rewarded careful reflection but instead required immediate reactions (often escape reactions), and who thus developed as a cognitive miser; who attended violent and grossly inferior schools and enjoyed almost no success there. This person may meet minimal competence standards, and certainly can make choices and act. But there is a profound and obvious contrast with the child of loving parents and adoring grandparents and supportive aunts and uncles, who was read to every night and whose efforts at careful sustained thought were praised and supported and even celebrated, who was lovingly shaped to be strong in powers of self-control and deferred gratification, who attended excellent schools and was constantly challenged and encouraged there. Those differences have become even more obvious as we have learned more about the effects of lead poisoning, the early development of powers of deferred gratification, the importance of reinforcing childhood efforts, and the many other biological and psychological and social factors that impact our development.

Though we may strive to close our eyes to such differences, and pretend that on the plateau of competent moral responsibility everyone is basically equal, the force of the obvious contravening facts is too strong to ignore. If we refuse to consider junking the entire system of moral responsibility and just deserts and criminal justice—because doing so would "threaten human dignity," or because the changes are too great to contemplate—then one "solution" is to keep the problem confined within a narrow and controllable sphere. That is precisely what the U.S. criminal justice system has done: Take the concerns about dramatically different capacities and abilities among competent persons, and concerns about the detailed causes operating on those who commit criminal acts, and focus those concerns and debates on a rigidly limited question. That tightly restricted question is the question of *mitigation* in cases of first degree murder.

As soon as we look closely, it is obvious that the restrictions on this investigation are arbitrary and unjustified. As Stephen J. Morse has noted concerning the doctrine of considering diminished capacity for murderers—and exclusively murderers—when deciding criminal sentences:

> Limiting the doctrine's application to the crime of murder makes little sense. One can understand that in Britain the "diminished responsibility" doctrine is useful to avoid the mandatory term of life imprisonment for murder (and, in the past, to avoid the death penalty), but the logic of the doctrine applies with equal force to all crimes. As a result of mental abnormality, one can be less responsible for burglary or assault, for instance, as well as for murder. . . . If the rationale for the doctrine is that criminal responsibility is lessened by extreme emotional disturbance, a disturbed defendant who commits any crime is not fully blameworthy. (1984, 22, 24)

When a person charged with murder is placed on trial, then—unless there is a question of insanity, in which the defendant is regarded as utterly incompetent—there can be no evidence concerning the defendant's brutal childhood or traumatizing war experiences or deep depression: such evidence is inadmissible when considering whether the defendant is guilty. But once the defendant has been found guilty of first degree murder, then—and only then—can such considerations be raised for the purposes of *mitigation*, to show that the defendant does not justly deserve the death penalty.

But once you have recognized "mitigating factors" in cases of capital punishment, only willful blindness can prevent one from seeing their relevance in other cases as well. The Supreme Court's justification for allowing mitigation *only* in capital cases was stated by Chief Justice Burger: "the imposition of death by public authority is . . . profoundly different from all other penalties." (*Lockett v. Ohio*, 438 U.S. 586; 1978) Capital punishment is a special sort of punishment, of course: it is the ultimate punishment, and mistakes can't be corrected. But mistakes can't be corrected when we lock someone in a cage for years. We can ultimately release the wrongly convicted prisoner, but we cannot restore those years or wipe out the suffering or (at least in many cases) fix the psychological damage. Even if we agree that capital punishment is "profoundly different," that in itself cannot justify the consideration of mitigating factors in capital punishment cases but not in other criminal cases. That capital punishment is different is no justification, *unless* there is something unique about capital punishment that makes mitigation *relevant* in capital cases but irrelevant in all other cases (including cases in which prisoners may be locked in prison cells for decades). What that relevant difference could be I cannot imagine, and the Court never suggests any possibilities. Once we recognize mitigating factors, it is difficult to avoid recognizing that there are *always* factors beyond one's control.

So what is the real reason for allowing the consideration of "mitigating factors" in cases of capital punishment, but excluding them from all other criminal proceedings? One reason is that in capital cases, the causal factors become too obvious to ignore; the second is that it is a way of confining and controlling the discussion of mitigating causal factors, which can quickly get out of hand: it leads to deeper examination of all the causal details and undermines belief in just deserts and moral responsibility, and ultimately destroys the shaky foundation of the criminal justice system. That is not to suggest that those who argue for mitigating considerations in capital punishment cases are playing some manner of devious trick; to the contrary, the campaign to take seriously and even enlarge the mitigating factors that count against the imposition of the death penalty is carried out by people deeply and sincerely disturbed by the grotesque spectacle of mentally retarded persons and children dragged into an execution chamber and killed (as they were in the United States until comparatively recently, when a majority of Supreme Court Justices prohibited such cruel and unusual punishment, over the strong objections of a minority who favored allowing states to continue executing children and the severely retarded).

Allowing the consideration of mitigating factors to prevent capital punishment—but only *after* the person has been convicted of first degree murder—softens somewhat the ugliest elements of the criminal justice system: those most *obviously* suffering from the harshest histories and problems are locked away in cages, but are not subject to execution. Thus allowing the very *limited* consideration of mitigating factors makes the criminal justice system seem more humane, and deflects some of the objections to the most blatant punitive injustices: the concerns are boxed within a clearly defined area of inquiry, and not allowed out to cast doubts on the legitimacy of the entire system. But while limiting such mitigating inquiries within a narrowly confined sphere does serve to ameliorate some of the most disturbing aspects of the system, that amelioration comes at a price: Once we begin to seriously inquire into the causes of criminal behavior, any stopping point seems—and is—arbitrary. Deeper inquiry reveals causes—detailed causes that undercut claims of morally responsible choice—for a much broader range of murders, and not only of murders but also of other crimes; and when such inquiries continue to reveal causes of which we had been unaware and which undercut claims of moral responsibility, it becomes difficult to deny that there are many important and deep and detailed causes of which we were ignorant. Probing further and deeper raises serious doubts concerning moral responsibility and the justice system built on that foundation.

These sustained inquiries reveal something very disturbing about those who commit terrible crimes; in the words of a great bluegrass song by Pete Wernick, "let me tell you, my friend, he's just like you," made of the same flesh with similar genes and subject to the same sorts of causes and conditioning, and if you and I had been subjected to the same conditions—instead of having the good *luck* to avoid lead-poisoning and learned helplessness and the failure to learn self-control, and the good *luck* to have a loving family and supportive teachers and a fortunate childhood and positive rather than negative peer pressure—then you and I could have been the ones committing terrible crimes rather than living lives of success and comfort. That is not an easy idea to accept. It is easier to blame, and accentuate the differences, and pretend that they are differences in kind. But unless one has recourse to a miracle-working God-given free will—that transcends all prior and contemporary causal influences—then it is absurd to suppose that there can be a *fair* system of justice that systemically excludes such considerations. Nonetheless, that is precisely what our system of justice does in order to continue functioning in its traditional manner.

Preserving the system of moral responsibility—whether in the philosophy seminar room or the halls of justice—not only results in a distorted view of free will; it also blocks the deeper inquiries that reveal the rich structure of natural free will, that discover impediments to the development and exercise of free will, and that find ways of enlarging and enhancing free will. A better and broader understanding of free will requires unlimited study of the depths and details of free (and unfree) behavior. That understanding is valuable to philosophers, bakers, and candlestick makers; but it is crucial to those being ground up in the implacable machinery of our system of justice.

Chapter 7

Psychological Free Will

Richard Double (1991, 9) argues that the whole notion of free will is incoherent, and must be abandoned: Too many elements are regarded as essential properties of free will, and there is no way those supposedly essential elements can be integrated into a workable unity. Even a brief perusal of the startling variety of views that claim to be true accounts of free will (Zimmerman 2011, 100; Wright 2014, 227–8) offers powerful evidence that Double is correct. For Pico della Mirandola, the essence of free will is a special power of first-cause choice which offers open opportunities that range from the lowest beastliness all the way to immortal deity. While William James does not insist on quite such a panoply of open choices, he does insist that genuine free will can operate only in an open, rather than a closed (determined) universe: free will must afford choices among new and radically open paths and possibilities. C. A. Campbell concurs and postulates the remarkable power of contra-causal free will to guarantee such open choices. Robert Kane agrees that free will must involve open choices among alternative paths, but insists that such choices are possible within a scientifically naturalistic nonmiraculous world view. In contrast, Frankfurt argues that free will does *not* require open alternatives; and Susan Wolf goes even further, insisting that an agent who has the possibility of taking a different path has less than perfect freedom. For Wolf, genuine free will requires following the single narrow path that tracks the True and Good, and that basic model of single path free will has a long history: one strong Christian tradition insists that the only perfect freedom consists in complete and willing enslavement to God, and that in the eternal bliss of Heaven when we are directly in the presence of God there will be no inclination whatsoever to deviate from the path of righteousness and single-minded worship, and that is the highest degree of perfect freedom. Dostoyevsky begs to differ: unswerving adherence even to the true rational

115

path would destroy freedom, and humankind would go mad rather than be deprived of open alternatives:

> So one's own free, unrestrained choice, one's own whim, be it the wildest, one's own fancy, sometimes worked up to a frenzy—that is the most advantageous advantage that cannot be fitted into any table or scale and that causes every system and every theory to crumble into dust on contact. . . .
>
> Now, you may say that this too can be calculated in advance and entered on the timetable—chaos, swearing, and all—and that the very possibility of such a calculation would prevent it, so that sanity would prevail. Oh no! In that case man would go insane on purpose, just to be immune from reason. (1864/1961, 110, 115)

According to the free will account offered by one neuropsychologist, Michael Gazzaniga, the *more* genuinely open possibilities one can consider the greater the freedom: "Our freedom is to be found in developing more options for our computing brains to choose among" (2014, 73).

Another psychologist, Roy Baumeister, at one time saw little or no benefit to such multiplication of open alternatives, instead viewing the capacity to accept one's societal role and follow the rules as the key to free will: "Free will evolved, in part, to enable people to follow rules." (Baumeister, Crescioni, and Alquist 2011, 2); however, Baumeister—an honest and conscientious scientist—recently changed his view, in light of additional research (Baumeister 2014, 246–7).

We get reason in Plato, Kant, Wolf, Nelkin; a more modest commitment to reason joined with strong will in John Fischer; greater emphasis on will in Frankfurt, but still with higher order reflection; much stronger commitment to will in Pico and William James; and anti-reason combined with super will in Dostoyevsky and Sartre.

Open alternatives are essential, open alternatives are superfluous or even undesirable; free will is natural, free will is miraculous; free will must be rational, free will must be able to escape the bonds of rationality; free will must include the possibility of radical choices among dramatically different paths, free will requires only modest guidance control, real free will requires enslavement to the single true path; free will is enhanced by profound commitment, free will must be free of any constraining commitments; almost everyone enjoys free will (except when locked in chains), only a very few perfectly rational persons have free will. If all of these remarkably diverse and conflicting accounts of free will point toward a single entity, then it must be a fabulous creature indeed.

Richard Double is correct that these divergent and even contradictory accounts cannot pick out something identifiable as free will, but that does not imply that there is no workable account of free will. Finding that account requires returning to a free will unencumbered by burdens it was never equipped to carry.

FREE WILL WRIT LARGE

The fundamental problem in our understanding of free will occurred when humans claimed exclusive dominion over free will. It is not surprising that this happened. It *is* surprising that this monopolistic megalomania has endured for two millennia; and it is amazing that it continues more than 150 years after Darwin published *On the Origin of Species*. Michael Ruse notes that:

> Darwinism insists that features evolve gradually, and something as important as morality should have been present in our (very recent) shared ancestors. Furthermore, if morality is as important biologically to humans as is being claimed, it would be odd indeed had all traces now been eliminated from the social interactions of other high-level primates. (1986, 227)

That is good Darwinian advice for our understanding of morality, and the same principles apply to our understanding of free will. It is likely that morality became advantageous when larger groups of animals—many of them distant relations at most—began to live together for mutual benefit. But by that time, free will was already well-established in animals considerably less social. Rather than claiming that free will belongs exclusively to humans, and struggling to find ways to separate human free will from anything occurring in animal behavior, we must recognize that free will is valuable to humans for the same reasons that make it valuable to other species. It took us a long time to recognize that those from other cultures and tribes and ethnic groups are not that different from us. Sadly, it is a lesson easily forgotten. Racism and ethnic prejudice and religious bigotry and tribal allegiance can still overwhelm recognition of our common nature and result in horrific acts, as witnessed in the Balkans and Rwanda and Iraq. But of course no one living in the United States or Europe need look to distant lands to find evidence of the power and resiliency of racism. When we are killing and exploiting our fellow humans, we do it more comfortably if we convince ourselves that they are "not like us," that there is some essential difference between "them" and "us"; and that belief can be remarkably powerful (the brilliant and "enlightened" Thomas Jefferson could regard his own *children* as legitimate objects of enslavement). When we treat the members of other species as objects of our blood sports, as objects to be raised in cruel conditions for the pleasures of our palates, as appropriate subjects for painful experiments to test our cosmetics, that is easier when we regard them as profoundly *different* and *distinct* from us. Most of us manage to maintain that attitude, even when we realize that much of what we know about our *own* physical and psychological make-up was derived from studies on other species. So the question seems a natural and unproblematic one: What is it about humans that makes them radically different from all other species? There must be *something*, after all, for otherwise our treatment of other species would raise deeply disturbing questions.

Even today, in our post-Darwinian world, well-informed Darwinians often emphasize the *differences* between humans and other species more than the commonalities. Thus Daniel Dennett, a brilliant philosopher steeped in Darwinism, writes eloquently of the special difference between humans and other creatures:

> Our human brains, and only human brains, have been armed by habits and methods, mind-tools and information, drawn from millions of other brains which are not ancestral to our own brains. This, amplified by the *deliberate, foresightful* use of generate-and-test in science, puts our minds on a different plane from the minds of our nearest relatives among the animals. (1995, 381)

Dennett's account is precisely right. This relatively small difference between the brains of humans and the brains of even our nearest relatives has resulted in an enormous cultural difference. But the difference between humans individually and other animals is not nearly so great. The great mass of our cognitive processes are very closely related to those of other primates, and our behavior is shaped in ways that parallel behavioral shaping in other species. Collectively, our rational processes result in the world of scientific inquiry and an enormous range of understanding; individually, we are still subject to rational limits and cognitive flaws, as Daniel Kahneman (2011) makes clear. Free will is not a product of our enormous cultural advances in science or mathematics or the arts; rather, it is something we share with other species, and its basic nature is better understood by examining the common elements. Those common elements of free will—when combined with the special adaptive advantages of language—have made possible the remarkable advances Dennett describes.

Dennett rightly emphasizes the great power of the generate-and-test method of inquiry—"the *deliberate, foresightful* use of generate-and-test in science, puts our minds on a different plane"—and this bedrock of scientific inquiry is indeed a powerful means of exploration. But while the development of scientific method and the elaborate scientific refinements of the generate-and-test method are a remarkable human achievement, the generate-and-test method is not the exclusive property of scientists, nor is it confined to the human species. It is the basic method employed by chimpanzees, white-footed mice, pigeons, and perhaps even bees and fruit flies. It is basic for free will, and it is basic for scientific inquiry; but that basis runs much deeper than human scientific inquiry.

The white-footed mouse and the white-coated lab scientist are employing a very similar method. The lab scientist has a marvelous "domain of expertise" to bring to bear on the problem, as well as a systematic method of eliminating failed hypotheses; but the white-footed mouse also has substantial cognitive resources for exploring possibilities and avoiding bad options (it avoids predators and does not chew on rocks). While its method of eliminating failed hypotheses is not as sophisticated as that of the scientist, it is still effective. Both will nonconsciously winnow out many unpromising options.

Scientific research is "deliberate and foresightful," as Dennett notes; but the white-footed mouse is also deliberate in its use of generate and test; and while it is not as "foresightful" as the scientist's "domain of expertise," it is certainly foresightful in the sense of having testing mechanisms to sort out the generated alternatives. After all, neither the scientist nor the white-footed mouse knows the answer without generating possibilities that are not known to be true. And if we examine a less exalted level than rigorous science (rigorous science is not a large part of human thought, and is not the only sort of thought engaged in by scientists) we find convenient but limited heuristics doing the sorting, in ways that look a lot like white-footed mouse sorting. No one denies the difference between the scientist and the white-footed mouse; but we may gain more by starting from the common elements rather than the differences.

Science is the exclusive property of humans; but the generate-and-test method that lies at the foundation of science (and many other forms of human creativity and discovery) was in use long before the development of scientific method, and indeed long before humans arrived on the scene. The generate-and-test procedure continues to provide benefits to many species, and to scientists and nonscientists alike. Donald Campbell (1960, 1974) offers the best-known statement of the model, though (as Campbell acknowledges) Alexander Bain (1868) had proposed the basic model a century earlier. In Campbell's model—which he notes is similar to Popper's (1959, 1963, 1972) approach to scientific discovery—there is a two-stage process of discovery and learning: the stages of "blind variation" and "selective retention," which together constitute what has come to be known as the BVSR model.

ACTIVE EXPLORATION OF ALTERNATIVES

The process of blind behavioral variation (BV) is essential. There is considerable debate concerning the nature and degree of the "blindness," but for present purposes the key is *variation*: animals *vary* their behavior and *explore* alternatives in an active rather than a passive process. The default state is not a passive waiting for stimuli that will prompt a reaction; rather, animals are naturally *active*—constantly active—in their behavioral processes. As Brembs (2014) notes:

> Traditionally, the neurosciences have been working under the assumption of the sensorimotor hypothesis, namely that the main function of brains is to compute motor output from sensory input. At the same time, ecologists have known for a long time that such passive strategies are not evolutionarily stable. Instead, animals must be constantly active, exploring, probing the environment with spontaneous actions and planning future actions by learning from behavioral consequences.

Such activity does not always result in overt behavior, but instead occurs as active neurological processes, many of which never rise to the level of consciousness.

This active behavior ranges from the exploratory behavior of honey bees to the nonconscious exploratory behavior in Poincaré's mathematically brilliant brain—after Poincaré has put aside an unsolved mathematical problem to pursue a new one—which ultimately results in Poincaré's conscious recognition of the breakthrough to the solution that his conscious thought had not discovered. On a more mundane and familiar level, we make a conscious struggle to remember the name of an old friend or an actor or a movie watched years ago; our efforts fail, and we stop thinking about it. Or rather, we stop consciously thinking about it, but the wheels continue to turn nonconsciously, until hours or even days later the answer "pops up" in our conscious thought. Long after an intense argument—when we have long since "stopped thinking about it"—the perfect rebuttal to an opponent's claim emerges into consciousness: Nonconscious argument development continues grinding out better arguments. Even when we have no reason to continue pursuing the answer and no conscious desire to solve a problem, our nonconscious thought continues to generate new ideas and possible solutions (Snyder, Mitchell, Ellwood, Yates, and Pallier 2004).

Whether the process is conscious or nonconscious, it is rarely inactive (including when we sleep), and outside stimuli are not required to keep the process moving. Marcus E. Raichle reviews a range of studies on the high level of energy consumption by the brain, noting that "it is clear that the brain's enormous energy consumption is little affected by task performance" (2010, 180) but instead results from a constant high level of activity (even when we are not conscious of exerting cognitive efforts); thus "it is probable that the majority of brain energy consumption is devoted to functionally significant intrinsic activity" (2010, 180).

This is not some mysterious uniquely human process, but a process that occurs in species ranging from fruit flies to humans. It does not require special powers (unless they are powers shared with many other species). It is not magical or supernatural; rather, it is a process that is deeply entrenched and valuable for survival in a changing world. It is hardly surprising that the value of alternative behavioral possibilities would be a deeply ingrained value, and a valuable element of free will. Rather than seeking godlike human powers that mysteriously generate open alternatives, we gain a better perspective when we start with what we have in common that has proved its value for many species. As George Sugihara (a researcher on behavioral variability in fruit flies) stated concerning an experiment by Maye, Hsieh, Sugihara, and Brembs (2007):

> We found that there must be an evolved function in the fly brain which leads to spontaneous variations in fly behavior. The results of our analysis indicate a mechanism which might be common to many other animals and could form the biological foundation for what we experience as free will. (Quoted in Brembs 2014)

One of the most striking demonstrations of this power to spontaneously generate alternative paths is found in research on flies. Björn Brembs and his colleagues at the Free University of Berlin conducted an experiment in which a fly was tethered inside a blank white cylinder in conditions of complete "stimulus deprivation": that is, no environmental cues were present to provoke a behavioral direction. If behavioral variation were the product of external influences, then lacking an external stimulus the fly would move in no patterned direction; instead, the fly explored its immediate area, then attempted to execute large jumps to other areas. That is, the fly—without external stimuli—actively engages in localized exploratory behavior followed by spontaneous forays into different environs (Maye, Hsieh, Sunihara, and Brembs 2007).

This *apparently* random behavior—generated without being under the control of external stimuli—was once regarded as a frustrating problem for researchers, defying their best efforts to develop experimental methods that would eliminate such behavioral "errors." It prompted a rather whimsical but exasperated "law" among those operating learning labs, the "Harvard Law of Animal Behavior": "Under carefully controlled experimental circumstances, the animal behaves as it damned well pleases." J. Lee Kavanau, who devoted much of his career to the study of learning processes in feral white-footed mice, noted the frustration that can result from such stubborn variability: "Investigators sometimes are puzzled by the fact that once an animal has learned a discrimination well, it nonetheless still makes some 'incorrect' responses" (1967, 1628). But after reflecting on this phenomenon, Kavanau reached an important insight:

> Actually, these responses are incorrect only from the point of view of the investigator's rigidly prescribed program, not from that of the animal. The basis for these responses is that the animal has a certain degree of variability built into many of its behavior patterns. This variability is adaptive to conditions in the wild, where there are many relationships that are not strictly prescribed. . . . The habit of deviating fairly frequently from stereotyped "correct" responses, together with a high level of spontaneous activity, underlie the remarkable facility with which white-footed mice can be taught to cope with complex contingencies. (1967, 1628)

Animal behavior—including the behavior of mice, chimpanzees, and humans—stems from a dual process of variation and selection, and that selection of behavior parallels the process that occurs in evolutionary natural selection. The latter does not require a special and unique intelligence to guide it. Neither does the former.

OPEN ALTERNATIVES

For foraging animals in a changing and challenging environment, the first and vitally important element of free will is the generation of open behavioral alternatives. This is an endogenous and ongoing activity. Many analyses—by philosophers, economists, and even psychologists—go astray at that initial stage. On the one hand, there is a common tendency (shared by existentialists, source-libertarians, rational-man-economists, some psychologists, and many of the "folk") to grossly exaggerate both the range and the nature of those open alternatives. (Among sophisticated compatibilist philosophers there is a tendency to *under*estimate or even deny the importance of such open alternatives, but that approach will be considered later.) The spontaneous generation of varied alternative possible behaviors requires nothing exotic, much less anything miraculous; but its importance is enormous. As noted above, Kavanau is well aware of its importance to the well-being of white-footed mice:

> The habit of deviating fairly frequently from stereotyped "correct" responses, together with a high level of spontaneous activity, underlie the remarkable facility with which white-footed mice can be taught to cope with complex contingencies. (1967, 1628)

It also, of course, underlies "the remarkable facility" with which white-footed mice—and other species—can cope with complex contingencies in their natural environments. The process of "deviating fairly frequently" opens new possibilities—some of which are positively reinforced and may lead to very beneficial results—that would not have been discovered had the mouse confined itself to a single optimum path. Complex patterns or sequences of behavior can be mastered, as the animal learns one beneficial response and then follows it by a variety of other responses; when one of those responses is reinforced in combination with the earlier response, the more complex behavior pattern emerges, and it can become increasingly complex as more elements are added.

Animals that steadily follow the same behavioral path become predictable and easy prey for predators, just as predators that rarely vary their hunting paths and techniques are easier for potential prey to avoid. The importance of such behavioral variation is emphasized by Björn Brembs (2010):

> Beyond behaving unpredictably to evade predators or outcompete a competitor, all animals must explore, must try out different solutions to unforeseen problems. Without behaving variably, without acting rather than passively responding, there can be no success in evolution. Those individuals who have found the best balance between flexible actions and efficient responses are the ones who have succeeded in evolution. It is this potential to behave variably, to initiate actions independently of the stimulus situation, which provides animals with choices.

Choices are an essential element of animal free will, including the free will of human animals. But when we start our examination of free will with a narrow focus on *human* free will, there is a tendency to distort and exaggerate the nature of such choices. At the most extreme, some suppose that the choice must be removed from the natural world altogether, and transformed into something godlike. The natural choices available to animals are quite various indeed, and neither mysteries nor miracles are required to generate them. They can involve variation in location, in time, in sequence of behaviors, in the manner in which a behavior is performed (swiftly or stealthily, tentatively or forthrightly), and so forth. But they are not—thankfully, for our successful functioning—unlimited, nor are they miraculously independent of our environmental circumstances.

The variation element of free will is vitally important to animals, humans and otherwise. But there is another element: the choosing among alternatives. Alternatives without workable powers of choice is not freedom. In particular, simply enlarging our options does not enhance our freedom; to the contrary, it may undermine our animal free will. Choices among an excessive number of alternatives is disturbing, even paralyzing, as we realize we are unlikely to make the best choice and that we lack the resources for making the best choice: "More choices, and possibly more options, may be better than fewer, but only up to a point" (Patall, Cooper, and Robinson 2008, 297; see also Vohs, Baumeister, Schmeichel, Twenge, Nelson, and Tice 2008; Reed, Kaplan, and Brewer 2012).

We know that multiplying alternatives is not always good, as dramatically illustrated by Bernard Williams:

> An effective way for actions to be ruled out is that they never come into thought at all, and this is often the best way. One does not feel easy with the man who in the course of a discussion of how to deal with political or business rivals says, "Of course, we could have them killed, but we should lay that aside right from the beginning." It should never have come into his hands to be laid aside. (1985, 185)

If I am considering how to remove a stump, I might consider dynamite, but not nuclear weaponry. It is important to have some order and limits on alternatives: the white-footed mouse does not attempt to fly; the scientist does not invoke miracles; the competent police investigator will not seek the services of a "psychic."

The breadth and depth of valuable alternatives should not be exaggerated. There is a tendency to suppose that if a choice among 10 alternatives is good, a choice among 100 alternatives must be better. It is not surprising that we think that way; after all, we have a strong tendency to suppose that human rational powers are unlimited, that we can always think harder and longer and better when it is in our interests to do so, and that our interests are well-defined and transparent. Those are the underlying principles of "rational man" economics, and its obvious implausibility notwithstanding it remained an article of faith until behavioral economists demonstrated its falseness as a model of human economic behavior. According to rational choice theory, a wider range of alternatives from which to choose is always advantageous, because it allows the person to find an optimum (or at least a better) match between one's final choice and one's known and defined preferences (Hotelling 1929). Adding more options can never be negative, because additional options increase the probability of finding a better fit with one's preferences. Even insightful contemporary psychologists fall into this error. Dean Keith Simonton writes that:

> free will tends to increase as k [the number of open alternatives] increases. . . . A student who selects from prospective 100 majors has more freedom than one who "selects" from only one. (2013, 379)

And a student who selects from only three or four alternatives must enjoy less freedom than one who selects from 100. But in fact too many choices results in a less than optimum choice opportunity (especially if one is lacking in knowledge or cognitive self-efficacy.) It might be great for reasoners of unlimited cognitive resources and godlike cognitive confidence; but it is not great for human animals.

The belief that more choices is always better is a deep and widespread belief. As Sheen S. Iyengar and Mark R. Lepper note:

> It is a common supposition in modern society that the more choices, the better—that the human ability to manage, and human desire for, choice is infinite. From classic economic theories of free enterprise, to mundane marketing practices that provide customers with entire aisles devoted to potato chips or soft drinks, to important life decisions in which people contemplate alternative career options or multiple investment opportunities, this belief pervades our institutions, norms, and customs. (2000, 995)

This tendency to equate greater freedom with more options is powerful. Michael S. Gazzaniga's extensive studies of the operations of the brain have resulted in important insights into the operation of free will, but even Gazzaniga—under the influence of deep beliefs about the special nature of human cognitive powers—can be led into exaggeration. He rightly emphasizes the human need for active exploration, but treats human freedom as based on an almost limitless process of enlarging our choices and options: "Our freedom comes from gaining more options to act upon as we relentlessly explore our environment" (2014, 60). And behind this claim is the deep belief in human uniqueness:

> We humans are about becoming less dumb, about making better decisions to cope and adapt to the world we live in. That is what our brain is for and what it does. It makes decisions based on experience, innate biases, and much more. Our freedom is to be found in developing more options for our computing brains to choose among. As we move through time and space, we are constantly generating new thoughts, ideas, and beliefs. All of these mental states provide a rich array of possible actions for us. The couch potato simply does not have the same array as the explorer. New experience provides the window into still more choices, and that is what freedom truly means. (2014, 73)

White-footed mice are also "about becoming less dumb," and about finding better ways to "adapt to the world we live in," and discover options that will enhance their likelihood of survival in a changing world. But neither humans nor mice benefit from adding more and more options, unless we can effectively control those options; and neither humans nor mice have infinite resources for such control. Gazzaniga is profoundly aware of both the powers and the limits of "our computing brains," and no doubt he would qualify his statement in various respects; but his emphasis on "gaining more options" as the essential way of enhancing free will is an indication of the power of that image: an image more appropriate for the unlimited powers of super rationality than the very limited powers of human reason.

While humans often express a preference for more and more options, our behavior shows that increases in options can be frustrating, and can result in less rather than more satisfaction with one's final choice. In one interesting experiment, supermarket shoppers were given an opportunity to sample a jam selected from a display of six varieties of Wilkin & Sons jams, and were given a coupon for one dollar off the purchase price. In alternate hours, shoppers were invited to sample a jam from among twenty-four varieties produced by Wilkin & Sons, and were also given a coupon. Shoppers were more likely to stop and sample at the larger display (60% as opposed to 40% who stopped at the smaller display); but 30% of the shoppers who sampled from among the six varieties actually bought jam, while only 3% of shoppers who sampled from the larger display made a purchase. The results of this study (together with several other studies along similar lines) led Iyengar and Lepper to conclude that while people typically *prefer* larger sets of choices, they are often less satisfied with their choices than when they are choosing among more limited alternatives, and that having choices among very large sets of alternatives typically results in reduced rather than enhanced motivation. In their discussion of their results, Iyengar and Lepper reach an apparently paradoxical conclusion:

> Even when choices are self-generated, it is possible that overly extensive choices may have demotivating consequences. Because people seem to enjoy extensive-choice contexts more than limited-choice contexts, they may sometimes prefer to make available to themselves many more choices than they can possibly handle. (2000, 1004)

Like other successful foraging species, we evolved with a strong preference for open alternatives and behavioral variety, preferences that served us well in a changing environment and a variety of conditions. Genuine open alternatives were not easy to come by: the problem was finding enough workable alternatives, rather than too many. Path A is blocked by a fierce aggressive predator, path B passes through the jealously guarded territory of a large and powerful rival, and path C is flooded. It was a rare and wonderful thing when we were confronted with a rich variety of choices. There was no need and little opportunity to develop a means of limiting an excessive number of options. That becomes a problem in our contemporary world which often offers (to humans) options in spectacular profusion: walk into a large supermarket and contemplate the varieties of mustard on offer. An enormous range of choices may be fine for gods and other perfectly rational beings who can be sublimely confident of invariably choosing the best of all possible worlds, but it is not always beneficial for humans.

Why would we suppose that more choice is always better? Because we evolved in settings of limited choices, not in supermarkets; and because now we adopt the "rational man" view in economics and in philosophy, and we forget that our rationality is not infinite but instead quite limited, and sometimes very limited indeed. For the perfectly rational man of economic fantasy, more choices can never be a disadvantage; for the real man of behavioral economics and psychological reality, more choices can be a major problem. This is particularly true if—as is often the case—we have abundant choices and meager information. We do want open alternative paths; but these are not real alternatives if we are not sure how to effectively pursue those alternatives and we are incapable of gaining workable knowledge of the nature of those paths. Paths that must be traveled in the dark, as well as alternative paths where all the possible paths are tragic (Botti, Orfali, and Iyengar 2009) feel like coercion rather than choices under our effective control.

Having open alternatives is important and beneficial, for humans, white-footed mice, and many other animals. For gods, there is perhaps no upper limit on the desirability of more alternatives; for humans and other animals, there is. We may still *like* the idea of 400 colleges, or majors, or job applicants, or automobile models to choose from; but the task of choosing from an enormous variety of alternatives—particularly if many of those alternatives are quite similar (almost all the applicants are in the right area of specialty, have glowing references, and received outstanding teaching reviews)—can be disheartening, and leave one less confident of and more dissatisfied with one's choice. At the extreme, the choosing process may be sufficiently unpleasant to produce lethargy and avoidance. When confronted with a choice situation that is difficult—because the number of choices offered is overwhelming, or the differences among the items to be chosen are unclear, or because the items under consideration are particularly complex (as is often the case in deciding among various medical options)—then decision makers are more likely to forgo choosing altogether (Chernev 2003; Botti and Iyengar 2006; Iyengar, Jiang, and Kamenica 2006), even though not choosing may have very bad consequences (as when one delays or avoids choosing among treatment options for a cancer that is more likely to metastasize if left untreated). When they do choose, people are often less satisfied with the choice they made, and experience more regret over the choice (Brenner, Rottenstreich, and Sood 1999; Carmon, Wertenbroch, and Zeelenberg 2003; Iyengar, Wells, and Schwartz 2006; Sagi and Friedland 2007). This problem of "choice overload" is a well-known phenomenon in psychological studies.

In addition, there are cases where choices are inherently distressing. When all the available options are painful, this may seem more like "coerced choosing" rather than genuine choice. Perhaps the most disturbing example of such a "choice" is the case of "Sophie's Choice," made famous by the novel and film depicting a woman, Sophie, who is held prisoner by the Nazis and forced to make a choice of which one of her two children will be killed (if she refuses to choose, both will be killed). For anyone with children, it is difficult to imagine a more horrific "choice." Less monstrous but still deeply disturbing are the choices parents sometimes must make between continuing painful and probably futile treatment for an infant or small child, or instead stopping treatment and allowing the child to die more peacefully. Such "tragic choices" do not seem like free choices; and having the choice is typically much more disturbing than not having that choice. A study of such tragic choices (Botti, Orfali, and Iyengar 2009) found that parents wanted all the information they could get about their child's condition and prognosis, but that parents who were themselves required to make the choice between stopping and continuing treatment (as was typically the case in American hospitals) suffered greater psychological distress both at the time of the decision and later, while parents who were kept informed but did not make the final decision (in France, the physicians make the decision whether treatment of the child should continue or be halted) reported less distress and less feeling of guilt. Aversion to such a "choice" is a special case in which both options are awful: the child continues painful treatments but may well die in any case and in the unlikely event of survival will be severely disabled, or the child dies more swiftly. Not only does such a "choice" feel coercive, but being faced with such a terrible choice—where all the possibilities are bad for a beloved innocent child—has a shattering effect on our deep (but often unrecognized) belief that the world is generally *just*.

As already noted, open choices are vitally important for our psychological well-being, and having a workable range of choices typically enables choosers to find a better path than would have been available with fewer or no choices. But in some circumstances, choices can be very unpleasant, even debilitating. One such case, noted above, is when the number of options is so large as to be overwhelming and unmanageable. Another such situation is when the chooser has a weak sense of self-efficacy, or an actual lack of sufficient knowledge to make an intelligent choice (Rodin, Rennert, and Solomon 1980; Bandura 1989). One study (Woodward and Wallston 1987) found that many older patients were reluctant to make their own health care choices; however, older patients with a strong sense of health self-efficacy—patients with confidence in their knowledge and ability to make effective health care decisions—showed a much higher preference for making their own decisions.

We have ways of limiting our choices: When the white-footed mouse is choosing among different paths, it does not choose to fly over the predator, nor to attack the fox that blocks one path, nor does it endeavor to burrow through the solid rock at its back. None of these are options that come into play. And our deeply ingrained cultural values may also limit our choices, in ways that we generally find beneficial and typically do not even notice.

In some circumstances we can handle and appreciate more options (when, for example, it is easy to sort them into smaller categories). Auto manufacturers who offer views of various models of cars and trims and colors on their website do not offer the overwhelming choice among several hundred vehicles of various sizes, trims, colors, and accessories; instead, they offer choices among a limited number of models, then go to styles among those models, then to trim lines, then to colors, and finally to accessories. Eventually you have chosen from among several hundred possibilities, but not in a manner that overwhelmed your resources and discouraged you from choosing.

There are situations in which animals prefer fewer open behavioral alternatives, and animals can learn to adjust the level of variability in response to changing environmental factors. When a reliable source of reinforcement—for example, a reliable path to food—is readily and steadily available, variability of behavior is reduced: the steady positive reinforcement of a single behavioral option will eventually cause variation in behavior to diminish. Behavioral variation will not disappear, however, as Kavanau (1967) notes. Animals that are locked into one path are not only easier prey for predators, but are also ill-equipped to deal with environmental changes: when the steady source of food disappears, the lack of variability and of exploratory behavior will mean that the animal is unlikely to have ready replacements available. On the opposite tack, when a food source becomes less and less reliable, behavioral variability dramatically increases.

Humans and chimpanzees and honey bees vary in their need for open alternative paths of behavior: some individuals are much higher in sensation-seeking than are others. In addition—whether pigeon, rat, or human—under different conditions we vary in our need for and inclination toward open behavioral alternatives. When we have found a reliable source of rewards we tend to remain and exploit it, varying our behavior less (though variation does not disappear); and when the bar press that hitherto had delivered food now becomes less reliable, we engage in a greater variety of behavioral options. But need for alternatives and open paths remains a strong need throughout, and for good reason: it is one of our most adaptive characteristics, whether white-footed mouse or human.

ANIMAL FREE WILL

What is the psychological nature of free will, for humans and chimpanzees and white-footed mice? We want choices, and varying numbers of alternatives under changing conditions; and we want choices that are manageable, and are good enough, without overwhelming our capacity to choose with confidence: neither humans nor chimpanzees nor white-footed mice can benefit from choice-making in a "blooming buzzing confusion" of overwhelming alternatives. Robert Frost may enjoy selecting the "path less traveled" when a road forks; but he will not enjoy selecting a path when the road abruptly splits into hundreds of paths. If a prospective college student must choose among all the colleges and universities in the world, it is unlikely that the student will make the optimum choice, and unlikely that the student will feel confident in her choice. If she is instead choosing among major state universities in the Midwestern United States that have strong anthropology programs, she will have quite enough choices and likely be happier and more confident in the process of choosing.

The key point is that we do—in normal circumstances—want to *make choices*, and select among alternatives; and we value such choices whether we are humans, pigeons, rats, white-footed mice, or chimpanzees. Pigeons prefer tasks that allow for choosing among alternatives (Catania and Sagvolden 1980), and similar studies yield similar results for rats (Voss and Homzie 1970) and humans (Suzuki 1997, 2000): pigeons, rats, and humans prefer tasks that allow choices in behavior, even if the choice alternatives are equally effective. Indeed, Suzuki (2000, 113) found that subjects still preferred choice even when one of the alternatives was somewhat worse than the optimum. The psychological and physical benefits of choice have also been demonstrated in research with polar bears (Ross 2006) and pandas (Owen et al. 2005). Choice itself is (under most circumstances) inherently appealing (Morris and Royale 1988; Bown, Read, and Summers 2003). Choice is valuable; indeed it is so valuable that we have evolved to favor it for its own sake. This is not surprising, as Catania and Sagvolden note:

> Given that food supplies sometimes may be lost to competitors or may disappear in other ways, an organism that chooses patches of the environment in which two or more food supplies are available will probably have a survival advantage over one that chooses patches of the environment containing only a single food supply. (1980, 85)

Choice among open alternatives is the key element of free will, and was the key element long before the evolution of humans; and it was a valuable part of human free will long before humans distorted free will in a futile effort to justify moral responsibility.

The depth of the need and desire for choice is indicated by a study of the neural substrates that respond to the anticipated opportunity for making a choice. Leotti and Delgado "tested whether the mere anticipation of personal involvement through choice would recruit reward related brain circuitry, particularly the striatum" (2011, 1311); as they describe their results:

> In summary, we obtained behavioral evidence that choice is desirable, and, furthermore, we found that anticipating an opportunity for choice was associated with increased activity in a network of brain regions thought to be involved in reward processing. Collectively, the findings suggest that simply having the opportunity to choose is inherently valuable in some situations.
>
> These results provide empirical evidence supporting the hypothesis that the need for control—and the need for choice—is biologically motivated. (Leotti and Delgado 2011, 1314; see also Bjork and Hommer 2007)

And as Leotti, Iyengar, and Ochsner note concerning the location of the brain activity associated with choice and control:

> If the desire for control is imperative for survival, it makes sense that the neural bases of these adaptive behaviors would be in phylogenetically older regions of the brain that are involved in affective and motivational processes. (2010, 461)

The desirability of making choices—and maintaining open options for later choices—is sufficiently powerful that it can outweigh the greater immediate benefits of an option that would eliminate the possibility of future choices (Bown, Read, and Summers 2003), and can lead to continuing the choice-making process beyond the point at which it is beneficial (Botti and Iyengar 2004). From the perspective of our evolutionary history, this result is not surprising:

> We suggest that a preference for choice over no-choice is a heuristic that has emerged because, in evolutionary terms, it has usually led to the best outcome. Our ancestors would have quickly learned that it is better to hunt in an area where there is a choice of prey (both in number and species), than in an area where there is little if any choice. Indeed, it is likely that they would not have had to learn at all—the research showing that animals prefer choice over no-choice paths . . . suggests that the preference for choice may be a fundamental part of our natural endowment. (Bown, Read, and Summers 2003, 307)

Effective choice-making is valuable for and valued by humans and many other animals. The valuable choices are not the absolute choices of libertarians such as C. A. Campbell (choices that are made with contra-causal independence from environmental influences or formed character), nor are they the super rationalist "choices" that allow for neither variation nor alternatives. Animals—white-footed mice, chimpanzees, and humans—need choices that are generated by and adapted to the environments in which we live. Such choices may not enhance white-footed mouse moral responsibility, but they greatly enhance white-footed mouse survivability.

THE NEED FOR CONTROL

The philosophical popularity of compatibilist accounts of free will has resulted in philosophical neglect of the vital free will importance of open alternatives. But on the other hand, the importance of *control* has been clearly recognized, refined, scrutinized, and celebrated. Daniel Dennett has led the celebration of control, while at the same time making valuable and insightful inquiries into the place of control in free will. Dennett's *Elbow Room* (1984) is the classic examination of both the nature and importance of exercising control. That is not to suggest that Dennett ignores the importance of open alternatives for free will; to the contrary, his remarks on the importance of new possibilities are profound:

> The trajectory of a pinball . . . after bumping, say, twenty posts (in a few seconds) is unpredictable *in the limit*, far outstripping the limits of accuracy of any imaginable observation devices. Now this result is surely "just epistemic." What could it have to do with free will?
>
> Just this, I think: such chaotic systems are the source of the "practical" (but one might say infinitely practical) independence of things that shuffles the world and makes it a place of continual opportunity. The opportunities provided are not just *our* opportunities, but also those of Mother Nature. . . . (1984, 152)

While Dennett is obviously aware of the importance of open alternatives, his focus is squarely on the importance of exercising *control*. The bogeymen he banishes (1984, 7–10)—the invisible jailer, the nefarious neurosurgeon, the cosmic child whose dolls we are, the malevolent mindreader—are all threats to our power to exercise control; and in addition to reassuring us that such bogeymen are bogus, he makes clear the wonderful resources of control we actually have, and their importance to our well-being.

The genuine value of control—and the severe problems that result from loss of control—are clear to contemporary compatibilist philosophers, and they have been well-documented by psychological research (Thompson and Spacapan 1991; Lang and Heckhausen 2001; Leotti, Iyengar, and Oshsner 2010). The power to exercise effective control—even the belief that one can do so (Taylor 1983; Taylor, Kemeny, Bower, and Grunewald 2000)—prevents depression (Silver and Wortman 1980; Devins, Binik, Hollomby, Barre, and Guttmann 1981; Devins et al. 1982; Skevington 1983; Taylor 1983; Devins et al. 1984; Benassi, Sweeney, and Dufour 1988; Mirowsky and Ross 1990; Thompson, Sobolew-Shubin, Galbraith, Schwankovsky, and Cruzen 1993; Kunzmann, Little, and Smith 2002; Joekes, Van Elderen, and Schreurs 2007) and strengthens the immune system (Langer and Rodin 1976; Schorr and Rodin 1982; Rodin 1986; Bandura, Cioffi, Taylor, and Brouillard 1988; McNaughton, Smith, Patterson, and Grant 1990; Wiedenfeld et al. 1990; Kamen-Siegel, Rodin, Seligman, and Dwyer 1991; Rodin and Timko 1992). Numerous studies have shown that when people believe they can exercise some control over a painful stimulus (when, for example, a subject in a painful cold-pressor experiment is requested to bear the discomfort as long as possible but can stop whenever he or she chooses to do so) they suffer less and endure the suffering more easily and with less stress (Bowers 1968; Corah and Boffa 1970; Staub, Tursky, and Schwartz 1971; Langer, Janis, and Wolfer 1975; Averill, O'Brien, and DeWitt 1977; Pennebaker, Burnam, Schaeffer, and Harper 1977; Reesor and Craig 1987; Turk and Fernandez 1990; Arnstein, Caudill, Mandle, Norris, and Beasley 1999). It was feared that if patients could control their own use of analgesics that they would over-use them; instead, when patients were given the opportunity to immediately and effectively control their access to analgesics (through pressing a button on a pump), the patients required significantly less medication to achieve relief than did patients whose analgesics were dispensed by the nursing staff (Hill et al. 1990, 1991; Mackie, Coda and Hill 1991).

The importance of control has been demonstrated in many contexts, from the management of disease (Taylor 1983; Wallston 1993) to the life satisfaction of those in long-term care facilities (Langer and Rodin 1976; Schorr and Rodin 1982; Rodin 1986; Rodin and Timko 1992). It is important to the psychological well-being of those in challenging and changing social settings (Grob, Little, Wanner, and Wearing 1996) as well as to the physical and psychological health of those in lower socioeconomic conditions (Lachman and Weaver 1998). Control is valuable not only to human animals, but also to other species such as white-footed mice (Kavanau 1963, 1967), rats (Singh 1970; Joffe, Rawson, and Mulick 1973), laying hens (Taylor, Coerse, and Haskell 2001), marmosets (Buchanan-Smith and Badihi 2012), and monkeys (Hanson, Larson, and Snowden 1976; Mineka, Gunnar, and Champoux 1986).

Control involves being able to make things happen, being able to follow one's chosen course, living in an active rather than merely passive relation to one's social and physical environment. The effective exercise of control requires a great deal, and a great deal more than David Hume's condition that one not be in chains. The effective exercise of control requires not merely the opportunity to cause things to happen, but also the confidence that one can effectively carry out one's plans as well as the confidence that making things happen is in important ways within one's own power. At one extreme, consider the dog that has suffered repeated episodes of inescapable shock, and is then placed in a shuttle box in which it could easily escape shock by leaping a low barrier (Seligman 1975). When shocked again, the dog is incapable of exerting any effort to escape. It is in a state of severe learned helplessness, which destroys its capacity for control as effectively—perhaps more effectively—than chains. In order to exercise control, we must have confidence that we can perform well and achieve a desired result; that is, we require what Albert Bandura called a strong sense of "self-efficacy" (1977, 1982, 1997; Haidt and Rodin 1999). Some individuals are generally stronger in self-efficacy than are others, but considerations of self-efficacy are best applied to specific tasks and skills: one can be strong in mathematical self-efficacy while weak in basketball self-efficacy, strongly self-efficacious when it comes to catching a fly ball but weakly self-efficacious if the task is hitting a curve ball.

Effective exercise of free will requires more than a strong sense of self-efficacy; it also requires a strong *internal* locus-of-control (Rotter 1966, 1975, 1979, 1990). Those having a strong internal locus-of-control believe that they can exercise effective control over key events in their lives, while those who have an external locus-of-control (and obviously these come in degrees) believe that the important events of their lives are under the control of fate, or powerful others (perhaps deities), or some other force. A strong sense of self-efficacy cannot accomplish much if it is joined to a powerful belief in external locus-of-control: that is the situation for one who believes he really *could* be effective in making good things happen, but will never get the chance. Frustrating as that may be, it is probably preferable to having a strong internal locus-of-control combined with a weak sense of self-efficacy: What happens is up to me, but I don't know what the hell I'm doing.

BALANCING VARIATION AND CONTROL

The degree of blind variation in our behavior can vary significantly, from situations in which the variation is quite pronounced to others in which the variation is minimized and repetitive highly controlled behaviors dominate (Denney and Neuringer 1998; Neuringer 2004). Philosophers have tended to see these as opposite cases; examined from a larger animal perspective, they are points on a continuum. It is not surprising that these have become major philosophical positions (and often exaggerated and rendered extreme by philosophical dispute): libertarians focused on variation and alternatives while compatibilists emphasized authenticity and control. They are in fact the two poles of a process that is vitally important for all animals, and this process is manifested in a variety of ways. Björn Brembs describes the issue thus:

Animals need to balance the effectiveness and efficiency of their behaviours with just enough variability to spare them from being predictable. Efficient responses are controlled by the environment and thus vulnerable. Conversely, endogenously controlled variability reduces efficiency but increases vital unpredictability. Thus, in order to survive, every animal has to solve this dilemma. It is not coincidence that ecologists are very familiar with a prominent, analogous situation, the exploration/exploitation dilemma (originally formulated by March): every animal, every species continuously faces the choice between staying and efficiently exploiting a well-known, but finite resource and leaving to find a new, undiscovered, potentially much richer, but uncertain resource. Efficiency (or optimality) always has to be traded off with flexibility in evolution, on many, if not all, levels of organization. (2010, 2)

James G. March (cited by Brembs) describes this tension in the activities of organizations:

A central concern of studies of adaptive processes is the relation between the exploration of new possibilities and the exploitation of old certainties. . . . Adaptive systems that engage in exploration to the exclusion of exploitation are likely to find that they suffer the costs of experimentation without gaining many of its benefits. They exhibit too many undeveloped new ideas and too little distinctive competence. Conversely, systems that engage in exploitation to the exclusion of exploration are likely to find themselves trapped in suboptimal stable equilibria. As a result, maintaining an appropriate balance between exploration and exploitation is a primary factor in system survival and prosperity. (1991, 71)

This exploration/exploitation dimension has an important parallel in the evolutionary process. Just as we need to find a successful balance between variability and stability in behavior, we need a similar adjustment in genetic variability. As Donald T. Campbell notes:

In organic evolution, the variation process of mutation and the preservation of gains through genetic rigidity are at odds, with an increase in either being at the expense of the other, and with some degree of compromise being optimum. (1960, 391)

Several decades after Campbell emphasized the need for a process of balancing variation through genetic mutation with the preserved gains of genetic rigidity, researchers discovered in fruit flies a remarkable means of achieving that balance. A specific heat shock protein in fruit flies—Hsp90— typically blocks mutations from producing variation in the phenotype, thus allowing genetic variations to increase but without producing phenotypic changes in the flies having these increased genetic mutations. But when the fly is exposed to environmental stress, Hsp90 no longer blocks phenotypic expression, thus allowing for greater variation under special stressful conditions when such novel variations might prove most beneficial and most adaptive (Rutherford and Lindquist 1998; Queitsch, Sangster, and Lindquist 2002; Sangster, Lindquist, and Queitsch 2004).

Thomas Kuhn (1962) noted a comparable process in scientific discovery, between the periods of "normal" science (when scientists exploit a successful, broadly accepted, and highly productive theoretical framework) and "revolutionary" science (when difficulties and uncertainties prompt more adventurous proposals with much less confidence of success). Zuckerman notes something similar in successful societies, which require individuals of differing degrees of "sensation-seeking":

> Variation is a rule of nature, and within a species we generally find a certain range of biological and behavioral traits. The survival of species that live and move in groups is enhanced by having some members who are adventurous and others who are more cautious and orderly. The biological value of a Columbus to the species is incalculable, but for every Columbus there must be more cautious types who stay at home and keep the books, make the star charts, codify the laws, and plant the crops. (1983, 38)

While there are remarkable and valuable means of varying genetic diversity under changing conditions, the variability in behavioral diversity is obviously much greater. Some individuals will be consistently higher in sensation-seeking than are others, and the degree to which behavioral variability operates is also an effect of environmental conditions (as we see at the genetic level in fruit flies). As Roberts and Gharib (2006, 221) propose, the less expectation of reward, the more the variation; that is, in conditions of greater uncertainty, variations in behavior increase (Stahlman, Roberts, and Blaisdell 2010; Stahlman and Blaisdell 2011).

When the benefits of a path are substantial and reliable, and the risks on that path are few, then behavioral variability decreases. However, some degree of variability will remain. As the rewards of that path become less certain, behavioral variability increases. When benefits become rare, then the animal—whether pigeon, white-footed mouse, or human—increases the variability of behavior: rats and pigeons perform different behavioral sequences (Schwartz 1982; Cherot, Jones, and Neuringer 1996; Balsam et al. 1998), rats push a bar down longer (Roberts and Gharib 2006), pigeons increase the variation of the location of key pecks (Millenson, Hurwitz, and Nixon 1961; Ferraro and Branch 1968; Eckerman and Lanson 1969), and humans propose a greater variety of scientific models (Kuhn 1962).

The degree of behavioral variation changes as conditions change. It is not only the decreasing reliability of reward that prompts greater variability in behavior, but also new and uncharted conditions. Dean Simonton notes that "human creativity tends to be stimulated when individuals undergo exposure to novel, unpredictable, incongruous, or even random stimuli" (2011, 169); and a number of studies (Sobel and Rotherberg 1980; Rothenberg 1986; Finke, Ward, and Smith 1992; Proctor 1992; Wan and Chiu 2002) support that claim. The same phenomenon, not surprisingly, occurs when other animals are exposed to new and unpredictable situations. Whether rat, chimpanzee, or human, strange and uncertain environments stimulate greater behavioral variation, while variation tends to decrease as more reliably rewarded behaviors are reinforced.

Having real alternatives one can choose among and effectively and confidently pursue and control, together with the capacity to adjust pursuit of alternatives in relation to the degree of effective control: that is the core of free will, and it is a desideratum that is deep in our evolutionary history and a vital element of a psychologically healthy life. In contrast to a free will contrived to support moral responsibility, it is empirically plausible—and it provides genuine benefits for mice and marmosets, women and men.

Chapter 8

Restorative Free Will

The world is not just, it is not governed by a just God, humans are not God's special and unique creation, and moral responsibility claims cannot be justified in our natural world. When we take those points seriously, the most plausible account of free will looks less like something we share with gods and more like something we share with other animals. That is a positive development, since what we *share* with other species is a great deal more than what is *unique* to humans. Even our vaunted reflective reason is a comparatively recent addition: valuable, but not the dominant force philosophers like to suppose. As Jonathan Haidt notes, when linear reason developed, the swift and often nonconscious System 1 machinations did not go away, nor did they relinquish control:

> Automatic processes run the human mind, just as they have been running animal minds for 500 million years, so they're very good at what they do, like software that has been improved through thousands of product cycles. When human beings evolved the capacity for language and reasoning at some point in the last million years, the brain did not rewire itself to hand over the reins to a new and inexperienced charioteer. (2012, 45)

Human deliberative intelligence enlarges and enhances the human exercise of free will, but it does not establish a sharp distinction between human free will and the free will of other animals.

THE TWO ELEMENTS OF RESTORATIVE FREE WILL

What we want in free will—whether white-footed mouse or human—are options and control. We can mix these in different proportions—indeed, it is

essential that we do so—but without at least a modest portion of both there is
no free will. Free will requires the capacity to effectively explore open alternatives; that includes both the capacity to *explore* open alternatives, and to
effectively explore those alternatives. In addition, we must be able to vary the
levels of exploration and control in relation to varying environmental conditions. *Both* control and open alternatives, in effective and therefore variable
proportions, are the vital elements of the restorative free will that humans
share with many other species.

The dominant philosophical view of free will is compatibilism, which
insists—in stark opposition to the libertarian view—that free will does *not*
require open alternatives. Compatibilists have made important contributions
to our deeper understanding of free will, but on this point they are philosophically, psychologically, and biologically wrong. Animal free will—whether
manifested in white-footed mice, chimpanzees, or humans—requires open
alternatives and the power to choose among them. Psychologist Charles
Catania had it right: "Whatever else is involved in the concept of freedom,
it at least involves the availability of alternatives" (1975, 89). Free will does
not require absolute options: open alternatives that are chosen independently of all conditioned preferences and situational influences. Such *first
cause* (Chisholm) or "being-for-itself" (Sartre) or "causally inexplicable"
(Campbell) choices may be appropriate for gods; but human animals are not
gods. Neither foraging mice nor exploring humans need choices that are dis-
connected from the contingencies of our environment and from our needs and
interests and values. Human animals do not need alternatives that transcend
our conditioned characters and our environmental influences; to the contrary,
like other animals that evolved in and must survive in this changing world, we
need options that are closely tied to changing environmental contingencies.
Whether butcher, baker, or bonobo we require open alternatives generated by
our environmental conditions, and by our histories as animals living in that
environment.

Open alternatives are essential for free will, they are of great value to any
species that lives and forages in a changing environment, and the need for
open alternatives is built deep into our preferences and values whether we
are human children or adults, white-footed mice, rats, or monkeys. As Tiger,
Hanley, and Hernandez note:

> The phylogenetic perspective suggests that the probability of survival is higher
> for species that prefer choosing, and therefore this preference has been selected
> throughout our evolutionary history. For example, an animal that forages for
> multiple fruits in several areas would be more likely to survive a harsh sea-
> son than an animal that forages for one fruit in a single area. The ontogenetic
> perspective suggests that individual organisms have experienced that choosing

results in an improvement of some form, and therefore this preference has been selected from a personal history of improved outcomes associated with choosing. That is, choosing rarely results in selections among identical options. . . . Rather, a choice is usually between items of discrepant value, with the opportunity to choose ensuring procurement of the more valuable one. (2006, 15)

The strong preference for choice (for having alternatives to choose from, even if the alternative paths are equally rewarding) has been shown in children (Brigham and Sherman 1973; Tiger, Hanley, and Hernandez 2006), adults (Zuckerman, Porac, Lathin, Smith, and Deci 1978; Fisher, Thompson, Piazza, Crosland, and Gotjen 1997; Patall, Cooper, and Robinson 2008; Leotti, Iyengar and Ochsner 2010; Rost, Hemmes, and Alvero 2014), rats (Voss and Homzie 1970), polar bears (Ross 2006), pandas (Owen et al. 2005), monkeys (Suzuki 1999; Perdue, Evans, Washburn, Rumbaugh, and Beran 2014), baboons (Bronikowski and Altmann 1996) and pigeons (Catania 1975, 1980; Catania and Sagvolden 1980; Cerutti and Catania 1997).

At some point the genuine need for open alternatives became transmogrified (or apotheosized) into a desire for absolute first cause miraculous choices, and there were two sources for that change. First, a fear that determinism would take away all our choices, so the choices had to transcend any natural determining causal framework. This is a fear voiced by William James (1907) and William Barrett (1958), and the fear itself is real enough, though the peril is not. Our choices may be determined by our characters and situations and histories, but so long as the choice process does not "bypass" us (Mele 1995, 2006; Nahmias 2011) then we have all the free will we want or need, and a free will that can take us into new worlds. When the choice comes from ourselves and is a choice made by our own preferences among available alternatives and we make the selection that we favor, then we are not locked into a "block universe," but instead make choices as animals that evolved in a changing world to which we are constantly adapting. We have good reasons for not wishing to be manipulated by hidden purposeful controllers; but being moved by environmental factors is something entirely different. Those are factors for which we are well-adapted, and which are not controlling us for devious purposes (whatever may be imagined by those suffering from determinism-phobia). Nature generally influences us for our benefit: we evolved in those natural conditions, and they are largely user-friendly.

We want alternatives, but not too many: we do not benefit from having more alternatives than we can understand and control (Iyengar and Lepper 2000). Self-control is a way of enlarging options beyond the immediate ones—immediate attractive options are forgone in order to make later options available—and we are not the only animals that exercise it. Dedication and commitment (found in humans and other species) keeps options open that would otherwise be lost. One special enhancement of human free will is our capacity to explore new paths and possibilities without the risks of actually engaging in them: we can (in Karl Popper's phrase) "let our hypotheses die in our stead" (1972, 240); or as Roy F. Baumeister describes it: "Going through the process of trial and error mentally rather than physically saves considerable wear and tear on the body and probably prolongs life" (2014, 251). We can also profit from verbal accounts of desirable (and hazardous) paths we have not traveled. This is an enhancement of the human capacity for exploring alternatives, and thus an *enhancement* of human free will; but the basic elements of free will remain the same for humans, foxes, and hedgehogs.

The second essential element of free will is control; but again, this is not absolute control, the fixed control of perfect reason that locks us into the one true path. Rather, we want control that enables us to consider alternatives, place them in some workable order, and make our own choices. The terror of the Oedipus story is that for the major events of my life I am completely out of the causal loop. Daniel Dennett focuses on the importance of control, and he makes clear the vital role it plays in our lives and the profound fear generated when we suppose we might lose the capacity for control:

> What we fear—or at any rate a very important part of what we fear—in determinism is the prospect that determinism would rule out control, and we very definitely do not want to lose control or be out of control or be controlled by something or someone else—like a marionette or a puppet. We want to be *in control*, and to control both ourselves and our destinies. (1984, 51)

And as discussed in the previous chapter, the ability to exercise control is vital to our psychological and physical health.

There are many factors that can compromise effective control: a weakened sense of self-efficacy, a deeply ingrained orientation toward an external locus-of-control, inadequate powers of self-control (or "willpower"). As Burns and Bechara state:

> A full understanding of the operation of the process of choice will include the various states of mood, health and environment through which all human beings cycle. As is the case in most disciplines, there is likely to be a continuum of impairment in the exercise of willpower rather than a black-or-white state of dysfunction or health. (2007, 273)

This does not mean that the person weak in control has *no* control and no free will, but that person does have *less*: free will is not all or nothing, as moral responsibility requires it to be.

The basic need for both alternatives and control—and the capacity to adjust their relative strengths in changing circumstances—is the fundamental free will requirement and the constant challenge. Become too flighty, and you starve; become too stable, and you are easy prey, and more likely to starve when the current food supply is exhausted. No account of "free will as it is in itself" can be successful. That is, we cannot specify the "proper amount" of control or the "essential number" of available options required by free will; rather, we must understand free will as it functions in the world for foraging animals, and that means that the elements of free will must vary in their proportions in varying environments. Asking what is the *real* level of alternatives or control in free will makes no more sense than asking what is the *real* color of a chameleon, or the real pace of a horse.

RECONCILING LIBERTARIANS AND COMPATIBILISTS

Finding a workable balance between alternatives and authenticity—between open alternatives and preservation of favored paths—is essential for all animals that live in a changing environment: "every animal, every species continuously faces the choice between staying and efficiently exploiting a well-known, but finite resource and leaving to find a new, undiscovered, potentially much richer but uncertain resource" (Brembs 2010; see also March 1991). Finding that balance becomes difficult or even impossible when there is an effort to make human free will not only unique but also capable of carrying moral responsibility. Under those conditions, both the alternatives and the authenticity are grossly exaggerated, with the result that they are driven far apart into opposite extremes. On the libertarian (open alternatives) side, in order to make humans unique and justify moral responsibility we make the alternatives (or the choice among them) mysterious or even miraculous, and thus we make the choices useless for animals that evolved in a changing world and must respond to its contingencies. The libertarian problem is not the insistence on open alternatives, but the exaggeration of open alternatives in order to make free will the exclusive property of humans and the foundation for moral responsibility. This is the extreme of alternatives, just as perfect single-path rationality or deep self-sufficient self-approval is the extreme of authenticity. Both are designed to support human uniqueness and moral responsibility, and their competition to be the winning account of moral responsibility exacerbates the extremism. Free will viewed from the larger natural perspective of animal free will shows alternatives and authenticity to be complements rather than competitors. Neither libertarian alternatives nor perfect adherence to the single true path is of benefit for foraging animals; but both the open alternatives and the authenticity models make vital contributions to a balanced account of restorative free will.

With less control, we want more options, and (Taylor 1983) where we lack options in one place we seek them in another; when pressing the bar does not work, we (humans and mice and pigeons) increase the variability of behavior. When a chosen path is rich with rewards we feel a greater sense of control and reduce (but do not eliminate) the exploration of alternatives. Both choice among alternatives and deep devotion to favored paths are essential elements of survival for animals like ourselves (including white-footed mice and many other species), and they vary along a continuum, but—for healthy animals— neither control nor variability is total. Both random aimless motion and fixed immobility signal serious problems, not ideal states of free will.

Alternatives and authenticity—open alternatives and control—balance one another as conditions change: When the food source is reliable, the pigeon and the white-footed mouse continue to engage in some behavioral variability, but that variability is reduced while the control over a reliable food source is greater. As the reliability of that food source wanes, behavioral variability waxes: the pigeon pecks the bar more often and holds the bar down longer and engages in a greater variety of overall behavior; the white-footed mouse explores more alternative paths; the human tries new techniques, or new combinations of behavior, or proposes new paradigms.

Recent work on "secondary control" offers a clear example of the close relation between control and alternatives. "Primary control" is the control we exercise on our environments, whether building a nest (or home) or securing food or vanquishing a rival. But what happens when opportunities for primary control are lost? That is, what happens when we lose the capacity to exercise forms of control and accomplish goals in which we were once successful? This is a question that has been prominent in psychological research on life-span (Heckhausen and Schulz 1993) and on problems confronting the elderly (Schulz, Heckhausen, and O'Brien 1994; Verbrugge and Jette 1994). When sources of primary control are lost or diminished, an adaptive response—which prevents extreme loss of control, with its resultant apathy and depression (Seligman 1975; Abramson, Seligman, and Teasdale 1978)— is the modification of present goals or the substitution of new behavioral goals (new processes of control) in which the individual can be successful and can effectively exercise control. This process of "secondary control" is still a way of facilitating real control: "The major function of secondary control is to minimize losses in, maintain, and expand existing levels of primary control. . . . Secondary control plays an essential role in enabling the organism to select and focus on goals that expand existing levels of primary control" (Heckhausen and Schulz 1993, 286).[1] This involves avoiding the frustration and futility of pursuing unattainable goals and instead turning one's efforts to other goals that are achievable and that offer genuine opportunities for control.

For secondary control to function effectively, there must be open alternatives: different paths one can follow when formerly productive paths are no longer accessible. Vital to the effective exercise of control (and to maintaining motivation and avoiding helplessness and lethargy) is the opportunity to pursue paths that are genuinely productive, and that requires adjusting to changing conditions and having access to workable and controllable paths when a path that has been favored and that seemed (and perhaps was) productive is no longer beneficial or promising: "Striving for primary control requires a repeated adaptation of one's goal selections and control strivings to the objectively available opportunities and constraints in the given developmental ecology" (Heckhausen, Wrosch, and Schulz 2010, 38). When an individual recognizes that other genuine and attractive options are available, that facilitates the disengagement from failed or exhausted goals and opens the way to tasks on which the individual can exercise effective control (Aspinwall and Richter 1999; Wrosch, Scheier, Miller, Schulz, and Carver 2003). The animal—whether white-footed mouse or elderly human or philosophy graduate student—who narrows his or her focus to only one path, and refuses to consider or pursue other alternatives, lacks an essential element of effective free will.

Both alternatives and control are essential to animal free will, and animals that have free will must be able to adjust their proportions in relation to changing circumstances. But not only is there no fixed level of either alternatives or control for free animals; in addition, different individuals of the same species may require differing levels even when their situations are quite similar (for social animals, it is a great advantage if members of the group vary somewhat in sensation-seeking, so that in the same circumstances some want a higher degree of variation while others favor a higher degree of control). Though proportions can—indeed, must—vary, free will requires some degree of both. Alternatives with no control is frenzied madness; control with no alternatives is a fatal stagnation; neither is an exercise of free will.

PHILOSOPHICAL DISTORTIONS OF FREE WILL, AND THEIR VALUE

The two essential elements of animal free will—alternatives and control—are found in ideal but distorted forms in the competing views of libertarians and compatibilists. For libertarians, open alternatives are the essence of free will; and these alternatives must be free of all control, even the control of our own reason and desire. Dostoyevsky (1864/1961) embraces madness to keep the open options free from the control of mechanism and reason; Kane (1985, 1996, 2007) makes the open alternatives the product of pure randomness, in order to guarantee that they are perfectly free from external control; Campbell (1957) and Chisholm (1964) make the open choices a product of godlike creativity that transcends all worldly control and is inexplicable by any empirical inquiry. These are alternatives in their purest form—but in a form that is of no use for men or beasts, who need choices suitable to the world in which they evolved and for which they are shaped, not the absolute choices of gods. We want open options so that when one path is blocked, or the benefits of a favored path are exhausted, there will be other sources of food, other means of escape, other alternatives to try.

At the opposite extreme—also in pure but distorted form—are the compatibilists who deny the need for alternatives and rely completely on perfect control. Frankfurt (1969, 1971) develops a single path account of free will: you have free will when you reflectively approve of your effective will. The most famous contemporary philosophical case of single-path free will is Frankfurt's fascinating case of the willing addict. It is an important and instructive example, but it is not an example of free will, much less a case of an individual having "all the freedom it is possible to desire or to conceive" (1971, 17). To the contrary, it is a sad case of the destruction of free will, and the sort of case Frankfurt describes is painfully common. Frankfurt's "willing addict"—who has a narcotics addiction, but who reflectively approves of and identifies with his addiction—is a dramatic example, and Frankfurt's claim that such a willing addict enjoys maximum free will is a bold claim indeed. But Frankfurt's brilliant account notwithstanding, the addict's reflective approval of his addiction does not establish the addict's free will; instead it marks the addict as having reached a deeper depth of unfreedom, just as the "satisfied slave" (Chapter 4) has even less free will than the slave who struggles against bondage.

The "satisfied slave" is not a fanciful philosophical example, but a sad and all too common reality: the ambitious factory worker who finally gives up and embraces mind numbing repetitive labor; the spirited independent woman who ultimately "accepts her place" and embraces her subservience; the conquered and hopeless victims of an overwhelmingly powerful conqueror, for whom resistance is painfully and demonstrably futile and who finally come to identify with their rulers. Martin Seligman's dogs, vainly struggling to escape from the restraining harness and thus escape the painful shocks, are not free; but at the later stage, when having suffered repeated episodes of inescapable shocks the dogs no longer struggle against the shocks and make no effort to escape, they have not finally become free; to the contrary, they have become more profoundly unfree.

Devotion to a favored path may be valuable. In many cases such devotion keeps that favored path available as an option even when it is not immediately beneficial, and thus it may be an important element of genuine animal free will. But loyalty to a favored path is not the same as single path obsession or defeated acquiescence. It may be useful for societies to have some individuals who become consumed and unfree in devotion to a cause or theory, but not because those individuals are exemplars of freedom.

Setting aside cases of devotion to a lover or a theory, there are two situations when complete single-path devotion is prominent, and they lie at opposite extremes. First, for those powerless individuals in situations when all other possibilities have been destroyed beyond hope (the position of the willing addict and the satisfied slave); and second, at the opposite extreme, for those who are omniscient and perfect gods. The single narrow path may be a good fit for both self-sufficient omniscient deities and profoundly defeated and helpless animals; but it does not promote the well-being of exploratory animals such as humans and white-footed mice and chimpanzees. We can find cruelly damaged individuals who have been deprived of the capacity for exploration and now cling to a single path, but they are not paragons of free will. As William James noted, "There can be no doubt that when men are reduced to their last sick extremity absolutism is the only saving scheme" (1907, 140). Any model of free will that counts the willing addict or the profoundly abused and ultimately acquiescent slave as genuinely free is a model that stimulates the philosophical imagination but is a poor fit for animals who must live and prosper in a changing world. Typical Earthly cases of single path obsession are not cases of fortitude or devotion; rather, they are cases of despair, learned helplessness, and deep depression.

The willing addict is—supposedly—free: though he cannot take any path other than pursuit of drugs, he powerfully and reflectively approves of that single destructive path. But that makes not only willing addicts but also acquiescent slaves free; and close examination of the crippled capacities of the beaten-down slave swiftly undercuts any claim that the slave has now found freedom. But why should anyone imagine that this is freedom? Because—as Frankfurt makes clear—this is an account of free will that makes free will distinctively and exclusively human, by linking it with a *capacity* that is exclusively human: the capacity of second-order reflection:

> It is my view that one essential difference between persons and other creatures is to be found in the structure of a person's will. Human beings are not alone in having desires and motives, or in making choices. They share these things with the members of certain other species, some of whom even appear to engage in deliberation and to make decisions based upon prior thought. It seems to be peculiarly characteristic of humans, however, that they are able to form what I shall call "second-order desires" or "desires of the second order." (1971, 6)

Clearly Frankfurt regards it as a special advantage of his view that it makes free will exclusively human: "My theory concerning the freedom of the will accounts easily for our disinclination to allow that this freedom is enjoyed by the members of any species inferior to our own" (1971, 17). It is hardly clear that Frankfurt's theory *accounts* for that disinclination; the account of that disinclination runs much deeper, stretching back into ancient myths. To the contrary, Frankfurt has found a distinctively human capacity and—since free will is assumed to be distinctively human—he claims to have found the defining feature of free will. Second-order reflection is an important capacity, and it can indeed *enhance* human free will; but to make it the essential defining characteristic of free will runs headlong into the absurdity of the defeated slave who has reflectively embraced his slavery, cannot pursue or even desire better options, and now has become free.

This single-minded devotion to a single narrow path is even clearer in Susan Wolf. For Wolf, genuine human freedom requires an objective True and Good as well as the capacity to follow that straight track with no deviations: ". . . we can state the condition of freedom and responsibility more directly by referring outright to the ability to act in accordance with (and on the basis of) the True and the Good" (1990, 73). Swerving off the true path must be the result of ignorance or arbitrariness or even madness, and such swerves are the antithesis of genuine rational freedom:

> To want autonomy [in the open alternatives sense], then, is not only to want the ability to make choices even when there is no basis for choice but to want the ability to make choices on no basis even when a basis exists. But the latter ability would seem to be an ability no one could ever have reason to want to exercise. Why would one want the ability to pass up the apple when to do so would merely be unpleasant or arbitrary? (1990, 55)

Wolf regards such a capacity to act *ir*rationally and from ignorance as "a very strange ability to want, if it is any ability at all" (1990, 56).

We cannot reconcile Susan Wolf and Robert Kane; but they are two extremes on what should be a workable animal continuum. We are driven to extremes—of randomness or godlike first cause powers; or at the other extreme, single path devotion—when we fear either loss of alternatives or loss of control. Determinism can prompt fears of both, depending on the perspective from which we view it. When viewed from the perspective of Dostoyevsky and William James and William Barrett, determinism appears to close off all freshness and innovation and discovery: the universe is a closed, block universe, dull and repetitive, with nothing new under the Sun and no open alternatives, and this fear motivates an insistence on randomness or cause-defying miracles. When viewed from the perspective of Fischer and Frankfurt and Wolf, determinism threatens to place all control outside of us, in the inexorable deterministic process in which we are only small wheels in the vast deterministic machinery, wheels turned by forces independent of our efforts: thus the insistence on embracing and affirming the whole inevitable process as our own.

Why does it seem philosophically plausible (to the opposing libertarian and compatibilist camps) to treat either absolutely open alternatives or absolutely single-path authenticity as the defining mark of genuine free will? Partly because such extreme accounts are more easily viewed as exclusive to humans, and thus as plausible grounds for the deep belief in uniquely human free will (and also grounds for uniquely human moral responsibility). But there is a deeper reason why such extreme free will accounts seem plausible: Both libertarians and compatibilists focus on something genuinely important to the actual animal process of effective free exploration; but they focus narrowly on distinctly different parts of that process and—when considered separately and exclusively, and twisted into forms that attempt to make one essential element of free will carry out the functions that require *both*—the result is philosophical exaggeration. Free will is a difficult process, requiring an effective changing balance between exploration and exploitation (between alternatives and authenticity-control) in our constantly changing world; but when we try to make one element—whether alternatives or authenticity—carry the weight that can only be effectively handled by a finely adjusted balanced combination of both, then free will becomes impossible for animals (including human animals) and can only be achieved by beings made in the image of God.

Consider first the libertarian efforts to preserve open alternatives in the shadow of determinism. In some cases, the fear of loss of open alternatives becomes so strong that it obliterates any concern for effective control, as seen in Dostoyevsky and Sartre. Dostoyevsky embraces madness—the ultimate loss of control—in order to preserve open alternatives from what he perceives to be the inexorable assault of deterministic materialistic science:

> So one's own free, unrestrained choice, one's own whim, be it the wildest, one's own fancy, sometimes worked up to a frenzy—that is the most advantageous advantage that cannot be fitted into any table or scale and that causes every system and every theory to crumble into dust on contact. . . . All man actually needs is independent will, at all costs and whatever the consequences. (1864/1961, 110)

But if "all man actually needs is independent will" in the form of frenzied "choices," then the human species would be of very brief duration (had it ever evolved at all): choices are indeed essential, but without any element of control—or in complete defiance of control, even one's own intelligent control—choices are of no value (except, perhaps, in calming fears concerning the imagined perils of determinism). Sartre makes the free choices of "being-for-itself" (1946/1989) a uniquely human power that transcends all mundane circumstances and influences, and insists that such "choices" must be made with no guidance whatsoever, whether from others or from history or values or from one's own reflective powers; that is, these vital choices must be made as terrifying stabs in the dark. In the absolute determinism-transcending form favored by Sartre, it is hardly surprising that free will is something we are *condemned* to bear, rather than something that enhances our lives and prospects. "Free choices" that are forced upon us with no guides or understanding are not very appealing; nor are they of any value to natural animals (however valuable they may be to godlike existentialists).

ROBERT KANE'S OPEN ALTERNATIVES FREE WILL

When we turn to a more subtle, sophisticated, and rigorous libertarian such as Robert Kane, we find a serious concern with trying to preserve control while emphasizing the importance of free choice. Kane's dedication to preserving moral responsibility while also thwarting the imagined machinations of a super covert non-constraining controller drives him to place the power of free choice in splendid isolation; but his recognition of the need for *control* (along with absolutely unconstrained "choice") makes his account an instructive guide to some of the most challenging issues concerning free will.

Kane is well aware of the importance of intelligent control in our free choice making, and it is a cornerstone of his libertarian account. For Kane, genuine free will requires that we have intelligent *control* over our choices, and that we have intelligent control no matter which way our choices go. Such control requires what he calls *plural voluntary control*:

> Agents have plural voluntary control over a set of options . . . when they are able to bring about *whichever* of the options they will, *when* they will to do so, *for* the reasons they will to do so, *on* purpose, rather than accidentally or by mistake, *without* being coerced or compelled in doing so or willing to do so, or otherwise controlled in doing or willing so by any other agents or mechanisms. (2007, 30)

Kane insists that there is an element of genuine randomness in our pivotal "self-forming actions"—those special pivotal choices that help to establish our character and direction—so that after having willed *both* alternatives, then random particle motion moves the pointer to the alternative actually chosen. But no matter which choice the subatomic wheel of chance selects, that act is still our *chosen* act and our *own* act because we controlled the will-ing of it (since we willed *both* the alternatives prior to the random motion).

Kane is clear that we need *both* alternatives and authenticity, both open possibilities and genuine control, in order to have effective free will. But his desire for *ultimate* responsibility—a special grounds for moral responsibility—leads Kane to make the alternatives more absolute than needed, and the process more exotic:

> To have free will therefore is to be the ultimate designer of one's own purposes or ends or goals. And if we are to be the ultimate designers of our own purposes or ends, there must be *some* actions in our life histories that are will-setting, plural voluntary *and* undetermined by someone or something else. (2007, 22)

Kane's ultimacy requirement is met by randomness. When we are making the difficult and troubling decisions that pit our strongest desires against our sense of duty, and we genuinely will *both* of the conflicting alternatives, then our brains are in a state of troubled indecision. In those special situations parts of our brains may be in a state of chaos. In a state of chaos, tiny factors may exert a powerful influence. In that chaotic situation the *extremely* minute factors generated by quantum indeterminacy (a perfectly random process) might be amplified in such a manner that they result in *random* selection of one of the plural voluntarily willed alternatives, thereby resulting in a "self-forming action." The random element makes my decision *ultimate*, since the randomness precludes tracing the causal process deeper: the ultimate cause of choosing alternative A rather than alternative B (*both* of which were *willed*) lies in randomness, and no further causal explanation is possible. Therefore the ultimate responsibility buck stops with *me*, and not even a covert controller with omniscient understanding and enormous powers could manipulate my self-forming choices.

Kane is a remarkably innovative and insightful philosopher, and no one has done more to emphasize and elucidate the *essential* roles played by *both* open alternatives and control in free will. Kane also rejects any convenient appeal to special nonnatural powers (such as contra-causal free will or god-like first cause powers), insisting that a legitimate account of free will must stay squarely within the natural world: from the very beginning of his quest to develop a workable libertarian account of free will, Kane has refused to make any use of "mysterious accounts of human agency that are empty of explanatory content" (1985, 12). Kane remains true to his pledge to avoid any use of mystery in his account; but his insistence that an adequate account of free will must support moral responsibility leads him to complexities—and to a narrow focus on very special "self-forming choices"—that make the free will he offers of limited value for animals, including human animals.

Does Kane's wonderfully inventive and rigorous and complex model succeed in providing solid grounds for moral responsibility? I think not, and

Kane thinks so; but we have argued about that for three decades, in print (Kane 1985, 1988, 1996, 171; Waller 1988, 1990, 19–21, 1992, 2011, 35–7, 2015) and in person—in some of the most beneficial and enjoyable philosophical conversations of my lifetime—and I doubt that we will resolve our differences on that issue. But the present claim is that Kane's efforts to make free will support moral responsibility results in a free will account that is more cumbersome—and naturalistically less plausible—than it would be without that unfortunate appendage.

Kane, the most careful and judicious of philosophers, nonetheless exaggerates the sort of randomness required, since he is seeking a means of thwarting the machinations of a "covert non-constraining controller" of fearsome omniscient powers. But evolution did not equip us to deal with such powerful controllers; and the fact that we survived without such evolved equipment is a good indication that such omniscient covert controllers are not a major threat in the natural world in which we evolved and in which we now have our being. Rather, evolution equipped us to stay one step ahead of evolving predators and manipulators equipped with intelligence but not super powers. Kane is right that open alternatives—and the exploration of new paths, prompted by nonrational and unpredictable motives (unpredictable to natural predators, whatever their predictability to gods)—are essential to our wellbeing, whether human or white-footed mouse. Certainly we do not want to be covertly manipulated, and for good reason: manipulators rarely have our own best interests at heart. But rather than quantum indeterminacy amplified by chaos (the sort of apparatus we might have evolved if our survival required thwarting the malicious motives of omniscient demons), we require only the powers we share with white-footed mice.

Of course Kane is concerned with more than blocking the devious machinations of covert non-constraining controllers: his deeper motive is providing support for moral—or *ultimate*—responsibility that can legitimize just deserts. The insertion of a random element blocks any deeper efforts to trace the causes of behavior (the causes of our self-forming acts). Why did Anita choose to do X rather than Y? Because having willed *both*, her actual choice resulted from the random roll of the quantum dice; and since the result was random, deeper inquiry is impossible. But whatever its success or failure at blocking the deeper causal inquiries that undercut claims of moral responsibility, the costs of this elaborate model are substantial. First, it makes Kane's free will account—with its combination of quantum indeterminacy and the amplifying effects of chaos—more complicated than necessary, and thus more implausible as a product of natural evolution. All that is really required for free will (or at least for a free will unencumbered by moral responsibility) are the more modest open alternatives that provide rich benefits for white-footed mice and humans alike. Second, the concern with *ultimate* responsibility makes free will a rare and wondrous thing, requiring the combined operations of quantum mechanics and chaos and plural voluntary control. But psychologically satisfactory free will is not something reserved for special occasions; rather, it is a common process of choice and control in a world of changing conditions. As a wide range of psychological studies have made clear (Schulz 1976; Langer and Rodin 1976; Taylor 1983; Rodin 1986; Rodin and Timko 1992; Thompson et al. 1993; Wallston 1993), it is the daily mundane operation of free will—often on details that appear insignificant, and are certainly more modest than Kane's "self-forming acts"—that strengthen and sustain our vital sense of choice and control and prevent the depression that typically results from a sense of helplessness. Finally—a problem that plagues accounts of free will that endeavor to keep free will secure from outside influences—Kane makes the operation of free will fixed and constant, rather than variable; that is, on Kane's account the operation of free will always involves a fixed degree of dual process *control* balanced by a very modest measure of randomness. But animal free will, which operates in constant relation to a changing and challenging environment, requires different degrees of control and open alternatives under varying environmental conditions.

FISCHER'S TOTAL CONTROL FREE WILL

Kane recognizes the importance of having both alternatives and control in free will. In Dostoyevsky and Sartre we see the problems that result from an attempt to make open alternatives carry the full weight of free will, with no help from control: in such a model, we are "condemned to be free" and "free will" becomes a frenzied terror rather than something valuable and pleasurable—and adaptive—for many animals, including humans. At the other extreme, when philosophers endeavor to make *control* the total content of free will (with no element of open alternatives) then free will may not be as oppressive as Sartre's version, but it fails to provide much in the way of benefits for animals like ourselves. In Susan Wolf's account, our powers of reason give us complete control as we recognize the single true path, and open alternatives hold no charms; but rigid adherence to a single narrow path is not a policy of benefit to animals in a changing world. Once we make the perfect total control of perfect reason carry the full weight of free will, the value of open alternatives is squeezed out. Frankfurt winds up with an account in which the exemplars of free will are desperate drug addicts clinging to their addictions and brutalized defeated slaves who resign themselves to hopeless enslavement. Intelligent control is essential; but when it is treated as the whole of free will, then it closes off opportunities rather than enhancing our exploration of new possibilities. That may be a free will suitable for gods and angels who dwell in unchanging bliss, but not for foraging humans who evolved in a changing and perilous and uncertain world.

John Martin Fischer's creative and insightful account of free will is particularly instructive in showing the *limit* case in which alternatives are eliminated and control is expected to carry the entire free will load. Fischer's account—even in its early stages—was long on control and quite limited on alternatives. We may not have regulative control, which allows for genuine open alternatives; but we at least have guidance control, affording us the opportunity for variability in the *manner* in which we proceed down the prescribed path. But eventually even guidance control is challenged, and the door to open alternatives slams shut. During this process of *diminishing* open alternatives Fischer *increases* insistence on control, until—in the absence of all alternatives—control becomes a fixed and total affirmation. I could not have done it any other way, but I did it *my* way: I embrace every detail, not only the path taken but the manner in which I proceeded down that path. Whatever that style of proceeding was, it was *mine* and I would not have it *any other way* in the slightest detail. As alternatives diminish and finally disappear, control must become total:

> It may be that, just as there is a single line that connects the past to the present, there is only a single line into the future: a single metaphysically available path that extends into the future. In this case, what matters is how we proceed—how we walk down that path. There may be features that block access to alternative paths, but that play no role along the actual pathway. Thus, whatever it is that precludes access to alternative paths may not operate in such a way as to crowd out features in virtue of which we are robustly morally responsible. When we walk down the path of life with courage, or resilience, or compassion, we might not (for all we know) make a certain sort of difference, but we *do* make a distinctive kind of statement. For the semi-compatibilist, the basis of our moral responsibility is not selection in the Garden of Forking Paths, but self-expression in writing the narrative of our lives: it is not that we make a difference, but that we make a statement. In writing the stories of our lives, we connect the dots in a way that gives our lives a signature kind of meaning. (2007, 82)

As a semi-compatibilist, Fischer focuses on finding grounds for moral responsibility, rather than free will. I find it impossible to see how this account can provide support for moral responsibility; but the focus here is not on Fischer's justification of moral responsibility, but on his account of free will. And it is clear that Fischer does indeed have a rigorous and fascinating account of free will to offer.

In some contexts it may seem doubtful that Fischer is offering any account of free will whatsoever. True, Fischer does seem more concerned—in the absence of alternative possibilities—to preserve moral responsibility than to preserve free will. Furthermore, Fischer famously christens his own position "semi-compatibilism," meaning that he believes that moral responsibility can be justified even without belief in free will. But Fischer is always careful to note that the free will he rejects is any version of free will that requires genuine "alternative possibilities," and that he is not proposing a general rejection of free will:

> Causal determinism threatens our intuitive and natural view of ourselves as having free will in the sense that involves genuinely available alternative possibilities. It threatens the commonsense view that the future is a garden of forking paths. For all we know, causal determinism might turn out to be true. In this paper I have explored the question of what would be lost in a world without free will of this sort. (2006, 210)

But in rejecting a "free will of this sort," Fischer is not rejecting free will of a *compatibilist* sort. That is clear in this passage on the implications of what would follow if we learned that scientists had conclusively discovered the truth of determinism:

> I feel confident that this would not, nor should it, change my view of myself and other as (sometimes) free and robustly morally responsible agents—deeply different from other animals. . . . My basic views of myself and others as free and responsible are and should be resilient with respect to such a discovery. . . . (2007, 44–5)

Fischer's writings are delightful and clear, and his images are entertaining: who else would employ Frank Sinatra's "I did it my way" to describe his approach to free will? But Fischer's philosophical work is also rigorous, thorough, and systematic; and Fischer knows full well that *if* there are causes fixing for each of us a single path into the future, then those same causes would just as plausibly fix for each of us a single *style* of pursuing that path. If causal factors propel us along a single set path, they do not leave open the options of walking, sauntering, moseying, or marching down that path. And Fischer—as noted earlier—acknowledges precisely that, in his response to a comment by Michael Zimmerman:

> I think that Fischer's final rendition of his "new paradigm" would be improved if slightly reworded. To say that, even if there is just one path available into the future, I may be held accountable for how I walk down this path, suggests (to me, at least) that I have alternative ways of walking down that path open to me. . . . What I think Fischer should have said is this: even if there is just one available path into the future and just one available way of walking down it, I may be held accountable for walking down it in that way. (1996, 344)

Fischer agrees, stating "I gladly accept the interpretation" (2006, 28) offered by Zimmerman. So at this point, Fischer's model of free will leaves no space whatsoever for open alternatives, and the full weight of free will must rest upon *control* and authenticity. Fischer makes a heroic and creative effort to construct a version of control that will bear that full burden.

First, Fischer emphasizes the importance of full personal *endorsement* of the path taken and the style of taking that path: the path and style are my *own*, I do it *my way*, and I affirm it as my own. So Fischer is clear that he must have an account of free will that places the full weight of free will on control. But living my life "my way" seems a questionable foundation to support the extraordinary control that (in the complete absence of open alternatives) must carry the entire weight of free will (the brutalized and broken slave ultimately may embrace servitude as living his life "my way"); thus Fischer, ever resourceful, turns to another means of fortifying control: our capacity to make our lives into *stories*, into meaningful narratives, that will strengthen our control of our lives and enrich the idea of living my life my way:

> The value of acting freely, or acting in such a way as to be morally responsible, is the value of self-expression. When I act freely, I "make a statement," and the value of my free action is the value of writing a sentence in the book of my life (my narrative), rather than the value of "making a difference" (of a certain sort) to the world. I have not suggested that artistic self-expression is the only value, or a hegemonic one; rather, the suggestion was that the value of free action is the value, whatever that is, of artistic self-expression. . . . I shall contend that acting freely is what makes us the sort of creatures that live lives that have the characteristic features of narratives. Acting freely is what changes the depictions of our lives from mere characterizations to stories (or narratives). (2009, 145–6)

By fitting our life events into meaningful narratives we can gain some degree of control even over the *past* events in our lives (which at the time may have seemed totally beyond our control):

> It is a distinctive feature of narratives that later events can alter the "meaning" or "significance" of earlier events. . . . It is not that we can change the physico-causal past; but we can sometimes change its meaning and thus its contribution to the value of our lives overall. (2009, 147)

Fischer's account of narrative free will is uplifting, and certainly comforting: the problems I faced—even the injustices I suffered—are given meaning and purpose, and the world is well-ordered and just after all. It makes a nice story, but a false analysis: it gets things precisely backwards. Rather than acting freely being what changes our lives into stories, it is the depicting of our lives as stories that gives us the *sense* of acting freely (even in cases when we certainly did not act freely). In looking back into your narrative history, it may be possible to view even the darkest elements of your life as somehow making an essential contribution to a worthwhile whole. Every effort at escape and resistance not only fails, but brings brutal punishment. As resistance efforts weaken the shackles are reduced and meager comforts—slightly better food, a blanket against the chill—are provided. Other slaves who had kept a careful distance (lest they also suffer the overseer's well-known cruelties) offer some degree of comfort and companionship. Eventually the painful futility of resistance wears away even the hope and desire of liberation, and the slave accepts and even embraces and reflectively approves her enslaved status, teaching her children the "virtue" of meek acquiescence and their "proper place" as loyal slaves. The slave who is no longer capable of seeking freedom may—in this horrible system—be a happier slave than the slave who sustains fierce and futile efforts at resistance, and may fit all the horrible events of her brutalized life into a meaningful narrative that culminates in her reflective embrace of abject servitude; but this willing slave remains a vast distance from freedom and free will.

Several factors distort our "narratives" of our lives. First is the "illusion of control": "This illusion takes the form of people seeing their behavior as capable of influencing outcomes that are, objectively, determined by chance, such as the probability of a lottery ticket they selected being a winner" (Greenwald 1980, 604). Second, "people perceive themselves readily as the origin of good effects and reluctantly as the origin of ill effects" (Greenwald 1980, 605). A third factor is that "research suggests that individuals sometimes exaggerate their consistency over time when recalling the past" (Ross 1989, 347). As G. E. Vaillant (1977, 197) concluded from his study of adult development: "It is all too common for caterpillars to become butterflies and then to maintain that in their youth they had been little butterflies. Maturation makes liars of us all."[2] Our life narratives exaggerate the consistency between our present selves and our past history, exaggerate the impact of our own behavior, and exaggerate our own control over positive events; and since as the author of my own life narrative I am more like to cast myself as Batman rather than the Joker, my life narrative is likely to be a history of primarily *positive* events (which consistently contributed to the positive outcome which is *me*) and over which I exercised *control*. Fischer is certainly correct that looking back over our lives from the perspective of a life's story or narrative may give us a more positive view of our history, even the darkest moments of it, and that can be a psychologically positive exercise. But the fact that we are capable of such story telling—almost incapable of avoiding it—does not make us free, and does not make unfree elements of our histories into exercise of free will.

The problem is not in arranging the events of our lives into meaningful stories; rather, the problem is that we are all too capable of doing so. No matter what occurs, we place the event into a meaningful narrative (Gazzaniga 1985). When the neuropsychologist stimulates a part of my brain and causes me to look around, I have a ready explanation: I was looking for my slippers, or I heard a noise from that direction. The rain that falls was sent for the purpose of saving our wheat crop; the locusts that threaten my crops are a test of my faith; the sea gulls that arrive just in time to eat the locusts and save the crops were divine intervention. Indeed, we have developed a wonderful trick for fitting any event whatsoever into a meaningful narrative, even if we can make no sense of it and cannot connect it with any positive social or character development: the inexplicable event was clearly part of God's inscrutable will, and is perfectly planned for ultimate good, though our shallow minds cannot fathom God's profound ways and infinite wisdom; but we'll understand it better by and by:

Farther along we'll know more about it,
Farther along we'll understand why;
Cheer up, my brother, live in the sunshine,
We'll understand it all by and by. (Attributed to W. B. Stevens)

(Fischer famously employs song lyrics in his philosophical arguments—"I did it my way" is a marvelous example—and I was inspired to follow his example. It should be noted that while Fischer turns to Frank Sinatra and Sid Vicious for his musical inspiration, my help cometh from good old gospel hymns; but no conclusion whatsoever should be drawn from this striking difference.)

This deep inclination to meaningful narrative supports our powerful need to believe in a just world (as in the examples above); and when the need for meaningful narrative combines with the need to believe in a just world, their force becomes quite formidable. Jonathan Haidt suggests that our System 2 deliberative powers evolved in large part to supply us with a "public relations officer" who could readily provide a positive rationalization of any behavior (Haidt 2001, 820; Haidt 2007, 1000, 2012, 46; Haidt and Bjorklund 2007, 211). But whether our deliberative powers are primarily or secondarily equipped to arrange the events of our lives into positive and meaningful narratives, there is no question that they are well-equipped to do so. Of course those stories are notoriously inaccurate, and typically self-serving; but they do give us a sense of control. No doubt they are psychologically beneficial, and socially advantageous. The tendency would have been unlikely to become so strong and pervasive were they not. Whether they can provide a foundation for free will is another matter altogether.

Affirming an act as my own doesn't make it so; we might be the pawns of clever advertisers, or the slavish followers of fashions and trends, or the victims of devious manipulators; and even avoiding such perils, there might be nothing whatsoever distinctive in "my way" of following my own path, whatever I may believe to the contrary. But even so, the *sense* of being in control can still be very valuable: as described in the previous chapter, it enables us to better tolerate pain, for example, and is an important factor in avoiding depression. Whether real or illusory, this powerful sense of control is marvelous; but by itself, it is not sufficient for free will. The "happy slave" may include in his narrative a positive evaluation of the horrific and demeaning treatment he endured, and give it a positive spin because it led him to a humbled self-perception that facilitated his understanding of his proper abject relation to almighty God; but that will not make this profoundly enslaved person free, and it will not make the horrific elements of her history a positive story of real freedom (whatever the tortured and defeated slave may suppose to the contrary). Control is important, and no one celebrates control and the sense of control more insouciantly or brilliantly than Fischer; but vital as control is, it cannot carry the full weight of free will—except, perhaps, in fictionalized narratives.

John Martin Fischer gives up all other possibilities, rejects the regulative control that offers genuine alternative paths, and ultimately relinquishes even the guidance control that would empower him to pursue his fixed path with a distinctively different style. All that Fischer requires for free will is that I pursue my fixed path "my way"; that is, along a path and in a manner that I conclusively affirm and with which I firmly identify. If I am doing it *my* way, in a way that I endorse in every fixed detail, then I am genuinely and completely *free*. Certainly having a positive self-image, and a positive sense of self-worth and self-accomplishment, is a healthy and happy attitude; but Fischer's positive attitude goes well beyond what is beneficial for foraging exploratory animals. Perhaps when one is constructing one's life narrative (2009, 145–77), and looking back over one's life, it might be psychologically healthy to look upon that life with complete approval, not wishing to change the tiniest detail. After all, that selfish and mean-spirited and self-indulgent act you did in college was truly vile; but had you not done that vile act in that vile manner, your life would have traveled a very different track. Even small differences in trajectory could have had enormous long-term impact: you might not have discovered a love for philosophy, nor met your beloved spouse; your precious children would have been conceived at a different moment and so would have had different characteristics and been different persons (or might not have been conceived at all). All of this may be psychologically positive (though it may also contain the peril of being too accepting of causal factors that are harmful and that weaken the genuine exercise of free will).

Control alone, even buttressed by stories and narratives, will not suffice for animal free will. Determinism does not threaten the open alternatives required by free will, though certainly there are threats (some are real, while others—like Kane's covert constraining controller—are fabulous). When we are lied to, or otherwise deceived, our alternatives are compromised and our free will is diminished; and when we are manipulated by advertisers or con men or politicians into supposing we have real alternatives when we are actually being deprived of them, then our free will is undermined. The threats are real, both to the control and to the open alternatives that our natural free will requires. Supposing that free will can survive when one essential element is destroyed is not a promising means of contending with the genuine threats.

THE CHANGING BALANCE BETWEEN EXPLORATION AND EXPLOITATION

Kane, Fischer, Frankfurt, and Wolf champion distinctive views of free will, but they have something in common: They believe there is a fixed model of free will, that works in all weathers. This is because they all see an act of free will as an act we perform in splendid isolation: the act does not vary, because it comes from an independent and stable self, and is above outside influence. Of course we are subject to many influences; but when it comes to performing an act of free will, that act must come entirely from ourselves: it must be autonomous, an act from our fully self-sufficient free will (whether that free will is compatibilist or libertarian, miraculous or mundane, affirmed as part of our special narrative or embraced as an accurate step on the single path of the True and Good). In contrast, animal free will—restorative free will—must work in close concert with the environment and our changing circumstances: it must be capable of changing its dimensions. It ranges from high in variation and exploration to high in stable exploitation. Philosophers seek a free will that is fixed and unchanging in its dimensions; animals in the natural world require a free will that can vary with a constantly changing environment. There is no view from nowhere, and there is no free will from nowhere.

Philosophical accounts actually show the need for both variation and control, but because they insist on a *fixed* account they make one size fit every situation. Those who insist on greater variation are willing to forgo some control; those who want total control (Wolf) eliminate all variation; and as Fischer constantly cuts back on variation, he insists more and more on control. But though these views certainly vary in the degree of open alternatives and control they employ, whatever measure of each they apply—from zero open alternatives in Frankfurt and Fischer and Wolf, to modest but essential open alternatives in Campbell and Kane, to extreme open alternatives and zero control in Dostoyevsky and Sartre—they all hold their different levels of control and alternatives *constant*. Whatever the situation and circumstances in which free will is exercised, for Sartre the open alternatives are maxed out, for Fischer and Wolf the open alternatives are zero while the control is maximum, and for Kane the level of randomized open alternatives is significant but fairly low while the control is always relatively high. A constant and invariant free will makes sense for animals that are so special that they are insulated from the demands and dangers and advantages of a changing environment and changing conditions. But for animals that evolved and survive in a changing and challenging world, a steady state free will is not a functional free will. Animal free will must function in a world that sometimes requires extensive and variable exploration, and sometimes rewards more concentrated and steady exploitation, but always requires some of both, and constantly requires changes in their respective levels. What is workable free will in one context is distorted and inefficient free will under other environmental conditions. Free will under conditions of plenty is not effective free will under conditions of scarcity.

Both the open alternatives cherished by the libertarians and the devoted authenticity treasured by the compatibilists are important, even essential, for animal free will; but not in the extreme forms favored by libertarians such as Timothy O'Connor (2005) and C. A. Campbell and—at the other extreme—by single-track compatibilists such as John Fischer and Susan Wolf. The competing libertarian and compatibilist perspectives on free will mark—in philosophically exaggerated form—the basic problem that the evolved free will of foraging animals is adapted to solve: the balance between exploiting a present resource and exploring for new resources. The alternatives/authenticity struggle is the abstract philosophical representation of the exploring/exploiting struggle. In philosophy it is pushed to extremes by the desire to support human uniqueness and moral responsibility. At the extremes, we find Susan Wolf's perfect pursuit of the single true path (with perfect rational control and no alternatives needed or desired) opposite Dostoyevsky's fear of loss of all options and willingness to embrace madness and "noxious fancies" to preserve open alternatives from the imagined perils of determinism. But these philosophical extremes—completely open and chaotic options versus perfect single track reason—are not suitable for foraging animals, whether white-footed mice or humans. We *can* find special cases in which animals actually approach the extremes that philosophers champion, but those are extreme conditions of great stress and discomfort: Extreme conditioned obsession (when other options are blocked, as happens with white-footed mouse obsession with its bedding) or in obsessive-compulsive disorder (with its compulsion for hypercontrol and perfection, resulting in constant and excessive checking of details) and in conditions of extreme loss of control (which produces hypervariation of behavior, ultimately leading to learned helplessness). These extreme conditions are not the conditions in which free will flourishes, and not the conditions in which free will evolved.

COMBINING ALTERNATIVES AND AUTHENTICITY IN RESTORATIVE FREE WILL

The alternatives and authenticity approaches to free will have long been fierce competitors, and it seems there is no common ground on which they can meet. Either free will requires open alternatives (the libertarian view) or it does not (the compatibilist position). When we examine the impossible burdens of human uniqueness and moral responsibility that these competing free will accounts are designed to bear, it is not surprising that they get pushed to extreme positions with no room for agreement. Moral responsibility requires the extreme open possibility of choosing otherwise, of making self-defining choices by which we make our own destiny; otherwise, we are ultimately the product of forces that we did not choose or control, and thus we cannot be blamed for our flawed characters and the flawed behavior that flows from those characters. Or, at the other extreme, moral responsibility requires that we ourselves fully identify with who we are—I live and act *my way*, I reflectively approve of my own will and desires and character—and having genuinely open alternatives would imply that my choices were not totally the product of my own self-approved character and values and reason; deviations from my *own* deeply approved character would not then be under *my* control, would not be *authentically* my own.

The compatibilist and libertarian views seem plausible because both views have something profoundly *right*. Unfortunately, in trying to make their views strong enough to prop up moral responsibility, they have exaggerated and in some cases—such as Chisholm's claim that "we have a prerogative which some would attribute only to God: each of us, when we really act, is a prime mover unmoved" (1982, 32)—apotheosized the distinctly different but genuine elements of animal free will that each side celebrates. The exaggerations notwithstanding, both compatibilists and libertarians emphasize something true and important about the nature of free will.

First, free will—restorative animal free will—requires open alternatives. As noted, these are not the absolutely open alternatives of the libertarians; rather, they are the open alternatives of the foraging mouse and the hungry chimpanzee and the commuting human. We did not evolve with a need for alternatives having no connection to our interests and our changing conditions; rather, what is genuinely advantageous and adaptive is the capacity to vary our paths as conditions change, and vary our choices in such a manner that we discover and maintain open alternatives that will empower us to cope more effectively with changing conditions.

Second, as compatibilists argue, the choices we make must be *authentically* our own. Without that element, we may recognize that an event occurred, but we will not recognize it as our *own* choice that comes from our own values and wishes and will. C. A. Campbell's "creative" choices are not a product of our own desires and formed character, but instead happen through some inexplicable creative process resulting in behavior that may be totally out of character. It may be wonderfully creative, but it is difficult to see how those amazing choices can genuinely be my own. Campbell, of course, insists that when we introspect we cannot doubt that the choices and resulting behavior are truly our own; but in the circumstances as he sets them, the choices seem as likely to come from demon possession or chance as from my own personal character; and in any case, psychologists have long since demonstrated (Wegner and Wheatley 1999; Wegner 2002) how unreliable our introspection can be when it comes to determining whether an act or event is a product of my own character or behavior or efforts. Humans and other animals need the capacity to make choices that actually fit our needs and interests, choices that are generally beneficial. They need not be perfect, nor even optimum; indeed, our "mistakes" may be beneficial in making us less predictable to predators and more likely to discover valuable new possibilities. But the choices must not be random, and they must be regularly connected to genuine needs and goals if we are to live successfully. We must be capable of making minimally *effective* beneficial choices among available alternatives: without the capacity to exercise intelligent (not necessarily reflective or even conscious) control over our choices, the choices have little or no value. Authentic devotion to *my* path—when that path has been consistently productive—is a valuable trait, deeply entrenched in our vital capacity to learn by operant conditioning: when a behavior is reinforced, it tends to be repeated, and extensive reinforcement (particularly on a variable interval reinforcement schedule, which is quite common in nature) deeply entrenches the reinforced behavior and maintains that behavior for long periods in the absence of reinforcement (Ferster and Skinner 1957; Skinner 1953, 99–106). But far from being a competitor to open alternatives, the consistent favoring of a valuable path—even when the benefits of that path have diminished—keeps valuable paths open that would otherwise be abandoned. Even long beneficial paths and behaviors may ultimately be abandoned if they consistently yield no benefits; but the occasional following of a path that is now barren keeps that path available, and if the benefits of that path are restored—a new crop of berries is now ripening—this dedication to a temporarily nonproductive behavioral sequence will pay rich dividends. Higher-order reflective commitment can *enhance* that valuable process, but the process itself does not require uniquely human rational powers.

Free will does not require the godlike reason celebrated by Susan Wolf (and by philosophers from Aristotle to the Stoics to Kant). But human reasoning capacities do make a valuable contribution to our free will. Humans are a relatively bright species, though not as bright as we like to imagine. Our reasoning abilities are often employed for the purpose of rationalizing a choice made on deep emotional grounds, we are often unaware of the powerful effects of situations and priming on our thought processes, we operate in conditions of careful System 2 deliberation much less often than we suppose, our resources for such deliberation are exhausted more quickly than we generally believe as we slip into a state of ego-depletion, and even some of the most brilliant of our species who have studied cognitive errors their whole careers (such as Daniel Kahneman) acknowledge that:

> As I know from experience, System 1 is not readily educable. Except for some effects that I attribute mostly to age, my intuitive thinking is just as prone to overconfidence, extreme predictions, and the planning fallacy as it was before I made a study of these issues. I have improved only in my ability to recognize situations in which errors are likely. . . . And I have made much more progress in recognizing the errors of others than my own. (Kahneman 2011, 417)

All of those problems and limits notwithstanding, there is no question that human powers of reasoned inquiry are comparatively impressive. But when we try to make reason into a special definitive power of free will—a power that makes free will a uniquely human capacity—the result is a distorted picture of animal free will (together with an exaggerated picture of human reason). The role of reason in human free will is best understood in the larger framework of animal free will generally. Reason enlarges our realm of effective exploration, as does the eagle's capacity to soar, the wolf's olfactory powers, and the hawk's keen eyesight. In that context, human reason is a valuable enhancement of free will rather than a defining feature. Reason enables us to explore more paths with less risk: our hypotheses die in our stead. Reason sometimes enables us to make better choices among alternatives (though it is far from perfect in that regard, whatever philosophers and rational-man economists may suppose to the contrary). Nature equipped us to be explorers, to varying degrees (with varying levels of sensation-seeking); not perfect reasoners who find the final truth that brings a halt to inquiry.

Unvarying commitment to a single path may be valuable in some contexts. It may be valuable to society—and to science—to have some persons unswervingly committed to a theory or principle, who are not deterred by failure to detect the stellar parallax, not discouraged by calculations showing the Earth is too young for natural selection to have worked, or not daunted by the hardships of Valley Forge. It may keep an option open for the larger group or society, even at the expense of the individual. But the sacrifice such devotion requires is paid in free will. Not abandoning a temporarily unproductive path may preserve my options and enhance my freedom; but following a path no matter what is a sacrifice of freedom. It may be a worthwhile sacrifice; but only a rigid belief in value monism and a just world (in which genuine compromises and sacrifices are never required) could make this appear a preservation of freedom.

In Shakespeare's lovely sonnet, he insists that: "Love is not love which alters when it alteration finds, or bends with the remover to remove: O no; it is an ever-fixed mark, that looks on tempests, and is never shaken." A commitment that does not "alter when it alteration finds" is a commitment that exacts a considerable price in free will. Such commitments need not imply the complete sacrifice of free will. A commitment of friendship or love may play a large role in one's life, but it is not the whole of one's life; forsaking all other lovers in marriage does not mean forsaking all other friends, nor does it imply forsaking all artistic creation, philosophical exploration, and all other interests. Still, the price of powerful commitment is paid in limits on free will. In contrast, Gerald Dworkin insists that any adequate account of autonomy must not allow our valuable autonomy to conflict "with other significant values" (1988, 8) and thus there must be no conflict between autonomy and important values such as "emotional ties to others" and "commitment to causes" (1988, 12). Profound devotion is often genuinely valuable. It can be misplaced, and can result in great harm: the heartbreak of total devotion to a false or lost love is a standard source for country music ballads; and unconditional love that binds one to an abusive lover is clear evidence of the dangers of such commitments. We value deep devotion, though its cost may be paid in limits on open alternatives and free will. This may well be a cost worth paying, but it is still a cost. Unless we imagine we live in a perfectly just world—a world divinely ordered so that genuinely valuable goods are never in conflict with other genuinely valuable goods—that should not surprise us.

Both alternatives and authenticity are essential for restorative free will. Rather than competitors, they work in tandem and vary together to make the best of our changing world. The fundamental problem for foraging animals is maintaining the right balance between exploitation of currently rich resources and exploration of potentially valuable possibilities. In a resource rich setting, exploratory behavior is reduced and exploitative *authentic* behavior increases. The animal that stops exploring altogether is in great peril in a changing world; the animal that explores so much that it fails to take advantage of temporarily rich available resources is also at a significant disadvantage. Successful animals must be able to balance exploration and exploitation, adjusting the levels of each to changing conditions.

The pattern that works for the foraging efforts of white-footed mice can also be observed in the exploratory efforts of human scientists—as Thomas Kuhn (1962) describes that process. In periods of "normal science" there is widespread disciplinary agreement on the theoretical model, and scientists devote most of their efforts to exploiting the benefits of that model and pursuing research projects guided by that dominant model. When problems begin to proliferate—problems for which the current model has no promising solution—and the benefits of the current model become less reliable, there is a stronger inclination to propose new and different paths and revolutionary new scientific models. But even in the most comfortable and productive periods of normal science there are always a few scientists trying to break outside that box of rich results into radically new models. Those high in sensation-seeking look for new and better berry patches and those low in sensation-seeking exploit the obvious but perhaps less than optimum benefits: this grass is green, and should be exploited, even if there might be greener grass beyond. We need both types in our social groups; and in fact, every individual possessed of a well-functioning free will has a good measure of both, with changing proportions as the environment changes.

When we separate our need for open alternatives from our need for authenticity and control, then we try to make each element of free will do work that requires both working together. Compatibilists have an aversion to any loss of control, seeing loss of moral responsibility lurking in the shadows. But only gods have complete control; we don't need it, and we don't really want it (as Iqbal and James—noted in chapter 1—make clear). Or rather, we don't want it unless we are longing to be gods, and escape from the stress and strain of our changing and challenging world; or we are defeated, and wish to give up our own efforts and become perfect slaves; or we are seeking some special capacity that will support implausible claims of moral responsibility. And when control is such that only following a single narrow path—looking neither to the left nor the right, and eschewing all exploration of alternatives—is deemed acceptable, that control threatens the well-being of the animals who exercise it. On the other hand, absolute open alternatives in the traditional libertarian style would result in a blooming buzzing confusion, and in "choices" that are either arbitrary or capricious.

Restorative free will offers a positive integrated picture of libertarian and compatibilist positions that had been regarded as irreconcilable; it gives an account of free will that makes human free will continuous with the free will of other animals; and it recognizes human reason as an enhancement of free will, without exaggerating or dismissing its genuine contribution to both the enlargement of alternatives and the evaluation of those alternatives. The free will that is suitable for foraging animals is a free will that involves *both* open alternatives and considered controlled choices. If free will is to be optimally valuable in our changing world, then the crucial operating elements of free will—open exploration and dedicated exploitation—must be variable, rather than fixed: the proportions must vary in different settings. Free will is a flexible continuum between exploring alternatives and exerting control. When one extreme on that continuum is philosophically exalted while the other element of free will is abandoned, the result is no longer animal free will. It may be fine for gods, but it cannot meet the free will needs of mice and men.

NOTES

1. It should be noted that there are differences among psychologists about how "secondary control" should be understood; while there is certainly overlap in the usages among different researchers, there are also differences. For discussion of this issue, see Morling and Evered (2006), and Skinner (2007).

2. Quoted in Ross (1989, 347).

Chapter 9

Enlarging Ethics

The great impediment to a richer and broader conception of free will and of ethics—and of the animals that have free will and act ethically—is moral responsibility, and the assumption that having free will and acting ethically entails that one is morally responsible. Once we eliminate moral responsibility altogether then we can liberate free will and ethics from the human uniqueness grip of the moral responsibility system. In the absence of moral responsibility, attributing moral—and immoral—behavior to nonhuman animals is quite plausible. The infanticidal male chimpanzee is a morally bad individual, as is the infanticidal human stepfather; but neither is morally responsible. Obviously we should interfere with the stepfather. Should we interfere with the chimpanzee? That's analogous to asking whether we should interfere with a human culture that incorporates some horrific elements (such as slavery, or misogyny). These are complicated issues. We may well do more harm than good by interfering. But it doesn't change the fact that cultures that practice slavery, and chimpanzees that commit infanticide, are morally bad. That requires looking squarely at the fact that this is not a just world, and that a specific injustice may be (at least at present) ineradicable. But we are better off facing that fact, and recognizing that not every wrong can be remedied. That is not a reason to avoid making changes and improvements when we can (and when the changes will not cause more harms than they correct); but it does provide a reason for looking closely and carefully, rather than stumbling in without considering the circumstances and the consequences.

The anti-anti relativists in anthropology (Geertz 1984, 2000; Hatch 1997) offer wise counsel. We can reject relativism and believe strongly in the ethical principles we favor (whether we believe them to be objectively provable or not), and struggle to improve ourselves and our world, yet also

169

realize that the relativists make good points concerning the dangers of shallow understanding of other cultures and their complex structures and value systems. What may appear to us a wrong might be morally legitimate in the larger context of a very different culture. If an outside observer saw parents in our culture holding their small children while someone stuck needles in the children's arms, it might appear a horrific torture of defenseless children which cries out for intervention, when in fact it is the process of loving parents providing vaccinations to protect their children from deadly or debilitating diseases. In addition, many of the "morally required" interventions in other cultures are excuses for exploiting weaker groups: the U.S. interventions in Latin America that were ostensibly aimed at providing the benefits of Western technology for peasants were instead designed to drive small subsistence farmers off the plots of land that provided food for their families, so that those small plots could be combined into large plantations owned by international corporations; then the small farmers—who no longer had means of providing food for their families—would be forced to do the plantation labor under harsh conditions for very low pay.

Like the "anti-anti-relativists," it is important to remind ourselves that endeavoring to understand other cultures (and the behavior of other animals) may be more complicated than we suppose, especially if we view our own values as absolutes; and our motives for intervention—even when we imagine them to be pure—may be rationalizations for behavior that is primarily designed to suit our own selfish interests. When we consider the long history of cruel mistreatment of other species by humans, we should be particularly wary of interventions to correct the "bad acts" by members of other species. Perhaps we should remove the beam in our own eye before we start worrying about the immoral speck in the eye of a chimpanzee.

When a male chimpanzee commits infanticide—killing the infant of its new mate—it does not do so out of calculation that such a killing will enhance its own reproductive chances; likewise, when a human stepfather kills his stepchildren (a dreadful but too common occurrence) he does not do so on the basis of calculations of personal reproductive fitness. Both commit these acts intentionally (the human and the chimpanzee may both wait for a moment when the infant is not in the presence of its fiercely protective mother), even if neither makes explicit plans to carry out the murder. Both do something that is morally egregious. Not every male chimpanzee, nor every human stepfather, commits such vile acts; and it would be valuable to know the causal factors that distinguish those who commit infanticide from those who don't (and simply blaming the wrongdoers gets us no closer to that knowledge). The stepfather may have a capacity for second-order reflection that the chimpanzee lacks—but it will rarely come into play, and when it does it is more likely to provide rationalization than real reflection; and again, it would be useful to know why some stepfathers avail themselves of such reflective powers while many more do not.

At the opposite end of the moral spectrum, the chimpanzee is likely to react with horror at the danger of an infant falling to its death, and may even risk its own life to carry out a rescue. As Jane Goodall notes:

> Chimpanzees cannot swim and, unless they are rescued, will drown if they fall into deep water. Despite this, individuals have sometimes made heroic efforts to save companions from drowning—and were sometimes successful. One adult male lost his life as he tried to rescue a small infant whose incompetent mother had allowed it to fall into the water. (1990, 213)

This same deep inclination is precisely the one that Mencius used to support claims of a basic element of ethics: the sentiment of concern for conspecifics in danger, even strangers:

> Suppose a man were, all of a sudden, to see a young child on the verge of falling into a well. He would certainly be moved to compassion, not because he wanted to get in the good graces of the parents, nor because he wished to win the praise of his fellow villagers or friends, nor yet because he disliked the cry of the child. (1970, 82–3)

Film makers are well aware of this sentiment: the innocent person on the screen is a perfect stranger to you, but you recoil in horror when that person faces a dangerous threat. Such emotions are the basic elements of ethics: rules and deliberation can be a valuable enhancement, but they are not the core of ethics. One can act ethically—and unethically—without such rules; but as Damasio argues (1994) it is extremely difficult to act ethically with the rules but without the emotions. There may be a few exceptional humans who can achieve at least a minimal standard of ethical decency in the absence of emotion: Kant may have been one, and James Fallon—so he claims (Fallon 2013)—might be another. But those will be rare cases indeed, while those who act ethically without higher-level reflection on ethical rules are quite common. It is only an insistence on uniquely human moral responsibility that makes the *enhancement* afforded by higher-order reflection seem plausible as the essence of morality.

ETHICS WITHOUT MORAL RESPONSIBILITY

Frans de Waal was horrified when Luit—an older dominant male chimpanzee whom de Waal had long studied and particularly liked—was killed in a purposeful brutal attack orchestrated by Yeroen (who sought the alpha role held by Luit) and a young accomplice, Nikkie. De Waal struggles against passing moral judgment on Yeroen, but eventually bites the bullet and holds Yeroen morally responsible as a murderer:

> Yeroen was to blame. He was, and still is, the one who decides everything in the chimpanzee colony. Nikkie, ten years younger, seemed only a pawn in Yeroen's games. I found myself fighting this moral judgment, but to this day I cannot look at Yeroen without seeing a murderer. (1989, 69)

De Waal struggles against the conclusion he cannot avoid drawing, for he continues:

> Such sentiments should not be confused with facts, however. Nikkie must have been involved in the fight as much as Yeroen. Also, "murderer" implies an intent to kill, something impossible to prove or disprove in this instance. (1989, 69)

Perhaps Nikkie was a willing accomplice, but De Waal is probably right that Yeroen was the brains of the outfit; and whether or not Yeroen had an "intent to kill," there is little doubt that he had an intent to inflict serious injury, and the injuries resulted in death: that counts as murder. So why the struggle to avoid the conclusion de Waal cannot avoid? Yeroen is a murderer, who engineered a brutal and terrible attack on Luit; Yeroen did something morally wrong.

De Waal cannot separate the conclusion that Yeroen committed a very bad act—and is a devious and malicious murderer, who kills in pursuit of power and status—from the conclusion that "Yeroen was to blame." That is, de Waal assumes that if Yeroen is genuinely a murderer, and Yeroen is counted as doing something morally wrong, then Yeroen also must be morally responsible for the act. Of course if Yeroen had killed Luit accidentally—by bumping him into the water when he intended only to greet him, thus causing his death by drowning—Yeroen would not be a murderer, and would not have committed a morally egregious act. But Yeroen's attack on Luit was intentional, perhaps premeditated; it was carried out in the night when Nikkie was easily motivated to help and no other chimpanzees could interfere. De Waal is right: Yeroen is a murderer. But if we go the next step and insist that Yeroen is therefore morally responsible for murder, then the real problems start; and because we can look at this squarely—Yeroen is a chimpanzee, not a godlike human—we soon reach deeper causes that make Yeroen's moral responsibility implausible. But those deeper causes do not change the fact that Yeroen did a terrible thing, and is a vicious individual.

Perhaps that is why de Waal gets into trouble when discussing ethics with philosophers: if he separated free will from moral responsibility, many of the problems would disappear. When an infanticidal baboon kills infants, or severely bites an individual in his "harem" who wishes to leave, that is wrong; it may be just as "natural" as the violent behavior of a jealous human husband, but still wrong. Once we recognize that the world is not just, and the baboon is not morally responsible, then we must face the harsh nature of the world. Also, it does not mean we should interfere in baboon culture; and perhaps not in human cultures that allow coercive harems, vile though they are: interfering may do more harm than good. At the very least, we should interfere only with great caution. In cases where it would be a mistake to interfere, we can still recognize that the act is wrong, and that is worthwhile (it keeps us from supposing that brutality toward females is "natural" and thus "good"). Who says it is wrong? We do; and that may well be the best we can do, as Richard Rorty (1989, 1993), Herbert Feigl (1950, 1952), and Hans Reichenbach (1951, 291–2) claim. It's *our* ethics, and we need not apologize for that. But that raises metaethical questions far beyond the present issue, and the present issue is controversial enough without seeking more trouble.

Why are we so reluctant to recognize free will in other species? Because we don't want to assign moral responsibility. And we are right. We look carefully and deeply and without blinders at the causes of *non*human behavior, and we find it absurd to hold the members of other species morally responsible. But once we separate moral responsibility from free will, we can make sense of free will in nonhuman animals while avoiding the impossible problem of moral responsibility. The same problem that has kept us from recognizing the broader category of ethical behavior in other species has obscured recognition of ethical behavior in our own species. Was Huck Finn morally responsible for protecting a runaway slave? No. Did he behave ethically? Certainly. Could a chimpanzee have done the same? Yes.

Uniquely human capacity for ethical behavior, uniquely human free will, uniquely human moral responsibility—all existing in a just world—form a system (Waller 2015); if you wish to challenge one, you must challenge them all. When we challenge that system, and all the parts that make it function, then the possibility of a better system that is not only more fair but also a better fit with our natural nongodly world can begin to take shape.

THE DEEP BELIEF IN ETHICS AS A
UNIQUELY HUMAN CAPACITY

From Aristotle to Kant to the present, we define ourselves by what is exclusive to humans; and we are admonished to honor and maximize those features that make us "distinctively human" and that place us in an exclusive category. At one time that approach may have been plausible for distinguishing species (though DNA studies are now a better guide); and it is certainly plausible if we are artifacts of a divine creator, and our distinguishing features are the features that make us godlike. It is much less plausible in our post-Darwinian world. But it is a view that has held sway for so long—indeed, for millennia—that it is now difficult to recognize that there is little to recommend it and powerful reasons to abandon it.

The essential and central condition of free will is the special human power of deep deliberative reflection: that view has been examined already, and found wanting. But the place where that perspective exerts its strongest hold is in our view of ethics and ethical behavior. Ethics belongs exclusively to humans: only humans are capable of genuinely ethical—and genuinely unethical—behavior. Indeed, this belief is embodied in our best known creation myth: God (or the gods) create Adam and Eve, but those first humans—like the rest of creation—are innocents, with no knowledge of good and evil. Placed in the Garden of Eden, they are given only one commandment: Do *not* eat of the tree of the knowledge of good and evil: "And the Lord God commanded the man, saying, of every tree of the garden thou mayest freely eat: But of the tree of the knowledge of good and evil, thou shalt not eat of it" (Genesis 2:16-17). At that point in the story, everyone knows what will happen in the next act: there is only one commandment to break, and Adam and Eve shatter it. Eve looks at the tree, recognizes that it is "a tree to be desired to make one wise" (Genesis 3:6), and that the serpent is probably right: "For God doth know that in the day ye eat thereof, then your eyes shall be opened, and ye shall be as gods, knowing good and evil" (Genesis 3:5). And of course the serpent *was* right, as God acknowledges: "And the Lord God said, behold, the man is become as one of us, to know good and evil" (Genesis 3:22).

This story has fascinated humans for many centuries, and even among those who reject gods the basic idea of the story is deeply held: knowledge of good and evil is what makes humans different from the rest of the animal world, the capacity to make ethical decisions and act ethically is uniquely human. Obviously one can hold such a view, even while fully acknowledging that humans—like other animals—are a product of evolution and that we share common animal ancestors (and in the case of humans, chimpanzees, and bonobos, we are very close evolutionary cousins). Christine Korsgaard certainly believes all that—she is no friend of creationism, and she is well-informed concerning contemporary biological and primate research—yet she also holds, quite consistently, that ethics belongs exclusively to humans.

Korsgaard can consistently hold a Kantian view of ethics while believing wholeheartedly in the evolutionary origin of the human species. That only requires setting the standard for genuine ethical behavior (and genuine free will) very high; and there is nothing inconsistent nor empirically false in setting such a high standard. The question is which system works best for our purposes—and that, of course, may depend on our purposes. If our purpose is to preserve a special place of human uniqueness, the Kantian system is superior. But if our purpose is to gain a better understanding of the behavior of humans and other animals, the advantage tilts the other way.

The capacity of linear deliberative reflective reason—developed in special form among humans—offers an enrichment of ethics and ethical behavior. Though the contribution of reason is often exaggerated, there is no question that reflective reason can enhance human ethical understanding. Humans, and only humans, can reflect on and seriously question deep inclinations and longstanding behavioral patterns. Of course, not many humans do so; and the capacity to do so is much more limited and constrained than philosophers often imagine; but that capacity, with all its limits and mistakes, is uniquely human, and it occasionally opens remarkable ethical vistas. Peter Singer (1981) can reflect on whether the range of ethical consideration should be an "expanding circle," encompassing not only those humans of other cultures but also the members of other species. We should not exaggerate this capacity, nor exaggerate the extent of its use among humans: for every Peter Singer, we find crowds of people eating the flesh of intelligent and sensitive animals that often were raised in harsh conditions on factory farms, with little or no reflection on its ethical legitimacy. When humans do reflect on their values and obligations and ethical views, that reflection is more often to find a rationalization for their current views and practices than to seriously examine and critique those views.

The driving force behind ethical behavior is not reason, but emotion (Damasio 1994; Haidt 2001, 2012); and that is true whether the ethical actor is a human or chimpanzee or bonobo. The Iroquois could come together and stop the mourning wars—wars driven by deep retributive emotions, and a profound desire to "pass the pain along" (Barash 2005, Barash and Lipton 2011)—and reflectively find ways to control those emotions and live in greater harmony. Such reflectively inspired harmony is impressive (though even there the emotional elements remain vital); but it did not prevent the Iroquois from brutal treatment of those who fell outside their larger group, just as the Christian reflective teachings of "love your neighbor" did not prevent the brutality of Europeans toward the natives of the "New World" or against the "heretics" within their own religion. Reflectively derived principles can enhance kindness and inclusiveness; they can also enhance cruelty when they override generous sentiments, as Jonathan Bennett (1974) notes of Himmler.

THE ARGUMENT FOR A HUMAN MONOPOLY ON ETHICS

Christine Korsgaard finds the Kantian view plausible: "the form of self-consciousness that underlies our autonomy may also play a role in the explanation of some of the other distinctively human attributes" (2006, 116); and she continues:

If that is right, then the capacity for normative self-government and the deeper level of intentional control that goes with it is probably unique to human beings, And it is in the proper use of this capacity—the ability to form and act on judgments of what we ought to do—that the essence of morality lies, not in altruism or the pursuit of the greater good. (2006, 116)

De Waal, as Korsgaard notes, acknowledges that humans "have explicit teachings about the value of the community and the precedence it takes, or ought to take, over individual interests" (2006, 54); and he even concedes that: "Humans go much further in all of this than the apes, which is why we have moral systems and apes do not" (2006, 54). But that concession is not enough for Korsgaard:

> The difference here is not a mere matter of degree. And it isn't a small difference, that ability to be motivated by an ought. It does represent what de Waal calls a saltatory change. A form of life governed by principles and values is a very different thing from a form of life governed by instinct, desire, and emotion—even a very intelligent and sociable form of life governed by instinct, desire, and emotion. . . . We have ideas about what we ought to do and to be like and we are constantly trying to live up to them. Apes do not live in that way. We struggle to be honest and courteous and responsible and brave in circumstances where it is difficult. Even if apes are sometimes courteous, responsible, and brave, it is not because they think they should be. (2006, 117)

Very well: there is a difference here, an important difference. But it is not as large a difference as Korsgaard's idealized account suggests, and even in idealized form it is not enough to place the moral behavior of human animals on one side and all other animal behavior on the other side of that line, outside the realm of morality. In the first place, this "form of life governed by principles and values" is not quite such "a very different thing from a form of life governed by instinct, desire, and emotion" as Korsgaard suggests. The form of life "governed by principles and values" is still motivated by basic "instinct, desire, and emotion": by our deepest "intuitions," as Haidt (2001, 2012) calls them, which are not rationally derived; and by emotions, without which—as Damasio (1994) argues—the moral life fails to function. Of course humans do at times switch into more rigorous System 2 deliberation concerning what we ought to do (not nearly as often as rationalists suppose, but it does happen); but even then, we do not transcend the emotional roots of our ethical lives. Instead, we are struggling with which of our deep emotional "intuitions" should carry the greatest weight; or more likely, we are simply rationalizing what our desires are directing us to do: the primary function of our System 2 deliberations is not to reason dispassionately about ethical principles, but to act as a public relations agent finding rationalizations for our preferred behavior (Haidt 2012, 46).

But imagine the best possible case for the Korsgaard model: A case in which we genuinely deliberate about what we ought to do, considering principles and values and how they fit together or conflict, and not merely seeking a convenient rationalization. This move to serious higher-order reflection on our values and ethical choices is special, and a special and distinctively human capacity; and we might acquiesce in Korsgaard's insistence that "the difference here is not a mere matter of degree." But even in that best case scenario, does that make human ethical activity *different in kind* from the ethical behavior of all other animals? That remains an implausible claim: the basic emotion-driven element of ethics is the driving force of ethics; and that is what runs most human ethical behavior. Many humans never or very rarely engage in such higher-order ethical deliberation, but they continue to act ethically in their daily lives; and even those who do engage in such deep deliberation perform most of their ethical acts without such deep reflection. It is notorious that those engaging in the deepest ethical reflection (such as professional philosophers) are not notably better ethical actors than are those who do not.

Humans can and do struggle deliberatively with ethical quandaries. In most cases, these "struggles to decide what we really *ought* to do" are in fact struggles to find a rationalization for what we want to do; but in some—comparatively rare—cases, the struggle is a genuine deliberative struggle to decide what action one ought to do, which path of life one should follow, which of our values is more worthy. A brilliant young woman struggles between two job offers, one of which would make her quite wealthy but will involve work she believes would cause environmental damage which she deplores, and a second job which pays much less but involves work protecting the environment rather than damaging it. She may, of course, following years of graduate school poverty, opt immediately for riches and spend her powerful deliberative efforts in rationalizing her choice ("I will be able to provide comforts for my dear old mother, and anyway if I don't do the work someone else will"); but she may engage in a genuine deliberative struggle over the sort of person she really wants to be and the sort of life she believes is worthwhile. This genuine deliberative process will still involve deep emotional "intuitions" as well as powerful emotional concern: it is not a rational process that transcends emotions and operates with no emotional content and no emotional motivation, as the work of Haidt (2001, 2012) and Damasio (1994) makes clear (Kant's insistence to the contrary notwithstanding). It is—or at least can be, on rare occasions—a uniquely human process of ethical deliberation that enhances our ethical capacities. But is that rare and wonderful process the *essence* of ethical behavior, so that only such processes—and the decisions and actions that result from them—count as genuinely ethical acts?

Suppose that a second brilliant young woman is so deeply committed to protecting the environment that the high-paying job is something she will not even consider, and she engages in no deep ethical reflection (and perhaps did not do so at any point as her powerful views and values concerning protection of the environment developed and strengthened and coalesced into the value system she devotedly follows). She turns down the high-paying job offer (probably with contempt), and makes the same decision her indecisive friend ultimately reaches. But is the decisive environmentalist less of an ethical actor than her deliberative indecisive friend? Or even less plausibly, is the indecisive young woman an ethical actor while the acts of her decisive friend fail to qualify as ethical at all? Deep deliberation is—or can be—an enhancement of our ethical activity (though it can also be an impediment); but it is more plausible—it is philosophically and psychologically less extravagant— to view it as a special enhancement, not the essence of ethics. Counting deliberative reason as the key element of ethics (while emotions are trivial at best) is like counting the cherry as the essence of an ice cream sundae, and treating the ice cream as merely the scaffolding that holds the cherry high.

When de Waal says that "we have moral systems and apes do not" (2006, 54) that is true if it means only that humans have formal systems of moral rules while apes do not; but if he means more than that—that we behave in a genuinely moral manner, while ape behavior is merely "proto-moral" or only a stepping stone to *genuine* ethical behavior (of which only humans are capable)—then he concedes far too much. De Waal is right that there are some distinctive elements—special enhancements—that humans occasionally (or rarely) employ that are unique to human morality:

> The desire for an internally consistent moral framework is uniquely human. We are the only ones to worry about why we think what we think. We may wonder, for example, how to reconcile our stance towards abortion with the one towards the death penalty, or under what circumstances stealing may be justifiable. All of this is far more abstract than the concrete behavioral level at which other animals seem to operate. (2006, 174)

We should not exaggerate this special human "desire for an internally consistent moral framework"; it is more often manifested in philosophical treatises than in human behavior; indeed, it seems such a marginal desire that it is honored more by the breach than the observance. The very same human who wrote that "we hold these truths to be self-evident, that all men are created equal, that they are endowed by their Creator with certain unalienable rights, that among these are Life, Liberty, and the pursuit of Happiness" was a slave holder, who kept some of his own children in bondage; the same humans who visit the Statue of Liberty and become misty-eyed over the inscription by Emma Lazarus—"Give me your tired, your poor, Your huddled masses yearning to breathe free, The wretched refuse of your teeming shore. Send these, the homeless, tempest-tossed, to me: I lift my lamp beside the golden door"—show up at the Mexican border shouting ugly slogans and demanding that children be turned away and sent back to countries where they are likely to be killed; many of the people most vocal in their opposition to abortion rights are also vehemently opposed to providing prenatal care to protect the health of pregnant women in order to prevent miscarriages and promote the health of newborns. If commitment to "the desire for an internally consistent moral framework" is essential for genuine ethical agents, then genuine ethical agents will be rare indeed. Many of those rare agents will be philosophers. Certainly there are some wonderfully virtuous philosophers; but any model of ethics that casts philosophers as morally exemplary is a model of very doubtful plausibility.

It is tempting to suppose that only when one can effectively *reflect* on what one *ought* to do—what character one ought to develop, what ethical rules should govern one's behavior—is one acting ethically. But on careful scrutiny, that is no more plausible than supposing that one must reflect on the best way to run in order to count as a runner. Such reflection may (or may not) improve one's running technique; but deep reflection is not required in order to count as a runner. Indeed, there are great ethical traditions that regard ethical rule-following as—*at best*—a way of assisting novices to take the first stumbling steps toward genuine ethical action. Following rules may be useful when trying to learn a golf swing; but master golfers do not follow rules, but rather swing "naturally." A beginning chess player may need rules about protecting her queen, not overextending her pawns, being careful of forks; the chess master has no need of such rules. Do good not from rules, even self-formulated rules, but from deep affection for and empathy with other beings, with whom one feels deeply connected; "Love God, and do as you please," Augustine says (408/1888); and at that level, rules are not needed. Kant's "friend of mankind"—who takes pleasure in being kind and generous to others—may act ethically without ever reflecting on the nature or demands of ethics.

We may naturally feel a strong allegiance to our group, or our state; but is patriotism really a virtue? It is useful to have the capacity for deliberating about this issue; but those who do not are still capable of ethical behavior; and those who find it absurd for human affection and allegiance to be confined within arbitrary boundaries—and who feel this without long deliberation about the nature of patriotism and group attachments—may be profoundly virtuous. Of course it is possible to go the other way, and without reflection get caught up in nationalistic fervor which leads to horrific acts; and it is very useful to have the ability to step back and examine that profound but dangerous feeling. But that does not make it a necessary condition of ethics.

Considering the brutality he suffered at the hands of his alcoholic father, the pervasively racist society in which he grew up, and the harshness and ineptitude of the attempts to "civilize" him into a conscientiously "moral" person (by the standards of that racially and religiously intolerant society), Huck Finn was remarkably lucky to have emerged as a genuinely good and morally decent person. Huck (like many other unreflective humans and chimpanzees and bonobos) has a kind and empathetic nature. That certainly did not happen as a result of Huck's deep rational reflection on his moral duty. In short, Huck is *lucky* to be morally good; but morally good he is, and capable of morally good behavior. Huck doesn't follow ethical rules, nor does he reflect on ethical reasons and questions; he does not remind himself of the need to "do a good deed daily," but he does many good deeds; and he does not reflect on the golden rule to "do unto others as you would have them do unto you," and he does not follow such a rule; but he nonetheless lives a life that is in accordance with that rule. Huck is an ethical actor, and a very decent ethical actor; but he is not a reflective ethical actor.

Reflection can be important, and I would never disparage it: reflection can enable us to see that our retributive impulses—while deep and perhaps essential for our evolution and in some respects still valuable—are not appropriate ethical guides; but such reflection cannot float in the rationalist ether, devoid of emotional underpinning. It must ultimately turn to considerations of basic fairness (Waller 2011, 23–35), and such appeals depend on a basic fairness "intuition" (Haidt 2012) that is deep in our emotional nature.

Korsgaard overestimates the importance of reason in human ethical behavior, and she underestimates the cognitive elements in the behavior of nonhumans. She states:

> My point is not that human beings live lives of principle and value and so are very noble, while the other animals don't and so are ignoble. The distinctiveness of human action is as much a source of our capacity for evil as of our capacity for good. An animal cannot be judged or held responsible for following its strongest impulse. Animals are not ignoble; they are beyond moral judgment. (2006, 118)

This treats nonhuman animals as if they were wind-up toys. Nonhuman animals, like human animals, have a variety of impulses, and chimpanzees—and several other species—have a capacity for deferred gratification; and many animals make plans that involve multiple steps. Like humans, they act intentionally: sometimes they overcome profound fear in order to defend or rescue a member of the group. Saying that the behavior of a nonhuman animal is simply the product of "following its strongest impulse" is as plausible—or implausible—as the egoist's empty assertion that in all their behavior (including heroic rescues and generous aid) humans are really just following their own selfish desires. But the larger problem is one that Korsgaard passes by with little notice: "An animal cannot be judged or held responsible for following its strongest impulse." This is the old problem of making moral judgment inseparable from moral responsibility. It is ridiculous to hold nonhuman (and human) animals morally responsible; but making moral judgments of the behavior of humans and members of other species is a different matter altogether.

Chimpanzees may not know that what they are doing is acting ethically (or unethically); but that no more precludes their acting ethically than the fact that they don't know that they are using tools or transmitting cultural knowledge means that they do not know how to use tools or transmit cultural knowledge. If knowing requires knowing that we know, does knowing that we know require knowing that we know that we know? Chimpanzees know how to use tools, and they demonstrate that knowledge quite clearly. They also know how to perform ethical acts, and they likewise demonstrate that capacity. Knowing how to act ethically no more requires reflecting on ethical behavior than knowing how to use tools requires reflective consideration of tool use.

ETHICS WITHOUT HIGHER-ORDER REFLECTION

What is required for genuine ethical behavior? Immanuel Kant set the bar very high; so high, indeed, that very little human behavior counts as ethical, and few (if any) humans can qualify as ethical beings; but certainly no nonhumans, and perhaps no nondeities, can be genuinely ethical. That was fine with Kant. For Kant, genuine ethical behavior and genuine ethical actors are as rare as they are wonderful, requiring not only an extraordinary power of rationality but also a power of willing that can operate with no emotional support whatsoever; indeed, that can operate with no visible means of support, and is totally *causa sui*. It is a marvelous ethical system for deities, superhumans, and perhaps the angelic hosts, but not for natural animals, including human animals.

Jonathan Bennett's (1974) account of Huck Finn's emotional misadventures with his "conscience" offers a less exalted but more plausible account of human ethical capacities. Huck's reasoned "principles" lead him toward the egregious act of betraying his friend—Jim, an escaped slave—and returning Jim to slavery; but fortunately, Huck's deep affection for Jim wins out, and Huck deceives the slave catchers and aids Jim's escape to freedom. For Kant, Huck's act is *agreeable* at best, but has no ethical content whatsoever. But most of us celebrate Huck's deep decency and loyalty which enable him to resist a profoundly racist culture and act ethically for his friend.

Huck may not be a paragon of virtue, but when it comes to acting ethically, Huck appears to be better at it than Kant. As described in painful but brilliant detail by Rae Langton (1992), Kant's actual behavior was not always ethically exemplary. Maria von Herbert—a great admirer of Kant's work who had studied his writings assiduously and sought to order her life by his rigorous ethical demands—wrote to Kant seeking guidance. Von Herbert had deceived the man she loved ("though there was nothing unfavourable to my character" in the deception). She believed moral duty requires complete honesty, and that she was obligated to disclose the deception though it would imperil their relationship. After her disclosure the man had withdrawn his affection, and von Herbert was desperately unhappy (to the extent of contemplating suicide). Kant replied with a severe reproach for her dishonesty ("you have sought counsel from a physician who is no flatterer"), and advised her to focus on her duty and accept with composure her justly deserved punishment (both the punishment of her own self-reproach and the reproachful coldness of her beloved); and if in fact her beloved never again felt affection for her, then she shouldn't take it too hard. After all, "the value of life, insofar as it consists of the enjoyment we get from people, is vastly overrated."

Maria von Herbert writes back, again describing her miserable "vast emptiness," in which nothing attracts her. Devoid of feelings, she finds it easy to follow the Kantian moral law: no temptations distract her. But this only deepens her pain, because she has nothing for which to strive. She raises serious questions about potential problems in making such a life an ethical ideal, and seeks guidance from a philosopher she profoundly admires. Kant never replies, dismissing her as an "ecstatical little lady" who is driven by her passions (precisely the opposite of her real difficulty of being bereft of all passion and desire). Kant did not merely abandon her, but used her as an object lesson: he disclosed her personal letters to another, to be used as a warning against the "curious mental derangement" suffered by Maria von Herbert.

A stronger sense of sympathetic concern might have helped Kant in his relation to one of his followers who sought his advice, and then—with little concern for the crisis the person was facing—was used by Kant as an object lesson. The "moral law" may help one to see that an abstract person should not be used as an object, not even for a moral lesson; but without an empathetic concern, *real* ethical behavior becomes all but impossible. In the absence of empathetic resources, learning rules is better than nothing; but rules without empathy are not likely to be successful. Empathy with no capacity for rules places limits on one's ethical resources; but rules without empathy leaves one ethically empty.

In Kant's rational world, the moral law is supreme and perfectly ordered: neither moth nor rust corrupt, thieves do not break through nor steal, nor do genuine ethical quandaries trouble. But ethical life in our grubby natural Earth is very different from the ethics practiced in Kant's sublime heaven. In the case of Maria von Herbert, Rae Langton concludes that in order to progress toward a world in which all people are treated as ends and not as means, there may be circumstances in which we must act in ways that are generally wrong; thus, in Herbert's case:

> I think she may have a duty to lie. This is strategy, for the Kingdom's sake. Kant would not allow it. He thinks we should act as if the Kingdom of Ends is with us now. He thinks we should rely on God to make it all right in the end. But God will not make it all right in the end. And the Kingdom of Ends is not with us now. Perhaps we should do what we can to bring it about. (Langton 1992, 505)

Kant's ideal world is a just world; but as Langton forcefully states, the world in which we live is not just, and "God will not make it right in the end." The emotion of sympathy for struggling human animals faced with the trials and tribulations of this *non*just world is a vital ethical resource, and suppressing that emotion in order to "follow the moral law strictly through reason and will power" is to chart a course for ethical disaster.

Huck doesn't live up to his principles, but is guided instead by his affections; since his principles are bad and his affections are generous, the result is ethically positive. Kant also fails to live up to his principles: he treats Maria as an object, rather than the thoughtful and deeply reflective and profoundly troubled person she is; that is, Kant treats her as a means, and not an end in herself. Unlike Huck's principled commitment to slavery, Kant's principled commitment to treat everyone as equally valuable members of the "Kingdom of Ends" is good; but Kant combines that good principle with a principled rejection of all affection and empathy as legitimate motives for conduct, and strives to prevent feelings from exerting any influence. As a result, Kant's behavior toward Maria is ethically deplorable.

Huck was a good man; he might have been better with better resources for ethical reflection. Of course he might have been worse, having "reflectively" decided that slavery was justified and right, as many slave owners certainly did. Thomas Jefferson was a slave owner who proclaimed that "all men are created equal." Many slave owners were sincere Christians who believed the Bible to be the inspired word of God and thus believed Paul's clear statement that God "hath made of one blood all nations of men for to dwell on the face of the earth" (Acts 17:26); yet they insisted that a single drop of African blood placed one outside the category of persons with rights and made one worthy only of enslavement—even their own children, as in the case of Jefferson.

The essence of ethics is emotions, not reflective reason. Reflective reason, with all its limits and problems, can be a wonderful enhancement of ethics; but the essence of ethics remains emotions. We can act ethically without the aid of deliberative reason, as Huck does; but ethical actors devoid of sympathetic emotions are at best an extremely endangered species, Kant's dream notwithstanding. Emotions can lead to great cruelty, of course; but so can reflective reason. Consider the victims of the Inquisition and the Holocaust: these were policies justified by reflective reason. Of course we believe the reasoning to be profoundly flawed; but it was certainly reflective reason, and indeed sometimes reflective at an intense and highly developed level (the cruel policies of the Inquisition were crafted through elaborate reflective processes, as was the justification of slavery).

Reflection can enhance both ethics and free will; in neither case does it make ethics or free will exclusively human. When we acknowledge what we share with other animals, and appreciate the vital importance of what we share rather than treating it as "beneath our dignity," then we can also better appreciate what our more distinctive and even unique capacities can—and cannot—accomplish. For Kant, our uniquely human reason empowers us with knowledge of the moral law, and our super power of will enables us to follow that law with no aid from animal-like emotions. Small wonder that Kant's view was and is widely celebrated: it fits our self-congratulatory self-conception perfectly.

Huck Finn explicitly rejects deeper ethical reflection, resolving to simply "do what comes easiest at the time." That does not make him amoral: It *might* make him more limited in his ethical capacities (though Huck certainly acts more ethically than do many who reflect carefully and find a rationalization for slavery and torture and genocide, suppressing or deadening or even destroying their sympathetic emotions in the process). Humans have a rational enhancement of ethical behavior available, at least at times; but it is far from clear that it has made us a morally superior species. If we are looking for moral superiority, my money is on the bonobos. They are better at egalitarian living, they are less violent, they are not misogynist, they care for their unfortunates. They are not saints, but neither is the human species. We usually give our medal of honor to those who have been the most efficient killers; if bonobos had a medal of honor, it would probably go to the best lovers (though a "medal of honor" suggests an emphasis on individual honor and hierarchy that would have less appeal for bonobos). The "higher reason" of *homo sapiens* may turn out to be an adaptation like the Irish Elk's antlers: impressive, but ultimately not fitness enhancing.

Higher-order reflection on what one ought to do might be essential to *knowing* that you are ethical; it is not essential to *being* ethical. As Mark Rowlands notes, a person who lacks the higher cognitive resources to classify her action as prudential—"she is unaware that her motives are prudential, and lacks the metacognitive abilities required to categorize her motives in this way" (2012, 218)—may still engage in behavior that is rigorously and intentionally prudential. Higher-order reflection is no doubt an essential capacity for those who theorize concerning ethics, or scrutinize the comparative virtues of competing ethical systems; but it is not essential for the process of *acting* ethically. In order to do a good deed daily, you need not follow a rule that you should do a good deed daily and you need not be aware that you are doing a good deed daily. One who feeds a hungry stranger from compassion and empathy—without deep reflection (past or present) on whether one *ought* to feed hungry strangers—performs an ethical act. *Classifying* it as an ethical act may require careful reflection; but the person who feeds hungry strangers is performing ethical acts, not classifying them. Jesus of Nazareth counted feeding the hungry and caring for sick as among the most important ethical acts (as evidenced by his comments in "the Sermon on the Mount"), and he seemed to regard zealous concern for ethical rules as an impediment to living a good moral life. Frans de Waal uses the parable of the Good Samaritan—who stops and helps a stranger who has been robbed and beaten—to emphasize (as Jesus did) that an ethics of rules (an ethics "by the book") is often less trustworthy than an ethics of empathy and compassion; as de Waal states: "The biblical message is to be wary of ethics by the book, which as often as not offers excuses to ignore the plight of others" (2013, 141). Some Taoists hold a similar view: Rules can be useful for early guidance, but they are not essential and can easily become fixations that impede moral development and undercut ethical behavior. Rules may also be useful as an enhancement, when inclination gutters. Kant's "friend of mankind" who suffers hardship and loses the inclination to kindness may find great benefit from the rules; but that is an enhancement, and a rather desperate ethical measure when the basic emotional fuel of ethics has run low; it is not the essence of ethical behavior.

THE SYSTEM OF RATIONALIST ETHICS AND EXCLUSIVELY HUMAN FREE WILL

There is a standard move for taking capacities that are found in many species and claiming that humans enjoy exclusive title to them: take something that is a special human enhancement, and claim that it is the essential essence. That way only humans can have reason, only humans can have free will, and only humans can act ethically. There is no doubt that ethical rules can be a valuable enhancement of human ethical behavior, particularly when our sympathies are at a low ebb; but such rules lose their value and become detrimental—as Jonathan Bennett (1974) makes clear—when they take on such an exalted status that they push all sympathetic feelings out of the ethical life. And that is precisely the danger when we exaggerate the importance of ethical rules, and underestimate the importance of feelings and sympathies, in order to make ethics the exclusive property of uniquely special humans.

If Antonio Damasio (1994) is correct—along with David Hume (1738) and Adam Smith (1759)—freezing sympathetic feelings out of the ethical life destroys ethics at its roots and deprives it of essential nourishment. But if instead of being based in pure reason, ethics is based in emotions (emotions we share with other animals, and which we study equally in experiments on both human and nonhuman animals), then it is difficult to confine ethical behavior to humans and difficult to treat the capacity for ethical behavior as a clear mark of a dramatic difference between humans and other animals. Can nonhuman animals behave ethically? If Huck Finn behaves ethically (even though he never rationally derives basic ethical principles, and *a fortiori* does not follow his principles strictly from duty with no tinge of emotional support), then nonhuman animals do so as well. Whether we call the morality of nonhuman animals a proto-morality or a genuine morality, it is clear that the traditional wall between human and nonhuman is being battered down, brick by brick. In our post-Darwinian world there is little plausibility in a deep divide between humans and other species. But the belief in uniqueness—whether conscious or (like our belief in a just world) nonconscious—continues to exert a powerful hold.

The system of human uniqueness, special powers of free will, and rationalist ethics fits together, and its elements are mutually supportive. But it is under constant challenge from research in biology and primatology and psychology. The system that treats free will and ethical behavior as the common property of many species—and rejects belief in gods and moral responsibility and a just world—also fits together; and it is a better fit with our naturalistic post-Darwin world view. It acknowledges evolutionary continuity in free will and ethics, and rejects the stark line drawn by conceptions of free will and ethics that embrace moral responsibility; and it is s a better fit as we recognize how little our "true unbiased deliberation" really does, and why that is fortunate.

If one insists on drawing the boundaries of ethical action so narrowly that only humans—and very few of them—qualify as ethical actors, then one can do so: Humans seem to have a special need for belonging to exclusive clubs. But that will result in a narrow focus that neglects crucial aspects of ethical behavior. It is analogous to ornithologists ruling that only whooping cranes count as birds. Free will may well be linked to ethics: indeed, free will may be a necessary condition of ethical behavior. But neither ethics nor free will is the exclusively human, super rationalist process favored by many of the human chronic cognizers who write about ethics and free will.

Chapter 10

Why Keep Free Will?

The chapter on restorative free will argued that the restorative model offers the best account of free will. But even *if* one accepts that argument, there remains another tough challenge to restorative free will: why keep the idea of free will at all, given the enormous confusion and the great variety of uses? Doesn't "free will" obfuscate more than elucidate? Even *if* one grants that the restorative account of free will brings together the vital elements of free will into a cohesive and coherent whole, fits free will into a larger account of animal behavior, and explains why free will functions as it does; there remains the difficult question of whether accounts of free will have been so varied and jumbled and conflicting for so long that the notion of free will is hopelessly muddled. And there is yet another question closely related to the first: Is restorative free will sufficiently like our common understanding of free will (if there is anything that counts as a common understanding) to qualify as the best account of free will? So this final chapter must also deal with an objection from both philosophers and folk: The restorative account may be a coherent account of *something*, but it is not an account of free will.

FOLK FREE WILL

Contemporary philosophers generally have assumed that the folk believe in miraculous forms of libertarian free will; however, that assumption is subject to considerable dispute—and serious challenge—from experimental philosophers (Nahmias 2014a, 7). But even if it should be the case that the folk widely and steadfastly believe in some miracle-based model of libertarian free will, that does not imply that free will actually requires extraordinary first cause powers, nor that—in the absence of such powers—free will does not exist. The folk may also believe that humans are not closely related to other animals, and deny that the family group of bonobos, chimpanzees, and humans have a close common ancestor. If the folk believe that humans are the species created by God and are made in God's image and are radically distinct from all other species, that does not mean that humans are not close evolutionary cousins of other primates, much less that humans do not exist.

Experimental philosophy is valuable. As Tamler Sommers summarizes that value:

> There is no doubt that experimental work on the compatibility question has made numerous contributions to our understanding of free will and moral responsibility. The studies have raised serious doubts about the folk's pretheo-retic commitment to incompatibilism. They have illustrated the role of emotion in our moral responsibility judgments. They have revealed how factors such as personality differences, and the terms in which determinism is described (mechanistic or psychological, actual or possible) can influence our judgments on the compatibility question. (2010, 204)

Experimental philosophy not only reveals problems in philosophers' over-confident assumptions about folk beliefs concerning free will, but also shows that those beliefs are considerably more complex and nuanced than we had imagined (Nahmias 2006, 2014a; Nichols and Knobe 2007; Knobe and Doris 2010; Nichols 2011). Furthermore, the experimental philosophy studies form the essential groundwork for deeper examination of the psychological causes behind these beliefs, in work such as that of Shaun Nichols (2006). Its genuine virtues and importance notwithstanding, experimental philoso-phy concerning folk beliefs can no more tell us about what real free will is than it can tell us the truth concerning evolution. That is not a criticism of experimental philosophy; to the contrary, it is a fact acknowledged by some of the best and most creative researchers in the folk psychology field, such as Eddy Nahmias:

> Notice that contrary to some critics of experimental philosophy, neither Nichols nor I have suggested that discovering what the folk intuitions are (where that is possible) plays any decisive role in the substantive philosophical project. (2006, 216n.)

There is, however, a strong tendency to suppose that an adequate account of free will must remain a relatively close fit with the "folk" view of free will, and must not place undue stress on the "conceptual scheme" in which folk free will operates. In a more recent paper with Dylan Murray, Nahmias warns against free will accounts that diverge too far from the folk model:

"Free will" plays a central role in the conceptual scheme that we use to navigate the normative world via its connections to "moral responsibility," "blame," "autonomy" and related concepts. Theorizing about "free will" in isolation from the ordinary understanding of it thus risks being an academic exercise about some other, technical conception with understanding of it divorced from people's actual practices of assessing praise, blame, reward, and punishment, and from their understanding of themselves and their place in the world. (2014, 435–6)

The restorative free will account is not "in isolation from the ordinary understanding," but neither does it always adhere to the ordinary folk understanding; rather, it attempts to explain the ways in which the ordinary understanding of free will is based on the key elements of animal free will, and also attempts to understand *why* additional elements—not found in animal free will—were grafted onto the more plausible basic account of free will. Part of that explanation involves examining why humans developed a *distorted* "understanding of themselves and their place in the world." But requiring changes in human "understanding of themselves and their place in the world" has been a valuable project from Copernicus to Darwin to the present, and those changes do not mean that Copernicus was no longer talking about the Earth, that Darwin had abandoned discussion of the human species, or that the rich variety of studies by biologists, primatologists, and psychologists are studying something other than free will. We are not the center of the cosmos, nor the specially favored fixed species crafted by God, nor the only species having free will; but such changes, significant though they are, do not imply that we are no longer discussing free will.

Is the restorative account of free will a sufficiently close match with the ordinary understanding of free will to qualify as an account of free will? Exactly what is involved in the "ordinary" sense of free will is far from clear. If supporting moral responsibility and just deserts is the defining feature of free will, then restorative "free will" is not an account of free will. But the ordinary or folk understanding of free will is probably not sufficiently nuanced to make that determination. When experimental philosophers ask probing questions or present troubling scenarios, they are likely stimulating their subjects to contrive a more detailed and developed view of free will than the subjects have previously considered. As Murray and Nahmias state:

We find it unlikely that most people have any explicit theory of choice or the ability to do otherwise that contains substantive metaphysical commitments, just as we find it unlikely that most people have any explicit theory about the relation between free will and determinism. (2014, 459)

For ordinary daily life understanding of free will, the range of *human* acts of free will—acts of choice under my minimally intelligent and informed control that fit my own (nonobsessive) wishes and desires—is a workable match with the restorative model of free will.

There are profound differences distinguishing the compatibilist, libertarian, and restorative accounts of human free will; but when observing and classifying what falls into the category of human free will there is a substantial range of referential consistency. (Super rationalist accounts of free will, such as those of the ancient stoics and currently in the work of Susan Wolf, pick out a very different and much narrower set of persons acting with free will.) Differences arise when we ask *why* those acts count as free will and whether the acts justify reward and punishment.

IS RESTORATIVE FREE WILL REALLY FREE WILL?

The question is not what view of free will is held by the folk, nor—for that matter—what view of free will is held by philosophers. Rather, the important question is what view of free will fits with our best scientific understanding of animal behavior. We might, of course, conclude that free will is like phlogiston, and nothing fits. But if the restorative free will model makes sense of how free will confers selective advantages, incorporates key characteristics of both libertarian and compatibilist models, explains why such accounts developed and the points at which these accounts distorted our understanding of free will and why, and fits human free will into the larger framework of animal behavior, then that model can make a strong claim to being a legitimate account of free will—and a more successful and accurate account than can be found among the folk.

There are two questions here. One, does the restorative account make sense of the relevant aspects of free will (with part of that issue, of course, involving questions of what counts as relevant)? Second, does the account make enough connections with our basic understanding of free will to justify this as an account of "what free will really is," or does it instead turn free will into something like phlogiston which our best scientific accounts explain away? The claim is that restorative free will not only is the most plausible scientific naturalist account of free will but also an account that preserves what we best understand free will to be. This claim faces several challenges: one, free will has traditionally been associated with special godlike first cause (*causa sui*) powers; two, free will has been inseparably linked to moral responsibility; three, the restorative model cannot draw a clear line between animals that have free will and those that do not; and four, traditionally free will has been considered the exclusive property of humans.

If free will requires mysterious libertarian miraculous powers—the powers that Pico della Mirandola claims we were given by God, the powers that C. A. Campbell seems to attribute to us when we make contra-causal choices that are inexplicable scientifically, the power of being a *causa sui* or self-moved mover (which as Chisholm notes, is a power traditionally attributed only to God)—then there is no room in our naturalistic scientific system for free will. If such powers are essential for free will, then free will must be abandoned along with gods and miracles, and good riddance to the lot of them. However, there are good reasons for rejecting miracle-working powers as an essential element of free will; after all, the leading contemporary libertarian, Robert Kane, proposes a view of free will which abjures any appeal whatsoever to such powers; and compatibilists—the majority among contemporary philosophers—have no room for miracles in their accounts of free will. If miracles are essential for free will, then neither Kane's libertarian version nor any compatibilist account will be an account of free will. Certainly there are some who deny we can have free will unless we are blessed with godlike miracle-working powers. But few contemporary philosophers regard miraculous powers as an essential condition for free will.

Consider the second challenge to the proposed restorative account of free will: free will has often been linked with moral responsibility, and the restorative free will account rejects that linkage. There is no question that contemporary philosophers—and their forebears for generations past—have linked free will with moral responsibility. Indeed, the tradition has been so strong that the two are used almost interchangeably by many philosophers, and the assumption has been that in justifying free will one automatically provides a justification of moral responsibility. The claim that our best account of free will is one that severs the connection between free will and moral responsibility is obviously a contentious claim, and the objection that the restorative free will account cannot be adequate if it cannot support moral responsibility is a serious and substantial one; but that was an issue discussed in chapter 5.

A third objection to the restorative model of free will is closely related to the second: How low does free will go? Where do you draw the line? That is a complex question fallacy, that embeds a disputed assumption: The assumption that there must be a clear line between the presence and absence of free will. That is a holdover from the assumption that free will provides the grounds for having or lacking moral responsibility; there can be excusing and mitigating circumstances, but there must be a clear line between those who are and are not morally responsible, between those for whom the objective attitude rather than the reactive attitude is appropriate, between those who are on the moral responsibility plateau and those who are not, between those who justly deserve to be blamed and rewarded and those to whom just deserts do not apply. But that clear line is no more plausible when we are discussing the free will of evolved animals than when we are discussing the intelligence of such animals. As we study animal behavior, we find free will in crude and rudimentary forms, we find free will in more developed and effective forms, and we find free will in extremely sophisticated forms.

A better question: Why is it generally supposed that there must be a clear line dividing those who possess free will from those who do not? Because we commonly use free will to prop up moral responsibility, and moral responsibility needs clear lines: a dividing line like the line in the criminal justice system between the competent and the incompetent (a line that no one can even pretend is clearly marked, though we treat it as if it were). If we insist on moral responsibility, we are required to draw such implausible lines between the presence and the absence of free will; the natural world is under no such constraint. Roy F. Baumeister notes that for processes shaped by evolution, we should expect a continuum rather than a bright dividing line:

> A scientific theory about a human faculty would almost certainly describe it as something produced in stages by evolution and natural selection, which again points to the need to think of freedom along a continuum rather than an absolute, all-or-nothing matter. (2014, 236)

Eddy Nahmias (2014a, 21) also recommends that we recognize *degrees* of free will (though he seems to confine those degrees to humans, and one of his motives is the preservation of moral responsibility).

THE MUNDANE NATURE OF ANIMAL FREE WILL

The fourth challenge to the restorative account of animal free will is that free will traditionally has been regarded as belonging exclusively to humans. Though the restorative account of free will generates a decent match for the ordinary understanding of *human* acts of free will, it certainly does not match when it comes to *non*human free will. Where compatibilists, libertarians, and the folk see a null set, the restorative view sees free will in rich variety. But there are precedents for such an enormous extension of a narrower concept. The visible stars fixed in their places (on the most distant and nearly perfect sphere that circled our stationary Earth) were the totality of all the stars that exist; the billions of stars added to that number—by Galileo and his successors—far outnumber the stars once thought to hold exclusive title to that designation, but a better astronomical theory and better observation had no problem counting the billions of newly discovered lights in distant galaxies as stars. When we give up the pre-Darwinian idea of a clear line that separates human behavior from the behavior of all other species, we have no trouble extending our concept of free will far beyond its earlier limits. At one time it was believed that animals had no consciousness at all, and could not feel pain:

consciousness was the exclusive property of humans. When we acknowledged that animals are conscious of pain, that did not require us to give up our notion of consciousness; rather, we extended it more broadly. More recently, claims were made that the capacity for planning is exclusively human, that cultural transmission is exclusively human, that recognition of self and a sense of personal identity are exclusively human. When we discovered that other animals have such capacities, we did not decide that planning, or sense of personal identity, or cultural transmission no longer existed; rather, we enlarged the scope of what the concepts covered. That process of enlargement was facilitated by an understanding of evolution, and a resulting expectation of greater similarities between humans and other species than we had hitherto expected. When we dropped the idea that humans are uniquely made in the image of God, we did not lose our ability to identify humans. When we drop the comfortable belief that free will belongs exclusively to humans, we do not lose our capacity to recognize free will; to the contrary, we gain a richer understanding of free will by observing it writ large in the behavior of many species.

Philosophical efforts to block such an extension seem artificial and contrived: pivotal acts of free will must involve a decision which pits duty versus desire (C. A. Campbell 1957) or involve both rigorous moral deliberation and randomness (Kane 1985, 1996, 2007) or plumb our deepest reflective evaluations (Frankfurt 1971). That vigorous limiting of free will may be successful in confining acts of free will to humans, but it will be too successful by far; after all, many of our free choices—including many that are most vital to our psychological well-being—have nothing whatever to do with moral decision-making. Shall I stay for the last inning of this awful baseball game in hopes that the home team will rally from its nine run deficit, or leave a bit early and beat the traffic? (If the home team is the Boston Red Sox and Tamler Sommers is the fan, that might be regarded as an ethical quandary; but that is a part of Tamler's ethical code that few of us share.) Shall I take my bath this morning or this afternoon? Shall I sleep in for an extra hour and skip breakfast, or get up and join my friends? Shall I find a quiet place to read, or watch television? Shall I eat dinner at 6 or at 8? All of these are free choices and important acts of free will; they involve neither moral decisions nor deep reflection ("I desire to eat dinner at 8, but do I really want to have the desire to eat dinner at 8?"); and we do not realize how fundamentally important these mundane acts of free will are to our psychological and even physical well-being until we are deprived of such choices.

When captive white-footed mice have few opportunities for environmental control, they devote enormous and often repetitive effort to modifying the aspects of their environment which they can change:

Animals in the wild exercise a relatively high degree of control over the environment, for example, by selection of nest site, territory, food, and time and degree of activity and social contacts and by manipulation of many objects. But the activities of captive animals and the opportunities to interact with and modify the environment are restricted severely, with the consequence that their behavior becomes markedly distorted. A large amount of activity becomes channeled into "controlling the environment," that is, into manipulating, and altering relationships with, any susceptible environmental features. . . . When outlets are highly restricted, as is usual, virtually any opportunity to modify environmental variables is exercised repeatedly, in little apparent relation to the appropriateness of the act as a substitute activity. (Kavanau 1967, 1623)

For example, in one cage there was cotton that could be pulled through a crack, and the mice devoted great energy and time to that task:

At the rear of the nest is a small crack through which the cotton can be grasped from outside. Animals of both sexes spend hours reeling the cotton wad out through this crack, compacting the fluffy, strung-out mass with their forelegs and teeth, stuffing the wad back into the entrance to the nest, and then repeating the entire sequence hundreds of times day after day. (Kavanau 1967, 1624)

Something comparable occurs in the regimented confines of some long-term care facilities. "Difficult" residents (those who have not sunk into acquiescent learned helplessness) demand detailed control over trivial matters—exactly how dark her toast is, the precise consistency of his scrambled eggs, a salad with just the right amount of dressing (no more and no less), a specific chair in the lounge. Staff may become impatient with these insistent demands concerning irrelevant details; if there were more understanding of the pressing psychological need for residents to exercise greater control in other areas of their lives, then the free will of residents might be more respected and enhanced. When this is the only control available, it is of vital importance (Taylor 1983).

Long-term care facilities often deprive their residents of control, including control over the most mundane of activities: when to bathe, when and what to eat, when to go to bed, when to get up, when to socialize and when to be alone.

People are often placed in long-term care facilities against their wishes, and once there, they have little say in what they do; they are expected to allow the staff to make their life decisions. Meals are given at scheduled hours, baths are given only on certain days, and visiting hours are predetermined. All rooms are furnished alike. (von Bergen et al. 1999, 134)

Arthur Caplan forcefully describes the devastating effect this can have on residents who are deprived of the many mundane daily choices and exercise of control that are central to the basic operation of free will:

Those who live in nursing homes frequently feel that their control over the ordinary decisions of their lives, their autonomy, their dignity, even their sense of self is lost in the routines, policies, and constraints of nursing home life. Ethical questions about the loss of autonomy over the ordinary or routine decisions of daily living or about obligations on the part of those who are competent toward those who are not may seem to pale when viewed from the perspective of ethical issues concerning the use or cessation of lifesaving or life-prolonging medical care. But it is simply wrong to think that they are less momentous or deserving of careful thought and deliberation. (1990, 39)

The deprivation of such "trivial" control is strongly correlated with depression, greater vulnerability to infection, and a higher mortality rate (Bandura et al. 1988; Rodin 1986; Schulz and Hanusa 1978; Schorr and Rodin 1982).

This may explain why ancient belief in fatalism was not in fact a doctrine of helplessness and resignation. The gods might control the hour of your death, and perhaps various other important aspects of your life; but so long as you have control over the day to day living, you enjoy the exercise of a free will that is sufficient for the psychological well-being of human animals. Suppose that the hour of your death is indelibly recorded in the book of fate; would that deprive you of the vigorous exercise of free will? After all, we recognize that we cannot control the moment of our deaths: you may exercise and eat right and drive carefully and wear your seatbelt, but there are many factors you cannot control—the polluted air you breathe, your genetic heritage, the inebriated driver who swerves into your lane—that also play a part in writing the final chapter of your life; but that knowledge does not, for most of us, result in learned helplessness or loss of free will. You control how you teach your classes, which books and articles you will read, what you will have for dinner, the route you will take on your drive home, where you will go on holiday, whether or not you will go to the gym, whether to have a cup of coffee (and perhaps a muffin?), and many other daily mundane decisions that are of much greater free will significance than the momentous decisions (such as C. A. Campbell's contra-causal decisions between duty and desire, Frankfurt's higher-order reflective affirmations, and Kane's decisions concerning "life-forming actions") that philosophers sometimes celebrate as the essence of free will. Kane's life-forming choices are obviously important; but for an understanding of the basic benefits of free will for foraging animals (including humans), we must start at a more basic level.

Our sense of freedom depends more on our mundane choices—what Frankfurt dismisses as merely being "free to do as he pleases" (1971, 15)— than on whether we have "the will to want what we want to want." Shall I return to the ripe berry patch, or forage in a new area? Shall I take the usual path, or a new one? As in humans, most of the acts of free will by other animals are mundane rather than momentous, but they are no less essential for that. Such free choices usually do not involve profound deliberation, and our decisions may be powerfully influenced by factors of which we are not consciously aware, but that does not make such mundane choices less important to our psychological well-being, nor does it eject them from the realm of freely chosen acts. Shall I go to bed, or stay up and watch a late movie? Shall I go to sleep, or stay up and howl at the moon? The former may involve no more deliberation than the latter, and may involve no greater moral issue than the latter; and if the former is an act of free will, then consistency—within a post-Darwinian world view—should place the latter in the same category. No doubt many human choices are more complicated than those made by white-footed mice and wolves and chimpanzees. But many are not. One cost of insisting that only humans exercise free will is the systemic overestimation of the complexity of all human choice and a blindness to the genuine complexity of many choices made by nonhumans; but the most important cost is the neglect of the daily mundane choices—on the assembly line, on the farm, in our homes—that are the vital element of healthy free will. When we recognize the importance of the vast majority of free choices made by humans—mundane choices, but essential to a healthy sense of free control—then consistency requires that we recognize the importance of similar free choices in other animals. When we note the powerful factors that prevented us from acknowledging such parallels—belief that humans are the special and unique creation of God and totally different from all other animals, together with the belief that free will entails moral responsibility along with the recognized absurdity of holding dogs and cats and hamsters morally responsible—then acknowledging free will in nonhuman animals becomes plausible; and restorative free will comes much closer to a "common sense" view of free will.

One could insist that what is being described here—from the mundane choices of long-term care residents to the exercise of limited control by patients with fatal or chronic diseases to the exploratory efforts of the white-footed mouse—does not qualify as free will: it is merely "free behavior" or "freedom of action" rather than genuine exercise of free will. On that view, "real" free will is the rare and wonderful and semi-miraculous profound moral choice or life-altering decision that requires remarkable rational powers that are perfectly transparent to consciousness and which exist in a realm above and beyond the influence of visceral intuitions or System 1 heuristics or situational factors or priming forces. In contrast, restorative free will is closely linked with our deepest motives and our vitally important psychological needs. Restorative free will has room for careful deliberative reflective decisions, as a special enhancement of free will; in contrast, the opposing view must find ways of *separating* free will from the basic needs and psychological benefits that made free will adaptive for animals like ourselves. The opposing view is more complex; but that complexity comes at a steep price, in comparison to the more economical restorative approach.

THE ELIMINATIVIST CHALLENGE

Even if restorative free will qualifies as a legitimate account of free will, there remains a tough challenge. That basic challenge comes from free will *eliminativists* (Caruso 2012; Double 1991; Levy 2011; Nadelhoffer 2011; Pereboom 2001; Strawson 1986), who regard free will as falling into the same category as phlogiston (and immortal souls): a nonexistent element of a failed theory (or world view). There are solid reasons for abandoning the notion of free will altogether. The common belief in free will appears to involve miraculous and even incoherent powers of *ab initio* self-caused causes—though it is difficult to be confident of that description of the folk account of free will, since the folk seem quite willing to set different standards for free will in different circumstances (Knobe and Doris 2010), and as noted earlier there is considerable current dispute concerning the folk view of free will. The most common understanding of free will *appears* to require powers that are fundamentally inconsistent with scientific naturalism; so as good scientific naturalists, we should put free will in the same discard heap with deities and miracles and souls. There are, then, good reasons for the starkly eliminativist approach to free will. But there are also good reasons for preserving belief in free will; and by my lights, those reasons outweigh the genuine reasons for abandoning all talk of free will.

Free will as a miraculous power—a power that justifies holding transgressors morally responsible—does not exist. Likewise the fixed stars that revolved daily on their special crystalline sphere do not exist. However, the stars observed by those who believed in the Ptolemaic universe certainly do exist. The "wanderers" that the ancients called planets do not move in strange jerky orbits; but when William of Occam looked at Venus from his monastery window, he saw the same planet that Dan Dennett observes from his sloop. The "planets" took their name from their strange orbital paths, but when Kepler redrew those orbits as smooth ellipses, the planets remained the entities named and observed by the ancients. Among the ancients and the medievals, comets were miraculous messengers from God, announcing great wonders or dire warnings; they no longer deliver divine messages, but they are still comets. Likewise, we can identify the free will that the folk suppose justifies moral responsibility, even if we deny that it has that remarkable property.

THE PRACTICAL BENEFITS OF RESTORATIVE FREE WILL

Should we preserve or eliminate belief in free will? There are substantial advantages—or so I have argued (2011, 2015)—to eliminating belief in moral responsibility; but that is not the present issue. The question is: if we reject moral responsibility, should we keep free will, which (at least in modern times) has been closely connected with moral responsibility?

Shaun Nichols (2013) offers an insightful study of the plausibility of keeping a concept of free will, notwithstanding its association with the error of miracle-working powers; and he makes an excellent argument that we could plausibly opt *either* for eliminativism (discarding free will altogether) or revisionism (retaining free will in a revised form). Since both options are open, Nichols recommends that we consider the practical benefits of keeping or jettisoning free will, and weigh the practical benefits into our decision: "We might appeal to practical interests in deciding which convention to adopt and impose" (2013, 215). In his consideration of the practical benefits of retaining a revised notion of free will, Nichols sketches several practical advantages of belief in free will (advantages that are genuine, though Nichols is rather brief in his list of the advantages that accrue from retaining belief in free will). Then Nichols turns to the *dis*advantages of belief in free will; but there his argument goes astray. Adopting the common belief that links free will with moral responsibility, Nichols—drawing on the work of Tamler Sommers (2012)—notes some of the genuine and severe costs of belief in *moral responsibility*, and assumes that he is listing disadvantages of belief in free will:

> But there are also practical advantages to adopting eliminativism. As Tamler Sommers notes, the denial of free will can undercut an ugly self-righteousness: "Recognizing that all the people who we love, respect and cherish, including ourselves, do not deserve praise for being who we are may help to lessen the disdain and contempt we sometimes feel for those who are not fortunate enough to make it into this charmed circle." Sommers also suggests that denying free will can help to assuage pathological guilt, "the kind of morbid hand-wringing that keeps us awake all night thinking about what might have been." Indeed, invoking determinism is an explicit strategy in some prominent behavioral therapies. (2013, 215–16)

But those are advantages of abandoning moral responsibility, not free will; and that list of advantages could be lengthened many times over. Once we separate free will from moral responsibility, Nichols' scorecard for the practical advantages of keeping vs. eliminating free will turns out to be: Advantages for keeping free will, many; advantages for eliminating free will, zero.

Along similar lines Thomas Nadelhoffer and Daniela Goya Tocchetto (2013) offer a deep and insightful analysis of "the potential dark side of believing in free will (and related concepts)," noting a range of nasty attitudes (such as right wing authoritarianism) that are strongly associated with such belief. But because they are examining the possible effects of believing in free will *and related concepts* (and moral responsibility is central among the related concepts), it is quite possible that the "dark side" results from believing in moral responsibility, and is not a negative effect of believing in free will (except to the extent that people mistakenly treat free will and moral responsibility as inseparable).

Suppose we have agreed that moral responsibility is implausible in our contemporary naturalistic world view; should we—given the traditional link between free will and moral responsibility—also renounce free will? Of course we are renouncing miraculous versions of libertarian free will; but should we go further and deny free will altogether? There are three good practical reasons *not* to do so. First, denying free will provokes deep concern, and for good reason: loss of free will would be a severe loss indeed (and this fear is likely to be especially strong when moral responsibility is denied, since people typically believe that the demise of moral responsibility will pose serious threats to free will). Second, when free will is not distorted and darkened by its association with moral responsibility, then we are in a better position to study free will and understand how it actually functions; and we can see how the elements of free will that are of greatest psychological value are preserved in natural restorative free will. Third, along with the improved understanding of how free will functions we can find better ways to enhance free will and promote environments that will facilitate rather than undermine the exercise of free will.

The first practical advantage of preserving a concept of free will is in ameliorating the debilitating fear of *loss* of free will and loss of control. Eliminating moral responsibility does not result in loss of free will (Waller 1990, 2011); to the contrary, it strengthens free will. But eliminating moral responsibility exacerbates the *fear* of losing free will. When we abandon belief in moral responsibility, it is doubly important to emphasize that this does *not* threaten free will, and does not threaten what we really want from free will.

"To know all is to forgive all." True or false, that claim is not frightening. Some may regard it as naive, and others will view it as implausible or even foolish. But few will find it frightening. "No one has free will." That is a more chilling thought altogether. It conjures up notions of "peremptory puppeteers" pulling our strings for their devious purposes, the fates thwarting our best efforts, total constraint, complete helplessness. That is not only frightening, but psychologically and physically damaging. The belief that one cannot make choices, cannot exercise effective control, cannot escape coercive or devious control leads to depression, sickness, and even death (Seligman 1975; Rodin 1986; Schulz and Hanusa 1978; Schorr and Rodin 1982). Since we are certainly not *losing* free will by broadening and enriching our understanding of free will and placing it on a solid biological and psychological foundation, the fear of losing free will should be ameliorated rather than exacerbated. "You have genuine alternatives from which to choose, you can make your choices in accordance with your own values and preferences and understanding, and you can exercise genuine control over your own choices. You can't perform miracles; but you never really believed that you could. You can't make choices that are totally independent of who you are, and your character and values and history and circumstances; but if you could, it is hard to imagine that *you* would actually be making the choices, and difficult to see how 'your choices' would be of any benefit to you." What else would you want in the way of free will?

Of course there *are* those who want more. Some want a free will that makes them godlike. Others want a free will that will justify moral responsibility (and—correctly—they do not believe restorative free will can do the job). Finally, there are those who long to be the *ultimate* source of their own acts and accomplishments (but not because they want to claim exclusive *credit* for what they do). Robert Kane expresses this longing most clearly and eloquently: "The objective worthiness that concerns libertarians comes not merely from having in fact lived a good life or accomplished certain goals, but from the fact that you yourself were the independent source of the living of that life and of accomplishing those goals" (Kane 1996, 98–9). Kane's deep longing is not one I feel (which may only indicate that, as I have long suspected, Robert Kane has a nobler soul than I). It seems to me that Thurgood Marshall was a great man who accomplished great things, and that understanding the causes of his courageous and extraordinary behavior does not diminish the value of either Marshall or his accomplishments, nor does it compromise his uniqueness (Waller 2015, 180–2). Derk Pereboom draws a similar conclusion concerning the importance of our commitments and values, and their undiminished importance when we gain better understanding of their causes:

> Even independently of general considerations such as the plausibility of causal determinism one might wonder about the degree to which one's moral commitments are ultimately up to oneself, and not, say, due to upbringing and social context. When we come to see these commitments as due in large part to contributions by others, our reaction tends to be appreciative and not dispirited. (Pereboom 2014, 196)

That doesn't settle the question, of course; instead it marks a deep value disagreement between those who find compatibilist free will quite sufficient and those incompatibilists who value "a freedom requiring ultimate responsibility" (Kane 1996, 99). Those who genuinely value the "freedom requiring ultimate responsibility" might well find the denial of such free will discouraging, even depressing; but such a denial does not generate fear of complete helplessness, fear of being deprived of all choices and control. For some, then, restorative free will may not provide all they could possibly desire in the way of free will; but even then, restorative free will is not a scary prospect, while the denial of free will certainly is.

The second practical reason to maintain a strong concept of free will is that without the confusions of moral responsibility, we can now study free will more carefully, expand our study of free will to other species, and gain a better understanding of the factors that enhance and inhibit the exercise of free will. It is advantageous to study hearts in other species; of course, if there were no organ in other animals that functioned to pump the blood and keep it circulating, we would conclude that hearts are unique to humans; but we find parallel functions in other animals for both hearts and free will. Eliminating a rigid division (between humans who enjoy free will, and all the other species that do not) opens a clearer view and appreciation of the function and elements and varieties of free will. Not every animal has a heart shaped precisely like a human heart, but that does not mean that other animals do not have hearts, nor does it mean that we cannot enlarge our understanding of the heart by studying the hearts of other species.

Dogs (Seligman 1975) suffer debilitating effects when deprived of all power of control, and humans suffer similar effects when they are deprived of control and thus deprived of free will (whether in badly managed long-term care facilities or "highly efficient" supermax prisons). Years ago there was a memorable commercial for a headache remedy, in which a woman suffering from a headache is given unwanted assistance from her mother in a task that the woman prefers to carry out with no interference; the woman's exasperated rebuke of her mother became a popular culture catch phrase: "Mother, *please*; I'd rather do it myself!" White-footed mice know exactly what she means: when someone else starts the running wheel, they immediately stop it, and then start it themselves; when someone places them in the nest—which is where they wanted to be—they leave the nest and then return. White-footed mice are wise to resist such "help." A study of elderly persons given "coaching" and "help" in solving a puzzle found that those who received help performed worse on subsequent tests: the help conveyed the message that they were incapable of doing the puzzle on their own, and weakened their sense of "puzzle self-efficacy" (Avorn and Langer 1982). Humans—through cultural complexities—have developed methods and powers of exercising free will that are very impressive; but that is no reason to deny that the analogous methods and powers of exercising free will, that serve analogous functions for other species, are also instances of free will.

We have studied learning, depression, self-control and delayed gratification, need for control, group relations, altruism, aggression, reconciliation, problem solving, cooperation, sensation-seeking, and even culture in other animals; these studies did not change our meanings of these phenomena (much less imply that because we studied nonhuman manifestations of these capacities that we should no longer believe in them and eliminate them from our world view). When we recognize that free will is also present in other animals, that is not a reason to suppose that free will does not exist; rather, that recognition opens the way for a better understanding of free will, its general characteristics, and its special manifestations in various species. Rather than abandoning free will we should celebrate its value, recognize that it is a natural process that can be damaged or enhanced, and work to improve it. We ought to keep the term "free will," because then we can understand all the ways the notion of free will was distorted in trying to make it exclusively human and a support for moral responsibility, and we can understand what motivates our deep need for free will together with the elements that make up a genuine free will for animals like ourselves.

There is a third practical reason for maintaining belief in and commitment to free will, and it is closely connected to the second. With a broader and deeper understanding of why free will is valuable and how it functions, we are in a better position to promote and enhance free will. The insistence on linking free will with moral responsibility has had a particularly damaging effect on our commitment to the study of how free will capacities are developed, how they can be strengthened, and how they can be protected. Roy F. Baumeister makes a valuable point that the insistence on moral responsibility obscures and the plateau model of free will and moral responsibility desperately avoids recognizing: There are degrees of free will. As Baumeister notes:

> The question "Do people have free will" seeks a yes or no answer, but most psychological phenomena turn out to exist on continuums. Freedom probably comes in varying degrees rather than all or nothing. (2014, 235)

Baumeister does not draw out the further implications of this valuable insight: There are not only varying degrees of free will among humans, but also varying degrees of free will in different species (just as there are hearts of differing efficiency—the hearts of marathoners generally function better than the hearts of couch potatoes). There are also degrees of free will among members of the same species. Seligman's dogs have much less free will than does Bruno, our affectionate but fiercely independent and thoroughly self-confident poodle. Residents of a nursing home made significant free will gains in an experiment in which they exercised modest control: they were afforded the opportunity to control both the frequency and duration of visits by groups of undergraduates (a control group were visited with matching frequency and duration, but they were only informed when the visits would occur rather than controlling frequency and duration). The group that exercised control experienced both psychological and physical benefits; the control group did not (Schulz 1976). Unfortunately, once the experiment was over, the visits stopped; and those who had experienced increased control suddenly were faced with complete loss of control over what had become an important and satisfying element of their lives, and disastrous loss of free will—together with higher rates of depression and infection—resulted when the experiment ended (Schulz and Hanusa 1978). Even if we confine our attention to differences in levels and degrees and capacities of free will in humans, it is of great importance and benefit to recognize and study the varying degrees of free will, how those differences occurred, and how weaknesses in free will can be avoided or corrected and strengths in free will can be promoted. When (in order to support claims of moral responsibility) libertarians treat free will as mysterious and miraculous and compatibilists block deeper inquiry into behavioral causes, that does not promote deeper study and improved methods of enhancing free will.

Free will accounts that abjure miracles and mysteries may still promote obscurity and block inquiry when they are pressed into service for the support of moral responsibility. Consider the "plateau" or "threshold" argument for moral responsibility: everyone who reaches the plateau of basic competence has free will and can be held morally responsible (Dennett 1984, 2003; Metz 2006; Smith 2008). When we treat free will (that justifies claims of moral responsibility) as the equal capacity of all those who qualify as competent, we impose hard limits on our study of free will. We can study why some found it easy to reach the plateau, why some found it difficult, why some never made it, and perhaps why a few fell back over the edge and off the plateau. But we cannot study why some persons on the plateau are rich in free will resources while others are more limited, because admitting *differences* in free will capacities—among those competent ones dwelling on the plateau of free will and moral responsibility—destroys the usefulness of the plateau as grounds for moral responsibility. If Veronica's free will resources are superior to those of Wanda, then it is not surprising that Veronica acts virtuously while Wanda acts viciously: the differences in free will capacities can account for the differences in behavior. But the significant and substantial differences in free will capacities were the result of causes that neither Veronica nor Wanda chose or controlled. And this undercuts the function—supporting moral responsibility—that the plateau was designed to serve.

If we do not have to support claims of moral responsibility, then it makes perfect sense to examine why one has greater free will than another, and how those with weaker resources can be aided. Since everyone who is minimally competent and on the plateau of moral responsibility is assumed to have the full rich resources of free will, it makes no sense to concern ourselves with strengthening and enhancing free will. Since we are all morally responsible, we all must have a full and equal measure of free will, and so we need do nothing to nurture or support it. That prevents us from paying close attention to the many factors that enhance freedom (such as an internal locus-of-control and a positive sense of self-efficacy and effective powers of self-control) and inhibit freedom (ranging from lead poisoning to ego-depletion). And it is part of the idea that free will is self-sufficient, that it does not require a supportive environment, that it does not need a nurturing environment to develop, that it does not require the right environment to flourish. This is part of the "rugged individualism" free will (Waller 2015, 228–31) that makes catchy political slogans and harsh public policy, and that promotes "benign neglect" of the actual factors required for effective development and exercise of free will.

CONCLUSION

For the folk, free will means following your own preferences and making your own choices (including bad and intemperate choices). For day to day living—untroubled by inquisitive experimental philosophers—the common belief in free will works fine: I'm doing what I want to do, and could have done otherwise if I had wished. That's free will enough (and the exact nature of that "could have done otherwise" need not be scrutinized). That, of course, is good basic standard issue compatibilist free will, and a good match with restorative free will.

By what right can restorative free will claim the title to genuine free will? It is part of our best explanation of the range of phenomena, including the best explanation of the distortions; it incorporates what is really desirable in free will (open alternatives and control); it fits better with our natural understanding of the world and of animals and of the evolutionary process; and it explains why both the alternatives (libertarian) and authenticity (compatibilist) views flourish and what important elements they have right, and reconciles them. It is a coherent model of the sum of phenomena, in a way that views of free will incorporating human uniqueness and moral responsibility cannot manage. Restorative free will denies that free will is the special and uniquely human power that sets humans apart from all other species, denies that the natural free will enjoyed by humans can support moral responsibility, denies that the world is just, denies that all genuine values can be fitted together in such a manner that nothing of real value is lost, and insists that human free will is continuous with the free will found in closely related species. In sum, it is a better fit with our contemporary naturalistic world view.

For a naturalistic world view that eliminates miracles and rejects limits on inquiry, restorative free will makes sense; for pre-Darwinians, it does not. Many of our most important discoveries concerning the physical and psychological nature of humans were originally made by study and observation of nonhuman animals: from the circulation of the blood to major causes of depression, from the schedules of reinforcement that shape behavior in rats, pigeons, and humans to the structure of the strike-back mechanism (Barash 2005; Barash and Lipton 2011) shared by humans and chimpanzees and rats. If we want to *understand* human free will (rather than treating it as a mysterious prop for moral responsibility that we dare not examine too carefully) then the comparative study of free will in other species is a valuable resource. When we learned that humans are a lot like our nearest relatives and have common ancestors, we did not conclude there are no real humans. When we discover that free will in humans is a lot like free will in other animals, we should not conclude there is no free will.

Rather than give up free will, we should give it back: back to the animals in which it first evolved, long before imperialist humans came along to stake an exclusionary claim. There is plenty of free will to go around. By sharing it with other species, we do not deprive ourselves of free will; to the contrary, we understand our own free will better, and are less tempted by miracles and mysteries and moral responsibility. We can face squarely the fact that we must sometimes employ punishment, and acknowledge the injustice entailed by such punishment; we can face the fact that this is not a just world, and avoid blaming those who were not as lucky as we have been; and we can acknowledge that we did *not* "make it ourselves," with no help, though we certainly can and do make important contributions to many worthwhile projects. There is such a thing as luck. There is also effort and accomplishment, and we should value and strengthen them. But we should avoid imagining that we did it all ourselves, and that we are different in kind from those who are less lucky and from other species with other ways of acting freely.

When we liberate free will from the burden of moral responsibility and study it writ large in the behavior of other species, we are in a much better position to understand how it works and why it is valuable—and adaptive—for many species: species including but not limited to humans. Now that researchers have opened a clearer way of studying and understanding free will, and we can liberate free will from the burdens and obfuscations of moral responsibility, this is not the time for philosophers to insist that free will does not exist. Forty years ago E. O. Wilson suggested that "The time has come for ethics to be removed temporarily from the hands of the philosophers and biologicized" (Wilson 1975, 562). Free will should not be removed from the hands of the philosophers; to the contrary, philosophers have made remarkable contributions to the understanding of free will, including Daniel Dennett's insightful work on the importance of control, Robert Kane's strong insistence on the importance of *both* open alternatives and control, Harry Frankfurt's demonstration of how higher-order reflection can enhance human free will, John Fischer's profound account of the psychological importance of the authenticity-control element of free will, as well as the work of many others. But it is time for philosophers to better appreciate and incorporate biological research when formulating a comprehensive account of free will; and it is certainly time for philosophers to take seriously the evolutionary process that produced free will in humans and many other species, and to take note of the many essential elements of free will shared by philosophers, chimpanzees, and white-footed mice. When we appreciate the exercise of free will in other species, we also discover better ways of protecting and enhancing free will in our own.

Bibliography

Abramson, L. Y., M. E. P. Seligman, and J. D. Teasdale. 1978. Learned helplessness in humans: Critique and reformulation. *Journal of Abnormal Psychology* 87:49–74.

Allen, J., M. Weinrich, W. Hoppitt, and L. Rendell. 2013. Network-based diffusion analysis reveals cultural transmission of lobtail feeding in humpback whales. *Science* 340:485–88.

Aristotle. 1925. *Ethica Nicomachea.* Trans. W. D. Ross. Volume 9, *The Works of Aristotle.* Oxford: Clarendon Press.

Arnstein, P., M. Caudill, C. Mandle, R. Norris, and R. Beasley, R. 1999. Self-efficacy as a mediator of the relationship between pain intensity, disability and depression in chronic pain patients. *Pain* 80:483–91.

Aspinwall, L. G., and L. Richter. 1999. Optimism and self-mastery predict more rapid disengagement from unsolvable tasks in the presence of alternatives. *Motivation and Emotion* 23:221–45.

Athanassoulis, N. 2000. A response to Harman: Virtue ethics and character traits. *Proceedings of the Aristotelian Society* 100:215–21.

Augustine of Hippo. 408/1888. 7th Homily on 1st John. From *Nicene and post-nicene fathers, First series*, vol. 7. Trans. H. Browne. Edited by P. Schaff. Buffalo, NY: Christian Literature Publishing Company.

Averill, J. R., L. O'Brien, and G. W. DeWitt. 1977. The influence of response effectiveness on the preference for warning and on psychophysiological stress reactions. *Journal of Personality* 45:395–418.

Avorn, J., and E. Langer. 1982. Induced disability in nursing home patients: A controlled trial. *Journal of the American Geriatrics Society* 30:397–400.

Bain, A. 1868. *The senses and the intellect.* 3rd edition. London: Longmans, Green, and Co.

Balsam, P. D., J. D. Deich, T. Ohyama, and D. Stokes.1998. Origins of new behavior. In *Learning and behavior therapy*, ed. W. O'Donohue, 403–20. Boston: Allyn & Bacon.

Bandura, A. 1977. Self-efficacy: Toward a unifying theory of behavioral change. *Psychological Review* 84:191–215.

Bandura, A. 1982. Self-efficacy mechanism in human agency. *American Psychologist* 37:122–47.

Bandura, A. 1989. Human agency in social cognitive theory. *American Psychologist* 44:1175–84.

Bandura, A. 1997. *Self-efficacy: The exercise of control.* New York: W. H. Freeman.

Bandura, A., and D. Cervone. 1983. Self-evaluative and self-efficacy mechanisms governing the motivational effects of goal systems. *Journal of Personality and Social Psychology* 45:1017–28.

Bandura, A., D. Cioffi, C. B. Taylor, and M. E. Brouillard. 1988. Perceived self-efficacy in coping with cognitive stressors and opioid activation. *Journal of Personality and Social Psychology* 55:479–88.

Bandura, A., and D. H. Schunk. 1981. Cultivating competence, self-efficacy, and intrinsic interest through proximal self-motivation. *Journal of Personality and Social Psychology* 41:586–98.

Barash, D. P. 2005. Redirected aggression. CPS Working Papers No. 8:1–12.

Barash, D. P., and J. E. Lipton. 2011. *Payback: Why we retaliate, redirect aggression, and take revenge.* New York: Oxford University Press.

Barrett, W. 1958. Determinism and novelty. In *Determinism and freedom in the age of modern science*, ed. S. Hook, 46–54. New York: New York University Press.

Baumeister, R. F. 2014. Constructing a scientific theory of free will. In *Moral psychology, volume 4: Free will and moral responsibility*, ed. W. Sinnott-Armstrong, 235–55. Cambridge, MA: The MIT Press.

Baumeister, R. F., E. Bratslavasky, M. Muraven, and D. M. Tice. 1998. Ego depletion: Is the active self a limited resource? *Journal of Personality and Social Psychology* 74:1252–65.

Baumeister, R. F., A. W. Crescioni, and J. L. Alquist. 2011. Free will as advanced action control for human social life and culture. *Neuroethics* 4:1–11.

Bazelon, D. L. 1976. The morality of the criminal law. *Southern California Law Review* 49:385–405.

Bazelon, D. L. 1987. *Questioning authority: Justice and criminal law.* New York: Alfred A. Knopf.

Bechara, A., H. Damasio, D. Tranel, and A. R. Damasio. 1997. Deciding advantageously before knowing the advantageous strategy. *Science* 275:1293–5.

Bechara, A., S. Dolan, and A. Hindes. 2002. Decision-making and addiction (Part II): Myopia for the future or hypersensitivity to reward? *Neuropsychologia* 40:1690–705.

Benassi, V. A., P. D. Sweeney, and C. L. Dufour. 1988. Is there a relationship between locus of control orientation and depression? *Journal of Abnormal Psychology* 97:357–66.

Bennett, J. 1974. The conscience of Huckleberry Finn. *Philosophy* 49:123–34.

Beran, M. J., and T. A. Evans. 2012. Language-trained chimpanzees (*Pan troglodytes*) delay gratification by choosing token exchange over immediate reward consumption. *American Journal of Primatology* 74:864–70.

Beran, M. J., and T. A. Evans. 2006. Maintenance of delay of gratification by four chimpanzees (*Pan troglodytes*): The effects of delayed reward visibility, experimenter presence, and extended delay intervals. *Behavioural Processes* 73:315–24.

Beran, M. J., T. A. Evans, F. Paglieri, J. M. McIntyre, E. Addessi, and W. D. Hopkins. 2014. Chimpanzees (*Pan troglodytes*) can wait, when they choose to: A study with the hybrid delay task. *Animal Cognition* 17:197–205.

Von Bergen, C. W., B. Soper, G. T. Rosenthal, S. J. Cox, and R. Fullerton. 1999. Point of view: When helping hurts: Negative effects of benevolent care. *Journal of the American Psychiatric Nurses Association* 5:134–36.

Bjork, J. M., and D. W. Hommer. 2007. Anticipating instrumentally obtained and passively-received rewards: A factorial fMRI investigation. *Behavioural Brain Research* 177:165–70.

Blackstone, W. 1769/1992. *Commentaries on the laws of England.* London: William S. Hein & Co.

Boesch, C. 2012. *Wild cultures: A comparison between chimpanzee and human cultures.* New York: Cambridge University Press.

Botti, S., and S. S. Iyengar. 2004. The psychological pleasure and pain of choosing: When people prefer choosing at the cost of subsequent outcome satisfaction. *Journal of Personality and Social Psychology* 87:312–26.

Botti, S., and S. S. Iyengar. 2006. The dark side of choice: When choice impairs social welfare. *Journal of Public Policy & Marketing* 25:24–38.

Botti, S., K. Orfali, and S. S. Iyengar. 2009. Tragic choices: Autonomy and emotional responses to medical decisions. *Journal of Consumer Research* 36:337–52.

Bowers, K. S. 1968. Pain, anxiety, and perceived control. *Journal of Consulting and Clinical Psychology* 32:596–602.

Bown, N. J., D. Read, and B. Summers. 2003. The lure of choice. *Journal of Behavioral Decision Making* 16:297–308.

Brauer, J., J. Call, and M. Tomasello. 2007. Chimpanzees really know what others can see in a competitive situation. *Animal Cognition* 10:439–48.

Brembs, B. 2010. Towards a scientific concept of free will as a biological trait: Spontaneous actions and decision-making in invertebrates. *Proceedings of the Royal Society B: Biological Sciences.* 1–10. [published online 15 December 2010]

Brembs, B. 2014. *The neurobiology of spontaneity.* Retrieved from http://brembs.net/spontaneous/. Accessed September 1, 2014.

Brenner, L., Y. Rottenstreich, and S. Sood. 1999. Comparison, grouping, and preference. *Psychological Science* 10:225–9.

Brigham, T. A., and J. A. Sherman. 1973. Effects of choice and immediacy of reinforcement on single response and switching behavior of children. *Journal of the Experimental Analysis of Behavior* 19:425–35.

Bronikowski, A. M., and J. Altmann. 1996. Foraging in a variable environment: Weather patterns and the behavioral ecology of baboons. *Behavioral Ecology and Sociobiology* 39:11–25.

Buchanan-Smith, H. M., and I. Badihi. 2012. The psychology of control: Effects of control over supplementary light on welfare of marmosets. *Applied Animal Behaviour Science* 137:166–74.

Burns, K., and A. Bechara. 2007. Decision making and free will: A neuroscience perspective. *Behavioral Sciences and the Law* 25:263–80.

Cacioppo, J. T., and R. E. Petty. 1982. The need for cognition. *Journal of Personality and Social Psychology* 42:116–31.

Cacioppo, J. T., R. E. Petty, J. A. Feinstein, and W. B. G. Jarvis. 1996. Dispositional differences in cognitive motivation: The life and times of individuals varying in need for cognition. *Psychological Bulletin* 119:197–253.

Call, J., B. Hare, M. Carpenter, and M. Tomasello. 2004. "Unwilling" versus "unable": Chimpanzees' understanding of human intentional action. *Developmental Science* 7:488–98.

Call, J., and M. Tomasello. 1998. Distinguishing intentional from accidental actions in orangutans (*Pongo pygmaeus*), chimpanzees (*Pan troglodytes*) and human children (*Homo sapiens*). *Journal of Comparative Psychology* 112:192–206.

Campbell, C. A. 1957. *On selfhood and godhood*. London: George Allen & Unwin, Ltd.

Campbell, D. T. 1960. Blind variation and selective retention in creative thought as in other knowledge processes. *The Psychological Review* 67:380–400.

Campbell, D. T. 1974. Evolutionary epistemology. In *The philosophy of Karl Popper*, ed. P. A. Schilpp, 413–63. LaSalle, IL: Open Court.

Caplan, A. L. 1990. The morality of the mundane: Ethical issues arising in the lives of nursing home residents. In *Everyday ethics: Resolving dilemmas in nursing home life*, eds. R. A. Kane and A. L. Caplan, 37–50. New York: Springer.

Carmon, Z., K. Wertenbroch, and M. Zeelenberg. 2003. Option attachment: When deliberating makes choosing feel like losing. *Journal of Consumer Research* 30:15–29.

Caruso, G. D. 2012. *Free will and consciousness: A determinist account of the illusion of free will*. Lanham, MD: Lexington Books.

Catania, A. C. 1975. Freedom and knowledge: An experimental analysis of preference in pigeons. *Journal of the Experimental Analysis of Behavior* 24:89–106.

Catania, A. C. 1980. Freedom of choice: A behavioral analysis. In *The psychology of learning and motivation*, vol. 14, ed. G. H. Bower, 97–145. New York: Academic Press.

Catania, A. C., and T. Sagvolden. 1980. Preference for free choice over forced choice in pigeons. *Journal of the Experimental Analysis of Behavior* 34:77–86.

Cerutti, D., and C. A. Catania. 1997. Pigeons' preference for free choice: Number of keys versus key area over forced choice in pigeons. *Journal of the Experimental Analysis of Behavior* 68:340–56.

Chernev, A. 2003. When more is less and less is more: The role of ideal point availability and assortment in consumer choice. *Journal of Consumer Research* 30:170–83.

Cherot, C., A. Jones, and A. Neuringer. 1996. Reinforced variability decreases with approach to reinforcers. *Journal of Experimental Psychology: Animal Behavior Processes* 22:497–508.

Chisholm, R. 1964. Human freedom and the self. The Lindley Lecture, University of Kansas. Reprinted in *Free will*, ed. G. Watson. New York: Oxford University Press, 1982.

Clark, C. J., J. B. Liguri, P. H. Ditto, J. Knobe, A. F. Shariff, and R. F. Baumeister. 2014. Free to punish: A motivated account of free will belief. *Journal of Personality and Social Psychology* 106:501–13.

Corah, N. L., and J. Boffa. 1970. Perceived control, self-observation, and response to aversive stimulation. *Journal of Personality and Social Psychology* 16:1–4.

Cotton, M. 2005. A foolish consistency: Keeping determinism out of the criminal law. *Public Interest Law Journal* 15:1–48.

Dalbert, C., and L. Yamauchi. 1994. Belief in a just world and attitudes toward immigrants and foreign workers: a cultural comparison between Hawaii and Germany. *Journal of Applied Social Psychology* 24:1612–26.

Damasio, A. R. 1994. *Descartes' error: Emotion, reason, and the human brain.* New York: G. P. Putnam's Sons.

Danziger, S., J. Levav, and L. Avnaim-Pesso. 2011. Extraneous factors in judicial decisions. *Proceedings of the National Academy of Sciences* 108:6889–992.

Darley, J. M., and C. D. Batson. 1973. From Jerusalem to Jericho: A study of situational and dispositional variables in helping behavior. *Journal of Personality and Social Psychology* 267:100–8.

Dennett, D. C. 1978. *Brainstorms.* Montgomery, VT: Bradford Books.

Dennett, D. C. 1984. *Elbow room.* Cambridge, MA: MIT Press.

Dennett, D. C. 1995. *Darwin's dangerous idea: Evolution and the meanings of life.* New York: Simon & Schuster.

Dennett, D. C. 2003. *Freedom evolves.* New York: Viking.

Denney, J., and A. Neuringer. 1998. Behavioral variability is controlled by discriminative stimuli. *Animal Learning and Behavior* 26:154–62.

Descartes, R. 1641/1960. *Meditations on first philosophy*, trans. L. J. Lafleur. Englewood Cliffs, NJ: Prentice-Hall.

Devins, G. M., Y. M. Binik, P. Gorman, M. Dattel., B. McCloskey, G. Oscar, and J. Briggs. 1982. Perceived self-efficacy, outcome expectancies, and negative mood states in end-stage renal disease. *Journal of Abnormal Psychology* 91:241–4.

Devins, G. M., Y. M. Binik, D. J. Hollomby, P. E. Barre, and R. D. Guttmann. 1981. Helplessness and depression in end-stage renal disease. *Journal of Abnormal Psychology* 90:531–45.

Devins, G. M., Y. M. Binik, T. A. Hutchinson, D. J. Hollomby, P. E. Barre, and R. D. Guttmann. 1984. The emotional impact of end-stage renal disease: Importance of patients' perceptions of intrusiveness and control. *International Journal of Psychiatry in Medicine* 13:327–43.

Doris, J. M. 2002. *Lack of character: Personality and moral behavior.* Cambridge: Cambridge University Press.

Dostoyevsky, F. 1864/1961. *Notes from underground.* Trans. Andrew R. MacAndrew. New York: New American Library.

Double, R. 1991. *The non-reality of free will.* New York: Oxford University Press.

Dworkin, G. 1988. *The theory and practice of autonomy.* Cambridge: Cambridge University Press.

Eckerman, D. A., and R. N. Lanson. 1969. Variability of response location for pigeons responding under continuous reinforcement, intermittent reinforcement, and extinction. *Journal for the Experimental Analysis of Behavior* 12:73–80.

Englich, B., T. Mussweiler, and F. Strack. 2006. Playing dice with criminal sentences: The influence of irrelevant anchors on experts' judicial decision making. *Personality and Social Psychology Bulletin* 32:188–200.

Epictetus. 107/1865. *The works of Epictetus*, trans. Thomas Wentworth Higginson. Boston: Little, Brown.

Evans, T. A., and M. J. Beran. 2007. Chimpanzees use self-distraction to cope with impulsivity. *Biology Letters* 3:599–602.

Evans, T. A., B. M. Perdue, A. E. Parrish, and M. J. Beran. 2014. Working and waiting for better rewards: Self-control in two monkey species (*Cebus apella* and *Macca mulatta*). *Behavioral Processes* 103:236–42.

Fallon, J. 2013. *The psychopath inside: A neuroscientist's personal journey into the dark side of the brain.* New York: Penguin.

Feigl, H. 1950. "De principiis non disputandum . . .?" On the meaning and limits of justification. In *Philosophical analysis*, ed. M. Black, 119–56. Ithaca, NY: Cornell University Press.

Feigl, H. 1952. Validation and vindication. In *Readings in ethical theory*, eds. C. Sellars and J. Hospers, 667–80. New York: Appleton-Century-Crofts.

Ferraro, D. P., and K. H. Branch. 1968. Variability of response location during regular and partial reinforcement. *Psychological Report* 23:1023–31.

Ferster, C. B., and B. F. Skinner. 1957. *Schedules of reinforcement.* New York: Appleton-Century-Crofts.

Finke, R. A., T. B. Ward, and S. M. Smith. 1992. *Creative cognition: Theory, research, and applications.* Cambridge, MA: MIT Press.

Fischer, J. M. 1994. *The metaphysics of free will: An essay on control.* Oxford: Blackwell.

Fischer, J. M. 2006. *My way: Essays on moral responsibility.* New York: Oxford University Press.

Fischer, J. M. 2007. Compatibilism. In *Four views on free will*, eds, J. M. Fischer, R. Kane, D. Pereboom, and M. Vargas, 44–84. Malden, MA: Blackwell Publishing.

Fischer, J. M. 2009. *Our stories: Essays of life, death, and free will.* New York: Oxford University Press.

Fischer, J. M. 2012. *Deep control: Essays on free will and value.* New York: Oxford University Press.

Fisher, W. W., R. H. Thompson, C. C. Piazza, K. Crosland, and D. Gotjen. 1997. On the relative reinforcing effects of choice and differential consequences. *Journal of Applied Behavior Analysis* 30:423–38.

Fouts, R. 1997. *Next of kin: What chimpanzees have taught me about who we are.* New York: William Morrow.

Frankfurt, H. G. 1969. Alternate possibilities and moral responsibility. *The Journal of Philosophy* 66:829–39.

Frankfurt, H. G. 1971. Freedom of the will and the concept of a person. *The Journal of Philosophy* 68:5–20.

Frede, M. 2011. *A free will: Origins of the notion in ancient thought.* Berkeley, CA: University of California Press.

Furnham, A. 2003. Belief in a just world: Research progress over the past decade. *Personality and Individual Differences* 34:795–817.

Furnham, A., and B. Gunter. 1984. Just world beliefs and attitudes towards the poor. *British Journal of Social Psychology* 15:265–69.

Garland, E. C., et al. 2011. Dynamic horizontal cultural transmission of humpback whale song at the ocean basic scale. *Current Biology* 21:687–91.

Gaylin, W. 1982. *The killing of Bonnie Garland.* New York: Simon and Schuster.

Gazzaniga, M. S. 1985. *The social brain.* New York: Basic Books.

Gazzaniga, M. S. 2014. Mental life and responsibility in real time with a determined brain. In *Moral psychology, volume 4: Free will and moral responsibility*, ed. W. Sinnott-Armstrong, 59–74. Cambridge, MA: The MIT Press.

Geertz, C. 1984. Anti-anti-relativism. *American Anthropologist* 86:263–78.

Geertz, C. 2000. *Available light: Anthropological reflections on philosophical topics.* Princeton, NJ: Princeton University Press.

Genty, E., and J.-J. Roeder. 2006. Self-control: Why should sea lions, *Zalophus Californianus*, perform better than primates? *Animal Behaviour* 72:1241–7.

Glannon, W. 1998. Responsibility, alcoholism, and liver transplantation. *Journal of Medicine and Philosophy* 23:31–49.

Goodall, J. 1990. *Through a window: My thirty years with the chimpanzees of Gombe.* Boston: Houghton Mifflin.

Gould, S. J. 1977. *Ever since Darwin: Reflections in natural history.* New York: American Museum of Natural History.

Greenwald, A. G. 1980. The totalitarian ego: Fabrication and revision of personal history. *American Psychologist* 35:603–18.

Grob, A., T. D. Little, B. Wanner, and A. J. Wearing. 1996. Adolescent's well-being and perceived control across 14 sociocultural contexts. *Journal of Personality and Social Psychology* 71:785–95.

Haidt, J. 2001. The emotional dog and its rational tail: A social intuitionist approach to moral judgment. *Psychological Review* 108:814–34.

Haidt, J. 2007. The new synthesis in moral psychology. *Science* 316:998–1002.

Haidt, J. 2012. *The righteous mind.* New York: Pantheon.

Haidt, J., and F. Bjorklund. 2007. Social intuitionists answer six questions about morality. In *Moral psychology*, vol. 2: *The cognitive science of morality*, ed. W. Sinnott-Armstrong, 181–217. Cambridge, MA: MIT Press.

Haidt, J., and J. Rodin. 1999. Control and efficacy as interdisciplinary bridges. *Review of General Psychology* 3:317–37.

Hanson, J. D., M. E. Larson, and C. T. Snowdon. 1976. The effects of control over high intensity noise on plasma cortisol levels in rhesus monkeys. *Behavioral Biology* 16:333–40.

Hare, B. 2014. Is human free will prisoner to primate, ape, and hominim preferences and biases? In *Moral psychology, volume 4: Free will and moral responsibility*, ed. W. Sinnott-Armstrong, 361–6. Cambridge, MA: MIT Press.

Hare, B., J. Call, and M. Tomasello. 2000. Chimpanzees know what conspecifics do and do not see. *Animal Behaviour* 59:771–85.

Hare, B., J. Call, and M. Tomasello. 2001. Do chimpanzees know what conspecifics know? *Animal Behavior* 61:139–51.

Hare, B., J. Call, and M. Tomasello. 2006. Chimpanzees deceive a human competitor by hiding. *Cognition* 101:495–514.

Harman, Gilbert. 1999. Moral philosophy meets social psychology: Virtue ethics and the fundamental attribution error. *Proceedings of the Aristotelian Society* 99:315–32.

Harper, D., and P. Manasse. 1992. The just world and the third world: British explanations for poverty abroad. *Journal of Social Psychology* 132:783–5.

Hatch, E. 1997. The good side of relativism. *Journal of Anthropological Research* 53:371–81.

Hayden, B. Y., and M. L. Platt. 2007. Animal cognition: Great apes wait for grapes. *Current Biology* 17:922–3.

Heckhausen, J., and R. Schulz. 1993. A life-span theory of control. *Psychological Review* 102:284–304.

Heckhausen, J., C. Wrosch, and R. Schulz. 2010. A motivational theory of life-span development. *Psychological Review* 117:32–60.

Herzog, W. R. 1994. *Parables as subversive speech: Jesus as pedagogue of the oppressed.* Louisville, KY: Westminster John Knox Press.

Hill, H. F., et al. 1990. Self-administration of morphine in bone marrow transplant patients reduces drug requirement. *Pain* 40:121–9.

Hill, H. F., A. M. Mackie, B. A. Coda, K. Iverson, and C. R. Chapman. 1991. Patient-controlled analgesic administration: A comparison of steady-state morphine infusions with bolus doses. *Cancer* 67:873–82.

Hillemann, F., T. Bugnyar, K. Kotrschal, and C. A. F. Wascher. 2014. Waiting for better, not for more: Corvids respond to quality in two delay maintenance tasks. *Animal Behaviour* 90:1–10.

Hotelling, H. 1929. Stability in competition. *The Economic Journal* 39:41–57.

Hume, D. 1738. *A treatise of human nature.* London.

Inesi, M. E., S. Botti, D. Dubois, D. D. Rucker, and A. D. Galinsky. Power and choice: Their dynamic interplay in quenching the thirst for personal control. *Psychological Science* 22:1042–48.

Iqbal, M. 1990/2000. *Tulip in the desert: A selection of the poetry of Muhammad Iqbal.* Edited and translated by Mustansir Mir. McGill Queens University Press.

Isen, A. M., and P. F. Levin. 1972. Effect of feeling good on helping: Cookies and kindness. *Journal of Personality and Social Psychology* 21:384–88.

Iyengar, S. S., W. Jiang, and E. Kamenica. 2006. The psychological costs of ever increasing choice: A fallback to the sure bet. Working paper, Graduate School of Business, Management Department, Columbia University.

Iyengar, S. S., and M. R. Lepper. 2000. When choice is demotivating: Can one desire too much of a good thing? *Journal of Personality and Social Psychology* 79:995–1006.

Iyengar, S. S., R. E. Wells, and B. Schwartz. 2006. Doing better but feeling worse: Looking for the "best" job undermines satisfaction. *Psychological Science* 17:143–50.

Jacobson, J. W., J. A. Mulick, and A. A. Schwartz. 1995. A history of facilitated communication: Science, pseudoscience, and anti-science. *American Psychologist* 50:750–65.

James, W. 1897. The will to believe. In *The will to believe and other essays in popular philosophy.* New York: Longmans, Green & Co.

James, W. 1907. *Pragmatism: A new name for some old ways of thinking.* New York: Longmans, Green & Co.

Joekes, K., T. Van Elderen, and K. Schreurs. 2007. Self-efficacy and overprotection are related to quality of life, psychological well-being and self-management in cardiac patients. *Journal of Health Psychology* 12:4–16.

Joffe, J. M., R. A. Rawson, J. A. Mulick. 1973. Control of their environment reduces emotionality in rats. *Science* 180:1383–84.

Kadish, S. H. 1968. The decline of innocence. *The Cambridge Law Journal* 26:273–90.

Kadish, S. H. 1987. *Blame and punishment: Essays in criminal law.* New York: Collier Macmillan.

Kahneman, D. 2011. *Thinking, fast and slow.* New York: Farrar, Straus and Giroux.

Kamen-Siegel, L., J. Rodin, M. E. P. Seligman, and J. Dwyer, J. 1991. Explanatory style and cell-mediated immunity in elderly men and women. *Health Psychology* 10:229–35.

Kametekar, R. 2004. Situationism and virtue ethics on the content of our character. *Ethics* 114:458–91.

Kaminski, J., J. Call, and M. Tomasello. 2008. Chimpanzees know what others know, but not what they believe. *Cognition* 109:224–34.

Kane, R. 1985. *Free will and values.* Albany, New York: State University of New York Press.

Kane, R. 1988. Free will and responsibility: Comments on Waller's review. *Behaviorism* 16:159–65.

Kane, R. 1996. *The significance of free will.* New York: Oxford University Press.

Kane, R. 2007. Libertarianism. In *Four views on free will,* eds. J. M. Fischer, R. Kane, D. Pereboom, and M. Vargas, 5–43. Oxford: Blackwell Publishing.

Kavanau, J. L. 1963. Compulsory regime and control of environment in animal behavior. 1. Wheel-running. *Behavior* 20:251–81.

Kavanau, J. L. 1967. Behavior of captive white-footed mice. *Science* 155:1623–39.

Kawamura, S. 1967. Aggression as studied in troops of Japanese monkeys. In *Aggression and defense: Brain function,* eds. C. Clemente and D. Lindsley, 195–224. Berkeley: University of California Press.

Kirchmeier, J. L. 2004. A tear in the eye of the law: Mitigating factors and the progression toward a disease theory of criminal justice. *Oregon Law Review* 83:631–730.

Knobe, J., and J. Doris. 2010. Responsibility. In *The moral psychology handbook,* ed. J. Doris, 321–54. New York: Oxford University Press.

Korsgaard, C. M. 2006. Morality and the distinctiveness of human action. In *Primates and philosophers: How morality evolved,* ed. F. de Waal, 98–119. Princeton, NJ: Princeton University Press.

Krutch, J. W. 1967. Epitaph for an age. *New York Times Magazine,* June 30, 1967.

Kuhn, T. 1962. *The structure of scientific revolutions.* Chicago: University of Chicago Press.

Kunzmann, U., T. Little, and J. Smith, J. 2002. Perceiving control: A double-edged sword in old age. *The Journals of Gerontology Series B: Psychological Sciences and Social Sciences* 57:484–91.

Lachman, M. E., and S. L. Weaver. 1998. The sense of control as a moderator of social class differences in health and well-being. *Journal of Personality and Social Psychology* 74:763–73.

Lang, F. R., and J. Heckhausen. 2001. Perceived control over development and sub-jective well-being: Differential benefits across adulthood. *Journal of Personality and Social Psychology* 81:509–23.

Langer, E. J., and J. Rodin. 1976. The efforts of choice and enhanced personal responsibilities for the aged: A field experiment in an institutional setting. *Journal of Personality and Social Psychology* 34:191–8.

Langer, E. J., I. L. Janis, and J. A. Wolfer. 1975. Reduction of psychological stress in surgical patients. *Journal of Experimental Social Psychology* 11:155–65.

Langton, R. 1992. Duty and desolation. *Philosophy* 67:481–505.

Leotti, L. A., and M. R. Delgado. 2011. The inherent reward of choice. *Psychological Science* 22:1310–8.

Leotti, L. A., S. S. Iyengar, and K. N. Ochsner. 2010. Born to choose: The origins and value of the need for control. *Trends in Cognitive Sciences* 14:457–63.

Lerner, M. J. 1980. *The belief in a just world: A fundamental delusion.* New York: Plenum Press.

Lerner, M. J., and D. T. Miller. 1978. Just world research and the attribution process: Looking ahead and back. *Psychological Bulletin* 85:1030–51.

Levy, N. 2011. *Hard luck: How luck undermines free will and moral responsibility.* New York: Oxford University Press.

Lewis, C. S. 1970. The humanitarian theory of punishment. In *Undeceptions.* London: Curtis Brown.

Logue, A. W. 1988. Research on self-control: An integrating framework. *Behavioral and Brain Sciences* 11:665–79.

Luther, M. 1525/1823. *The Bondage of the will*, trans. H. P. Cole. London.

Mackie, A. M., B. C. Coda, and H. F. Hill. 1991. Adolescents use patient-controlled analgesia effectively for relief from prolonged oropharyngeal mucositis pain. *Pain* 46:265–69.

March, J. G. 1991. Exploration and exploitation in organizational learning. *Organization Science* 2:71–87.

Maye, A., C.-H. Hsieh, G. Sugihara, and B. Brembs. 2007. Order in spontaneous behavior. *PloS one* 2:e443.

McKenna, M. 2008. Ultimacy and Sweet Jane. In *Essay on free will and moral responsibility*, eds. N. Trakakis and D. Cohen, 186–208. Newcastle upon Tyne: Cambridge Scholars Publishing.

McNaughton, M. E., L. W. Smith, T. L. Patterson, and I. Grant. 1990. Stress, social support, coping resources, and immune status in elderly women. *Journal of Nervous & Mental Disease* 178:460–1.

Mele, A. R. 1995. *Autonomous agents.* New York: Oxford University Press.

Mele, A. R. 2006. *Free will and luck.* New York: Oxford University Press.

Mencius. 1970. *Mencius.* Trans. D. C. Lau. New York: Penguin Books.

Metz, T. 2006. Judging because understanding: A defence of retributive censure. In *Judging and understanding: Essays on free will, narrative, meaning and the ethical limits of condemnation*, ed. P. A. Tabensky, 221–40. Burlington, VT: Ashgate.

Milgram, S. 1963. Behavioral study of obedience. *Journal of Abnormal and Social Psychology* 67:371–8.

Millenson, J. R., H. M. B. Hurwitz, and W. L. B. Nixon. 1961. Influence of reinforcement schedules on response duration. *Journal of the Experimental Analysis of Behavior* 4:243–50.

Mineka, S., M. Gunnar, and M. Chapoux. 1986. Control and early socioemotional development: Infant rhesus monkey reared in controllable versus uncontrollable environment. *Child Development* 57:1241–56.

Mirowsky, J., and C. E. Ross. 1990. Control or defense? Depression and the sense of control over good and bad outcomes. *Journal of Health and Social Behavior* 31:71–86.

Mischel, W., and E. B. Ebbesen. 1970. Attention in delay of gratification. *Journal of Personality and Social Psychology* 16:329–37.

Mischel, W., E. B. Ebbesen, and A. R. Zeiss. 1972. Cognitive and attentional mechanisms in delay of gratification. *Journal of Personality and Social Psychology* 21:204–18.

Mischel, W., Y. Shoda, and P. K. Peake. 1988. The nature of adolescent competencies predicted by preschool delay of gratification. *Journal of Personality and Social Psychology* 54:687–96.

Montada, L. 1998. Belief in a just world: A hybrid of justice motive and self-interest. In *Responses to victimizations and belief in the just world*, eds. L. Montada and M. Lerner, 217–45. New York: Plenum.

Montmarquet, J. 2003. Moral character and social science research. *Philosophy* 78:355–68.

Moore, G. E. 1912. *Ethics*. London: Oxford University Press.

Moore, M. S. 1985. Causation and the excuses. *California Law Review* 73:1091–149.

Moore, M. S. 1997. *Placing blame: A general theory of the criminal law*. Oxford: Oxford University Press.

Morling, B., and S. Evered. 2006. Secondary control reviewed and defined. *Psychological Bulletin* 132:269–296.

Morris, H. 1968. Persons and punishment. *The Monist* 52:475–501.

Morris, J., and G. T. Royale. 1988. Offering patients a choice of surgery for early breast cancer: A reduction in anxiety and depression in patients and their husbands. *Social Science & Medicine* 26:583–5.

Morse, S. J. 1984. Undiminished confusion in diminished capacity. *Journal of Criminal Law and Criminology* 75:1–55.

Morse, S. J. 1996. Brain and blame. *Georgetown Law Journal* 84:527–49.

Mostert, M. P. 2001. Facilitated communication since 1995: A review of published studies. *Journal of Autism and Developmental Disorders* 313:287–313.

Mucalhy, N., and J. Call. 2006. Apes save tools for future use. *Science* 312:1038–40.

Murray, D., and E. Nahmias. 2014. Explaining away incompatibilist intuitions. *Philosophy and Phenomenological Research* 88:434–67.

Nadelhoffer, T. 2011. The threat of shrinking agency and free will disillusionism. In *Conscious will and responsibility*, eds. W. Sinnott-Armstrong and L. Nadel, 173–88. New York: Oxford University Press.

Nadelhoffer, T., and D. G. Tocchetto. 2013. The potential dark side of believing in free will (and related concepts). In *Exploring the illusion of free will and moral responsibility*, ed. G. D. Caruso, 121–40. Lanham, MD: Lexington.

Nahmias, E. 2006. Folk fears about freedom and responsibility: Determinism vs. reductionism. *Journal of Cognition and Culture* 6:215–37.

Nahmias, E. 2011. Intuitions about free will, determinism, and bypassing. In *The Oxford handbook on free will*, 2nd edition, ed. R. Kane, 555–75. New York: Oxford University Press.

Nahmias, E. 2014a. Is free will an illusion? In *Moral psychology, volume 4, free will and moral responsibility*, ed. W. Sinnott-Armstrong, 1–25. Cambridge, MA: MIT Press.

Nahmias, E. 2014b. Response to Misilroy and Haggard and to Björnsson and Pereboom. In *Moral psychology, volume 4, free will and moral responsibility*, ed. W. Sinnott-Armstrong, 43–57. Cambridge, MA: MIT Press.

Nelkin, D. K. 2011. *Making sense of freedom and responsibility*. New York: Oxford University Press.

Neuringer, A. 2004. Reinforced variability in animals and people: Implications for adaptive action. *American Psychologist* 59:891–906.

Nichols, S. 2006. Folk intuitions on free will. *Journal of Cognition and Culture* 6:57–86.

Nichols, S. 2011. Experimental philosophy and the problem of free will. *Science* 33:1401–3.

Nichols, S. 2013. Free will and error. In *Exploring the illusion of free will and moral responsibility*, ed. G. D. Caruso, 203–218. Lanham, MD: Lexington Books.

Nichols, S., and J. Knobe. 2007. Moral responsibility and determinism: The cognitive science of folk intuitions. *Nous* 41:663–85.

Nietzsche, F. 1889/1954. *Twilight of the idols*, trans. W. Kaufmann. New York: Penguin Books.

Noad, M. J., D. H. Cato, M. M. Bryden, M. -N. Jenner, and K. C. S. Jenner. 2000. Cultural evolution in whale songs. *Nature* 408:537.

Northcraft, G. B., and M. A. Neale. 1987. Experts, amateurs, and real estate: An anchoring and adjustment perspective on property pricing decisions. *Organizational Behavior and Human Decision Processes* 39:84–97.

O'Connor, T. 2005. Freedom with a human face. *Midwest Studies in Philosophy* 29: 207–27.

Osberg, T. 1987. The convergent and discriminant validity of need for cognition scale. *Journal of Personality Assessment* 51:441–50.

Osvath, M. 2009. Spontaneous planning for future stone throwing by a male chimpanzee. *Current Biology* 9:R190–R191.

Owen, M. A, R. R. Swasigood, N. M. Czekala, and D. G. Lindburg. 2005. Enclosure choice and well-being in Giant Pandas: Is it all about control? *Zoo Biology* 24:475–81.

Packer, H. L. 1968. *The limits of the criminal sanction*. Stanford, CA: Stanford University Press.

Parrish, A. E., B. M. Perdue, E. E. Stromberg, A. E. Bania, T. A. Evans, and M. J. Beran. 2014. Delay of gratification by orangutans (*Pongo pygmaeus*) in the accumulation task. *Journal of Comparative Psychology* 128:209–14.

Patall, E. A., H. Cooper, and J. C. Robinson. 2008. The effects of choice on intrinsic motivation and related outcomes: A meta-analysis of research findings. *Psychological Bulletin* 34:270–300.

Pennebaker, J. W., M. A. Burnam,, M. A. Schaeffer, and D. C. Harper. 1977. Lack of control as a determinant of perceived physical symptoms. *Journal of Personality and Social Psychology* 35:167–74.

Perdue, B. M., T. A. Evans, D. A. Washburn, D. M. Rumbaugh, and M. J. Beran. 2014. Do monkeys choose to choose? *Learning & Behavior* 42:164–75.

Pereboom, D. 2001. *Living without free will*. New York: Cambridge University Press.

Pereboom, D. 2014. *Free will, agency, and meaning in life*. New York: Oxford University Press.

Pico della Mirandola, G. 1486/1948. Oration on the Dignity of Man, trans. Elizabeth Livermore Forbes. In *The renaissance philosophy of man*, eds. E. Cassirer, P. O. Kristeller, and J. H. Randall, 223–54. Chicago: University of Chicago Press.

Popper, K. R. 1959. *The logic of scientific discovery*. London: Hutchinson; New York: Basic Books.

Popper, K. R. 1963. *Conjectures and refutations*. London: Routledge & Kegan Paul; New York: Basic Books.

Popper, K. R. 1972. *Objective knowledge: An evolutionary approach*. Oxford: Clarendon Press.

Potegal, M. 1994. Aggressive arousal: The amygdala connection. In *The dynamics of aggression: Biological and Social processes in dyads and groups*, eds. Michael Potegal and John F. Knutson, 73–112. Hillsdale, NJ: Lawrence Erlbaum Associates.

Premack, D., and G. Woodruff. 1978. Does the chimpanzee have a theory of mind? *Behavioral and Brain Sciences* 1:515–26.

Proctor, R. A. 1992. Selecting an appropriate strategy: A structure creative decision support method, *Marketing Intelligence & Planning* 10:21–4.

Queitsch, C., T. A. Sangster, S. Lindquist. 2002. Hsp90 as a capacitor of phenotypic variation. *Nature* 417:618–24.

Raichle, M. E. 2010. Two Views of Brain Function. *Trends in Cognitive Science.* 14:180–90.

Reed, D. D., B. A. Kaplan, and A. T. Brewer. 2012. Discounting the freedom to choose: Implications for the paradox of choice. *Behavioural Processes* 90:424–7.

Reesor, K. A., and K. P. Craig. 1987. Medically incongruent chronic back pain: Physical limitations, suffering, and ineffective coping. *Pain* 32:35–45.

Reichenbach, H. 1951. *The rise of scientific philosophy*. Berkeley: The University of California Press.

Roberts, S., and A. Gharib. 2006. Variation of bar-press duration: Where do new responses come from? *Behavioural Processes* 72:215–23.

Rodin, J. 1986. Aging and health: Effects of the sense of control. *Science* 233:1271–76.

Rodin, J., K. Rennert, and S. K. Solomon. 1980. Intrinsic motivation for control: Fact or fiction? In *Advances in environmental psychology*, eds. A. Baum and J. E. Singer, 131–47. Hillsdale, NJ: Earlbaum.

Rodin, J., and C. Timko. 1992. Sense of control, aging, and health. In *Aging, health, and behavior*, eds. M. G. Ory, R. P. Abeles, and P. D. Lipman, 174–206. Newbury Park, CA: Sage Publications.

Rorty, R. 1989. Solidarity. In *Contingency, irony, and solidarity*, 189–98. Cambridge: Cambridge University Press.

Rorty, R. 1993. Putnam and the relativist menace. *Journal of Philosophy* 90:443–61.

Rosati, A. G., J. R. Stevens, B. Hare, and M. D. Hauser. 2007. The evolutionary origins of human patience: Temporal preferences in chimpanzees, bonobos, and human adults. *Current Biology* 17:1663–8.

Roskies, A. L. 2014. Can neuroscience resolve issues about free will? In *Moral psychology, volume 4, free will and moral responsibility*, ed. W. Sinnott-Armstrong, 103–26. Cambridge, MA: MIT Press.

Ross, M. 1989. Relation of implicit theories to the construction of personal histories. *Psychological Review* 96:341–57.

Ross, S. R. 2006. Issues of choice and control in the behaviour of a pair of captive polar bears (*Ursus maritimus*). *Behavioural Processes* 73:117–20.

Rost, K. A., N. S. Hemmes, and A. M. Alvero. 2014. Effects of the relative values of alternatives on preference for free-choice in humans. *Journal of the Experimental Analysis of Behavior* 102:241–51.

Rothenberg, A. 1986. Artistic creation as stimulated by superimposed versus combine-composite visual images. *Journal of Personality and Social Psychology* 50:370–81.

Rotter, J. B. 1966. Generalized expectancies for internal versus external control of reinforcement. *Psychological Monographs 80* (Whole No. 609).

Rotter, J. B. 1975. Some problems and misconceptions related to the construct of internal vs. external control of reinforcement. *Journal of Consulting and Clinical Psychology* 43:56–67.

Rotter, J. B. 1979. Individual differences and perceived control. In *Choice and perceived control,* eds. L. C. Perlmuter and R. A. Monty, 263–9. Mahwah, N.J.: Lawrence Erlbaum Associates.

Rotter, J. B. 1990. Internal versus external control of reinforcement: A case history of a variable. *American Psychologist* 45:489–93.

Rowlands, M. 2012. *Can animals be moral?* New York: Oxford University Press.

Ruse, M. 1986. *Taking Darwin seriously*. Oxford: Basil Blackwell.

Rutherford, S. L., and S. Lindquist. 1998. Hsp90 as a capacitor of morphological evolution. *Nature* 396:336–42.

Sagi, A., and N. Friedland. 2007. The cost of richness: The effect of the size and diversity of decision sets on post-decision regret. *Journal of Personality and Social Psychology* 93:515–24.

Sangster, T., S. Lindquist, and C. Queitsch. 2004. Under cover causes, effects and implications of Hsp90-mediated genetic capacitance. *Bioessays* 26: 348–362.

Sartre, J.-P. 1946/1989. Existentialism is a humanism, trans. Philip Mairet. In *Existentialism from Dostoyevsky to Sartre*, ed. Walter Kaurmann, 345–68. New York: Meridian.

Scalia, A. 2002. God's justice and ours. *First Things: The Journal of Religion and Public Life* 123:17–21.

Schlick, M. 1939. When is a man responsible? Trans. D. Rynin. In *Problems of ethics*, 141–58. New York: Prentice-Hall.

Schorr, D, and J. Rodin. 1982. The role of perceived control in practitioner-patient relationships. In *Basic processes in helping relationships*, ed. T. A. Wills, 155–86. New York: Academic Press.

Schulz, R. 1976. Effects of control and predictability on the physical and psychological well-being of the institutionalized aged. *Journal of Personality and Social Psychology* 36:1194–201.

Schulz, R., and B. H. Hanusa. 1978. Long-term effects of control and predictability-enhancing interventions: findings and ethical issues. *Journal of Personality and Social Psychology* 36:1194–201.

Schulz, R., J. Heckhausen, and A. T. O'Brien. 1994. Control and the disablement process in the elderly. *Journal of Social Behavior and Personality* 9:139–52.

Schunk, D. H. 1981. Modeling and attributional effects on children's achievement: a self-efficacy analysis. *Journal of Educational Psychology* 73:93–105.

Schwartz, B. 1982. Interval and ratio reinforcement of a complex sequential operant in pigeons. *Journal of the Experimental Analysis of Behavior* 37:349–57.

Seligman, M. E. P. 1975. *Helplessness: On depression, development, and death.* New York: W. H. Freeman.

Sher, G. 1987. *Desert.* Princeton, NJ: Princeton University Press.

Sher, G. 2009. *Who knew? Responsibility without awareness.* New York: Oxford University Press.

Silver, R. L., and C. B. Wortman. 1980. Coping with undesirable life events. In *Human helplessness: Theory and applications*, eds. J. Garber and M. E. P. Seligman, 279–340. New York: Academic Press.

Simonton, D. K. 2011. Creativity and Discovery as blind variation: Campbell's (1960) BVSR model after the half-century mark. *Review of General Psychology* 15:158–74.

Simonton, D. K. 2013. Creative thoughts as acts of free will: A two-stage formal integration. *Review of General Psychology* 17:374–83.

Singer, P. 1981. *The expanding circle: Ethics, evolution, and moral progress.* New York: Farrar, Strauss, and Giroux.

Singh, D. 1970. Preference for bar pressing to obtain reward over freeloading in rats and children. *Journal of Comparative and Physiological Psychology* 73:320–7.

Skevington, S. M. 1983. Chronic pain and depression: Universal or personal helplessness? *Pain* 15:309–17.

Skinner, B. F. 1953. *Science and human behavior.* New York: The Macmillan Company.

Skinner, E. A. 2007. Secondary control critiqued: Is it secondary? Is it control? Comment on Morling and Everent (2006). *Psychological Bulletin* 133:911–16.

Smith, A. 1759. *The theory of moral sentiments.* D. D. Raphael and A. L. Macfie, eds. Oxford: Oxford University Press, 1976.

Smith, A. M. 2008. Control, responsibility, and moral assessment. *Philosophical Studies*, 138:367–92.

Smith, M. D., P. J. Haas, and R. G. Belcher. 1994. Facilitated communication: The effects of facilitator knowledge and level of assistance on output. *Journal of Autism and Developmental Disorders* 24:357–67.

Snyder, A., J. Mitchell, S. Ellwood, A. Yates, and G. Pallier. 2004. Nonconscious idea generation. *Psychological Reports* 94:1325–30.

Sobel, R. S., and A. Rothenberg. 1980. Artistic creation as stimulated by superimposed versus separated visual images. *Journal of Personality and Social Psychology* 39:953–61.

Sommers, T. 2010. Experimental philosophy and free will. *Philosophy Compass* 5:199–212.

Sommers, T. 2012. *Relative justice: Cultural diversity, free will, and moral responsibility*. Princeton, NJ: Princeton University Press.

Sreenivasan, G. 2002. Errors about errors: Virtue theory and trait attribution. *Mind* 111:47–68.

Stahlman, W. D., and A. P. Blaisdell. 2011. Reward probability and the variability of foraging behavior in rats. *International Journal of Comparative Psychology* 24:168–76.

Stahlman, W. D., S. Roberts, and A. P. Blaisdell. 2010. Effect of reward probability on spatial and temporal variation. *Journal of Experimental Psychology: Animal Behavior Processes* 36:77–91.

Staub, E., B. Tursky, and G. E. Schwartz. 1971. Self-control and predictability: Their effects on reactions to aversive stimulation. *Journal of Personality and Social Psychology* 18:157–62.

Stetler, R. 2007. The mystery of mitigation: What jurors need to make a reasoned moral response in capital sentencing. *University of Pennsylvania Journal of Law and Social Change* 11:237–64.

Strawson, G. 1986. *Freedom and Belief*. Oxford: Clarendon Press.

Stump, E. 2006. Augustine on free will. In *The Cambridge companion to Augustine*, eds. D. V. Meconi and E. Stump, 166–86. Cambridge: Cambridge University Press.

Suhler, C. L., and Churchland, P. S. 2009. Control: Conscious and otherwise. *Trends in Cognitive Sciences* 13:341–7.

Suzuki, S. 1997. Effects of number of alternatives on choice in humans. *Behavioural Processes* 39:205–14.

Suzuki, S. 1999. Selection of forced- and free-choice by monkeys (*Macaca Fasicularis*). *Perceptual and Motor Skills* 88:242–50.

Suzuki, S. 2000. Choice between single-response and multichoice tasks in humans. *The Psychological Record* 50:105–15.

Taylor, C. 1976. Responsibility for self. In *Identities of persons*, ed. Amelie Rorty, 281–99. Berkeley, CA: University of California Press.

Taylor, P. E., N. C. A. Coerse, and M. Haskell. 2001. The effects of operant control over food and light on the behaviour of domestic hens. *Applied Animal Behavioral Science* 71:319–33.

Taylor, R. 1963. *Metaphysics*. Englewood Cliffs, NJ: Prentice-Hall, Inc.

Taylor, S. E. 1983. Adjustment to threatening events: A theory of cognitive adaptation. *American Psychologist* 38:1161–73.

Taylor, S. E., M. E. Kemeny, J. E. Bower, and T. L. Grunewald. 2000. Psychological resources, positive illusions, and health. *American Psychologist* 55:99–109.

Thompson, S. C., and S. Spacapan. 1991. Perceptions of control in vulnerable populations. *Journal of Social Issues* 47:1–21.

Thompson, S. C., A. Sobolew-Shubin, M. E. Galbraith, L. Schwankovsky, and D. Cruzen. 1993. Maintaining perceptions of control: Finding perceived control in low-control circumstances. *Journal of Personality and Social Psychology* 64:293–304.

Tiger, J. H., G. P. Hanley, and E. Hernandez. 2006. An evaluation of the value of choice with preschool children. *Journal of Applied Behavior Analysis* 39:1–16.

Tobin, H., and A. W. Logue. 1994. Self-control across species (*Columba livia, Homo sapiens*, and *Rattus norvegicus*). *Journal of Comparative Psychology* 108: 126–33.

Tobin, H., W. Logue, J. J. Chelonis, K. T. Ackermann, and J. G. May. 1996. Self-control in the monkey *Macaca fascicularis*. *Animal Learning and Behavior* 24:168–74.

Tomasello, M. 2009. The question of chimpanzee culture, plus postscript. In *The question of animal culture*, eds. K. N. Laland and B. G. Galef, 198–221. Cambridge, MA: Harvard University Press.

Turk, D. C., and E. Fernandez. 1990. On the putative uniqueness of cancer pain: Do psychological principles apply? *Behavioral Research Therapy* 28:1–13.

Vaillant, G. E. 1977. *Adaptation to life*. Boston: Little, Brown.

Valla, L. 1443/1948. Dialogue on Free Will. Trans. Charles Edward Trinkaus, Jr. In *The renaissance philosophy of man*, eds. E. Cassirer, P. O. Kristeller, and J. H. Randall, 155–82. Chicago: University of Chicago Press.

Van Inwagen, P. 1983. *An essay on free will*. Oxford: Clarendon Press.

Vargas, M. 2013. *Building better beings*. New York: Oxford University Press.

Verbrugge, L. M., and A. M. Jette. 1994. The disablement process. *Social Science Medicine* 38:1–14.

Virgin, C. E., and R. Sapolsky. 1997. Styles of male social behavior and their endocrine correlates among low-ranking baboons. *American Journal of Primatology* 42:25–39.

Vohs, K. D. 2006. The psychological consequences of money. *Science* 314:1154–6.

Vohs, K. D., R. F. Baumeister, B. J. Schmeichel, J. M. Twenge, N. M. Nelson, and D. M. Tice. 2008. Making choices impairs subsequent self-control: A limited resource account of decision-making, self-regulation, and active initiative. *Journal of Personality and Social Psychology* 94:883–98.

Voss, S. C., and M. J. Homzie. 1970. Choice as a value. *Psychological Report* 26:912–14.

De Waal, F. 1982. *Chimpanzee politics: Power and sex among apes*. Baltimore, MD: Johns Hopkins University Press.

De Waal, F. 1989. *Peacemaking among primates*. Cambridge, MA: Harvard University Press.

De Waal, F. 1996. *Good natured: The origins of right and wrong in humans and other animals*. Cambridge, MA: Harvard University Press.

De Waal, F. 2001. *The Ape and the Sushi Master: Cultural reflections by a primatologist*. New York: Basic Books.

De Waal, F. 2005. *Our inner ape: A leading primatologist explains why we are who we are*. New York: Penguin.

De Waal, F. 2006. *Primates and Philosophers: How morality evolved*. Princeton, NJ: Princeton University Press.

De Waal, F. 2013. *The bonobo and the atheist: In search of humanism among the primates*. New York: W. W. Norton & Company.

De Waal, E. van, C. Borgeaud, and A. Whiten. 2013. Potent social learning and conformity shape a wild primate's foraging decisions. *Science* 340:483–5.

Wagstaff, G. F. 1983. Correlates of the just world in Britain. *Journal of Social Psychology* 121:145–6.

Waller, B. N. 1977. Chomsky, Wittgenstein, and the behaviorist perspective on language. *Behaviorism* 5:43–59.

Waller, B. N. 1988. Free will gone out of control: A critical study of R. Kane's *Free will and values*. *Behaviorism* 16:149–67.

Waller, B. N. 1990. *Freedom without responsibility*. Philadelphia, PA: Temple University Press.

Waller, B. N. 1992. In defense of freedom without responsibility: Response to critics. *Behavior and Philosophy* 20:83–7.

Waller, B. N. 1997. What rationality adds to animal morality. *Biology & Philosophy* 12:341–56.

Waller, B. N. 2011. *Against moral responsibility*. Cambridge, MA: MIT Press.

Waller, B. N. 2015. *The stubborn system of moral responsibility*. Cambridge, MA: MIT Press.

Wallston, K. A. 1993. Psychological control and its impact in the management of rheumatological disorders. *Bailliere's Clinical Rheumatology* 7:281–95.

Wan, W. W. N., and C.-Y. Chiu. 2002. Effects of novel conceptual confusion on creativity. *The Journal of Creative Behavior* 36:227–40.

Watson, G. 1987. Responsibility and the limits of evil. In *Responsibility, Character, and the Emotions*, ed. F. Schoeman, 256–86. Cambridge: Cambridge University Press.

Wegner, D. 2002. *The illusion of conscious will*. Cambridge, MA: The MIT Press.

Wegner, D., and T. Wheatley. 1999. Apparent mental causation: Sources of the experience of will. *American Psychologist* 54:480–91.

Weinberg, R. S., D. Gould, D. Yukelson, and A. Jackson. 1981. The effect of pre-existing and manipulated self-efficacy on a competitive muscular endurance task. *Journal of Sport Psychology* 4:345–54.

Whiten, A. 2013. Humans are not alone in computing how others see the world. *Animal Behaviour* 86:213–21.

Whiten, A., and C. Boesch. 2001. The cultures of chimpanzees. *Scientific American* 284:48–55.

Whiten, A., J. Goodall, W. C. McGrew, T. Nishida, V. Reynolds, Y. Sugiyama, C. Tutin, R. W. Wrangham, and C. Boesch. 2001. Charting cultural variation in chimpanzees. *Behaviour* 138:1481–516.

Wiedenfeld, S. A., A. Bandura, S. Levine, A. O'Leary, S. Brown, and K. Raska. 1990. Impact of perceived self-efficacy in coping with stressors on components of the immune system. *Journal of Personality and Social Pscyhology* 59:1082–94.

Williams, B. 1985. *Ethics and the limits of philosophy*. Cambridge, MA: Harvard University Press.

Williams, B. 1993. *Shame and necessity*. Berkeley: University of California Press.

Wilson, E. O. 1975. *Sociobiology: The new synthesis*. Cambridge, MA: Harvard University Press.

Wilson, E. O. 2012. *The social conquest of Earth.* New York: Liveright Publishing.

Wolf, S. 1980. Asymmetrical freedom. *Journal of Philosophy,* 77. Page numbers as reprinted in *Moral Responsibility,* ed. J. M. Fischer, 225–40. Ithaca, NY: Cornell University Press, 1986.

Wolf, S.1990. *Freedom within reason.* Oxford: Oxford University Press.

Wolf, S. 2011. Blame, Italian style. In *Reasons and recognition: Essays on the philosophy of T. M. Scanlon,* eds. R. Jay Wallace, R. Kumar, and S. Freeman, 332–47. New York: Oxford University Press.

Woodward, N. J., and B. S. Wallston. 1987. Age and health care beliefs: Self-efficacy as a mediator of low desire for control. *Psychology and Aging* 2:3–8.

Wright, R. G. 2014. Pulling on the thread of the insanity defense. *Villanova Law Review* 59:221–42.

Wrosch, C., M. F. Scheier, G. E. Miller, R. Schulz, and C. S. Carver. 2003. Adaptive self-regulation of unattainable goals: Goal disengagement, goal reengagement, and subjective well-being. *Personality and Social Psychology Bulletin* 29:1494–508.

Zimbardo, P. 1974. On "Obedience to Authority." *American Psychologist* 29:566–7.

Zimmerman, M. J. 1996. Book review of John Martin Fischer's *The metaphysics of free will: An essay on control. Philosophy in Review* 16:340–4.

Zimmerman, M. J. 2011. *The immorality of punishment.* Peterborough, ON: Broadview.

Zuckerman, M. 1983. A biological theory of sensation seeking. In *Biological bases of sensation seeking, impulsivity, and anxiety,* ed. M. Zuckerman, 37–76. Hillsdale, NJ: Lawrence Erlbaum.

Zuckerman, M., J. Porac, D. Lathin, R. Smith, and E. Deci. 1978. On the importance of self-determination for intrinsically motivated behavior. *Personality and Social Psychology Bulletin* 4:443–6.

Index

About the Author

Bruce N. Waller grew up in rural north Louisiana, and drifted around for several years before landing in Chapel Hill and finishing his Ph.D. in philosophy at the University of North Carolina. He taught at Elon University for ten years before moving to Youngstown State University, where he has taught for the last twenty-five years. *Restorative Free Will* is his fifth monograph, and he has also written five textbooks and edited four anthologies. While much of his writing has focused on questions related to free will and moral responsibility, he has also published material on critical thinking (his textbook, *Critical Thinking: Consider the Verdict*, is now in its 6th edition), bioethics, ethical theory (*Consider Ethics*, a textbook on ethical theory, is currently in its 3rd edition), philosophy of psychology, philosophy of biology, and philosophy of social science.

In addition to his books, he has published several dozen journal articles and a number of articles in anthologies. Much of his published work has focused on three main goals (some would say obsessions): distinguishing free will from moral responsibility, and arguing that the widely assumed close connection between free will and moral responsibility is a mistake; arguing that moral responsibility and the entire moral responsibility system is implausible and has no place in our naturalistic world view, and that we are better off without that archaic belief and the system that supports it; and developing a thoroughly naturalistic understanding of free will, and establishing the value and importance of natural free will when it is divorced from belief in moral responsibility. It is that last goal that led to the writing of *Restorative Free Will*.